Nove~~

C000256048

PURSUING THE M

*David Michael Dixon*
*College of the Resurrection*
*Mirfield.*

In memory of

Christopher Gray (1964–1996)

who walked with the Mystery

and saw it in people

Also by George Guiver and published by SPCK

*Company of Voices*
*The Fire and the Clay*
*Everyday God* (Triangle)

# *PURSUING THE MYSTERY*

## WORSHIP AND DAILY LIFE
## AS PRESENCES OF GOD

\*

## George Guiver CR

First published in Great Britain 1996
Society for Promoting Christian Knowledge
Holy Trinity Church
Marylebone Road
London NW1 4DU

Biblical quotations are from the *Revised Standard Version*
of the Bible © 1971 and 1952.

*British Library Cataloguing-in-Publication Data*
A catalogue record of this book is available from the British Library

ISBN 0–281–04991–2

Typeset by The Midlands Book Typesetting Co., Loughborough
Printed in Great Britain by
The Cromwell Press, Melksham, Wiltshire

# CONTENTS

# PREFACE

THIS BOOK HAS had two births. I am very grateful to Canon Alan Wilkinson, Benedict Green CR, Brother Harold SSF, Christopher Irvine and others who read and commented on the first version. Outside events then forced an interval, and when I returned to the manuscript it turned into something different, and my thanks go to Dr Martin Klöckener and all the staff at the German Liturgical Institute in Trier, to Silvanus Berry CR, Nicolas Stebbing CR, Thomas Seville, Novice CR, Ian Burton, Margaret Selby, Benjamin Gordon-Taylor, Christopher Gray, David Peebles, Adrian Souter and others, for reading it and giving their very helpful comments, and to Sr Hilara OSB of Herstelle Abbey for her kindness. I am particularly indebted to Dom Burkhardt Neunheuser OSB, and to Dr Arno Schilson for making time to read the manuscript and give their invaluable comments, suggestions and encouragement; my sincere thanks go to these and all the other people from whom I have received invaluable advice and encouragement, not least the publishing department of SPCK.

# Part I

# ONE
# *Real Life*

VISITORS TO BRADFORD can easily find themselves visiting the National Photography Museum with its Imax cinema. Its screen is very big and very close, producing the sensation of our actually being in the picture. Sometimes they show the flight of the space shuttle. We go up in it, above the atmosphere. We now look down at the breathtaking spectacle of earth slowly revolving in a delicate mantle of air. Arabia fills the screen, then South America, and the little island called Britain is also spottable if you look hard enough. The sight is stunning. From this stupendous vantage-point our worries and struggles suddenly look totally insignificant, they are swept from our consciousness. Other realizations now completely occupy the mind: we are so small, earth is vast, beautiful and baffling, we are incredibly *lucky*. It is very difficult from outer space not to see the earth and its life as a unity splendidly at peace with itself. No conflicts, dirt or blood, but a serene unity filling us with speechless awe.

The show ends, and back to daily life we go, only to find that the ordinary is still there: we have not gained any protection from it. We have come down to earth again, to human life, where office workers yawn over their desks, families quarrel in back rooms, and the familiar round takes its routine course. It had seemed so far away: the grandeur and beauty of what we saw did not belong in any way with all this. Up there, not only were there no yawning clerks looking out at the rain, but it does not occur to us that governments down below are ill-treating their citizens, refugees are desperately trying to get from one small part of this beautiful surface to another, that international companies are working away at its disfigurement and maiming.

Which gives the truer picture? Does the astronaut's-eye-view put life in proportion? Pilots, mountain-climbers, and astronomers have often made that comment. Or does human life and death dwarf even the grandeur of the heavens? Poets have often said as much: human life and its sorrows can make even the sun and the stars fall from the sky. The question is exceptionally poignant and divisive for modern people, and particularly for Christians. Who are right? The Christians who are otherworldly or those who are this-worldly? Which is closer to the truth – the natural or the supernatural? If, like most Christians, you find yourself in the middle, what are you to make of those who lay great emphasis on the Church and its 'holy' things, and those, on the other hand, who put all their emphasis on everyday life? Are we to choose between them? Or are we to take both views seriously? Another way of putting this question is to ask, 'Where is Christ present?' Is he most present in holy places, holy rituals and holy things and writings? Or is he most present in the everyday things of life? There are two streams in Christianity today which are difficult to name, but in this book I will call them 'eternalism' and 'humanitas'. (I apologize for the jargon, but promise not to use it frequently.)

Eternalism is a stream in Christianity which attaches such importance to God's transcendence that worship, the Church, the Tradition, and what can be called the 'things of God' deserve the best of our attention and our energies, as a place of privileged encounter with God. Humanitas, on the other hand, gives overall importance to daily life and the contemporary world. It is *this* which deserves the best of our attention, because it is a place of privileged encounter with God.

These two kinds of passion relate to us in two ways: (a) as an object of attention, cultivation, delight; and (b) as a source for understanding and for wholeness. The Curé D'Ars delighted in pursuing the worship of God and in decorating the church building, and out of that flowed a passion for souls. On the other side is a certain kind of modern Christian who delights in the everyday, and is most proud of being involved in ordinary people's struggles, and sees such involvement as the main road to full humanity, and God's preferred way of being obeyed. This is not simply a policy for living, but also a source of attention and delight. The two streams are not alternatives, and in fact live happily side by side in most Christians today. Most of us want to take God and his worship seriously, and also want to learn what daily life has to teach us. There is a problem with this, however, because we are prone to hold the two side by side in a middling sort of way, our Church life suffering in consequence from a crippling anaemia. In order to see how we are to hold them together, we need to look at the witness of the 'extremists', those who are a bit more emphatic in holding to the one or the other. By taking both extremes seriously, we can discover a different kind of middle way: one that is full-blooded and vigorous, a middle way with teeth. I want to show why we should listen intently to the passionate ones, rather than doing what we often seem to do – shun apparent extremes in favour of a more reasonable middle ground. The view of earth from the space shuttle and that from a bus stop are incompatible views – yet we are compelled to hold them together, and when we do so, we see with a new kind of seeing. That may help us to realize that the same is true about being Christians. It may be that the passionately other-worldly and the passionately this-worldly Christian are both proper witnesses, on whom God calls us, with a certain amount of strain, to direct both our eyes at once. There is something which adds encouragement to my quest for this vigorous centre, rather than opting for a wishy-washy kind of middle: that is the Anglican tradition of the *via media*, and the bold way in which this term was also taken up by the Second Vatican Council. The Latin word *media* can mean 'central'. But it can also mean 'average' or 'middling', and if we end up with that, then we have lost the Christ of the New Testament.

In Part One we shall examine some of the implications of the presence of these two streams in us, and then in Part Two, with considerable help from the German theologian Odo Casel, I hope to show a way forward. For the rest of this chapter we shall take a closer look at the origins of what I have called 'humanitas'.

## RELIGIOUS DECLINE

It is a fascinating and too little remarked-upon fact that in this century humanity has 'come down to earth'. At a certain point in our recent history 'real life' began to look more vital and compelling than the 'heaven' proclaimed by the Christian Church.

No single cause can be identified, but many factors contributed to this change, such as scientific progress, the achievement of widespread prosperity, the revolution in our understanding of psychology. Until a few generations ago such a change would have been unthinkable. How can we explain it? The roots lie in fact in the gospel itself.

### The discovery of God in the everyday

The Jesus of the gospels cannot be pinned down: he is splendidly sovereign, ill at ease with the religion of his day, and an uncomfortable fit too with everyday life. In him is the power of another whom he calls his Father. Jesus is a messenger, and in a sense a presence, of the Father, who is the source of all that enables us to be human. Jesus cultivates his relationship with the Father, speaking to him as 'Abba', and to him he constantly directs people's attention.

At the same time Jesus sniffs out and revels in sheer humanity. Fisherfolk, tax-collectors, thieves, prostitutes, cripples, farmers, old and young, poor and rich, all crowd the gospels and fill them with the smells and sounds and passions of life. And the gospels are filled with life at its most prosaic – the exalted ones step onto this scene almost as outsiders to the plot. The poor, the naked, the fishermen, the women, hold the principal parts in this topsy-turvy drama. 'What you have done to the least of these you have done to me', says Jesus, implying that God is to be found not only in the everyday, but in what are thought to be some of its most unimportant aspects, and even among things and people who were shunned as tainted by sin. From this very strong strand in the gospels it is natural to deduce that daily life is holy, and that God is present in it. However, Jesus does not state this in so many words – he proclaims it loudly by his actions, but he never specifically spells it out except perhaps in the parable of the sheep and the goats ('as you did it to one of the least of these, you did it to me', Matthew 25.40). But neither does he state categorically anywhere that God is to be sought principally in prayer-rituals, although he gives us examples (for example, the Lord's Prayer, the Last Supper, the parable of the persistent widow, prayer in the desert and in the Temple). In the stories that relate to seeking God we find two poles, daily life and prayer, and he leaves his hearers to reflect and draw their conclusions. Jesus, it seems, was concerned both with attending to

God within the special structures of prayer, and also with being conscious of his presence in daily life.

In subsequent history two strands find their home in different people and places in the Church. The one is a preference for being positive about daily life ('world-affirming'). The other (and this too is fully a part of life in this world) is love for worship. The first can so concentrate on the world as to risk losing sight of God, while the other can tip over into a 'flight from the world', and this is a possible interpretation, for instance, of parts of the Johannine writings.

## Flight from the world?

For most of history, life for the many has tended to be burdensome, if not 'nasty, brutish and short', and so it is not surprising that there has been an inclination to concentrate on the life to come. St Augustine, for instance, could assume it in his sermons:

> What did [the Lord] want to teach us? That our desire and our expectation of the resurrection should be ardent, that we may detach ourselves from the things of this world, and be orientated towards God. Here below we are born and we die: let us not be attached to this life; let us separate ourselves from it through the charity with which we love God, and let us seek to reach our home above.[1]

In similar vein Gregory Nazianzen could say of himself and Basil of Caesarea that 'our single preoccupation and yearning was the pursuit of virtue, and a life strained towards future hopes, living as though we were exiles from the world, even before we had departed from this present life'.[2]

On the whole, the sermons of Augustine and his contemporaries are far from being life-denying, nor are they simply hooked on 'pie in the sky when you die'. This strand in Christian teaching is easily and frequently misinterpreted as denying the holiness of creation, while its main concern is, rather, the struggle for freedom from domination by our appetites and desires, a quest for that freedom which can be found only in God. There is no doubt, however, that for such authors as Augustine the world is to be treated with reserve, while one of the signs of holiness is aspiration beyond the world to heaven.

Combined with a positive appreciation both of the divine presence in creation, and a positive commitment to combat evil and fight for the good in daily life, this 'other-worldliness' is a classic component of the gospel. Worldliness and other-worldliness combine in the gospel to coax us beyond our simple certainties, in precisely the same kind of paradox as is embodied in the incarnation itself. We run into problems, however, through our constant danger of veering too far in one direction or the other. So we can meet a depressing capacity to be so centred upon God's holiness that human beings are treated as ciphers. There is among the legends of the desert fathers a very unpleasant little story of some young boys who taunt a monk, and for their impiety are drowned in the sea. Augustine was able to teach that unbaptized infants are consigned to limbo, even while their parents go to heaven. The ability to put ourselves in other people's shoes and 'feel with' them is something we have only gradually acquired, and we still have a long way to go. Such an undervaluing of creatures in relation to the Creator can carry with it an undervaluing of the goodness of the whole of creation. We can see this straight away by comparing ancient marriage liturgies. The Byzantine wedding rite has a wonderfully positive view of God's creation and of marriage itself. The same is the case with the old Mozarabic liturgy of Spain.[3] Such positive evaluation of creation often goes together with relative prosperity and well-being. The Roman tradition, however, which evolved in a period of economic and social collapse, and was to no small degree influenced by Augustine's pessimistic view of human nature, tends to look on marriage as an unfortunate necessity. The woman is associated with uncleanness, and the rite becomes something done to the woman rather than to and by the couple. Only the bride is blessed, and traditions even grow requiring the newly-weds to abstain from the marriage-bed for several days!

The tension inherent in such an approach to the good things of this physical world is seen in the hypocrisy of Victorian England, and to the inconsistencies of that world the Britain of the 1950s was a direct heir. Until our very own day this split has gone deep down into the Western soul, conditioning our expression of the gospel, and continuing to be part of people's moral formation even when the power and influence of the Church have melted away.

Not only in sex and marriage was there an unreal divide, but almost everywhere one looked. The Church's life and worship became a monopoly of the clergy, who themselves in the Middle

Ages were monasticized to a degree far beyond what was appropriate for them, while the monastic life itself came to be siphoned off as the 'perfect' way – there alone was it thought possible to be fully, uncompromisingly Christian. This scheme was duplicated in the secular world, where the life of the 'lower orders' was kept as far as possible out of sight, being less cultivated, less godly, less human, while the educated and better-off were the only real human beings (and still in early twentieth-century Britain, they were the only real 'Englishmen'). 'Ordinary life' was despised, the best kind of life was a rarefied one. The unconscious association of working people with the merely worldly, the unartistic, the insensitive, the untranscendent, must to some degree be responsible for the peculiar incapacity for religion in the British working class (so far as it is possible or happy to categorize each other in these terms today). In the world that evolved in the West, holiness was found in the sacred places, sacred people and things. The rest was profane, some parts of it more profane than others.

## The twentieth century

By the time we reach the twentieth century this tradition is in an advanced state of decay. Alan Wilkinson, in his book *The Church of England and the First World War*, shows how remote a decadent other-worldly religiosity had become from ordinary working men and women. There were occasional clergy such as 'Woodbine Willie' (G. A. Studdert Kennedy), who won soldiers' affection through attractiveness of character, but the message being proclaimed was out of touch and unreal. It spoke of Jesus as an abstract personage we can contact through the airwaves of personal prayer. It failed dismally to connect with work, sex, and the struggles of life, and had the additional disability of being presented in terms of an alien class culture, an alien accent, childish hymns, poor language, dismal visual and physical presentation, and a sentimental style serving further to discredit the whole thing. In the course of summarizing the ecumenical report *The Army and Religion* of 1919, Wilkinson says:

> There was practically universal respect for Jesus, whereas the churches were constantly criticized[4] . . . The Church was criticized on innumerable counts – it lacked reality and conviction: 'When you go to church the bloody thing they offer you is the most damned insipid thing imaginable', said one

officer. The divisions within and between the churches produced confusion and rivalry. The clergy were out of touch;
they were professional people, living in large houses, a cut
above the ordinary people. In a chaplain, personality counted
for everything; the fact that he was ordained counted for
nothing. The churches did not support social justice . . . The
churches seemed stuck in the 16th and 17th centuries, unable
to recognize the Spirit in contemporary movements . . .[5]

Clearly there was plenty here to rebel against, and nobody can
be surprised that the reaction, when it came, was strong. Many
people had developed a deep revulsion against such religion, or
came to find it ridiculous.

A key stage in the development of these questions in the Anglican orbit was marked by a range of late nineteenth-century
thinkers such as F. D. Maurice, B. F. Westcott, Henry Scott Holland and Charles Gore. The incarnationalism which evolved
from this school proclaimed the presence of God in daily life –
Christ was not a 'prisoner in the tabernacle', but was there in the
factory and in the terraced house, and in the work of the labour
movements. This concern to link the gospel with social action
was above all a product of the Tractarian movement, and
remained for a long time peculiar to the Catholic tradition in the
Church of England, giving birth to a typically Anglican emphasis on the incarnation.[6] Frank Weston, Bishop of Zanzibar, was
heard to say, 'you cannot claim to worship Jesus in the tabernacle if you do not pity Jesus in the slum'.[7] A story was told of
a boy who threw a stone at a stained glass window, hitting the
'e' in 'highest', so that the legend read: 'GLORY TO GOD IN
THE HIGH ST'.[8] In the same period in the ordination course of
the Society of the Sacred Mission at Kelham the ordinands were
studying 'what God was doing on the Somme, and at Westminster, and at Tilbury Docks'.[9]

By the time of the Second World War things were moving further. Dietrich Bonhoeffer had shown a great interest in rediscovering prayer, liturgy and a sense of the Church, and this appears
in his little book *Life Together*.[10] But his enigmatic last letters
from prison appeared to dream of a religionless Christianity, a
secular faith which would take its cue from life as it really is.
After the war various forms of 'secular Christianity' came to be
proposed. This line of thinking has by our own day become
firmly established in the consciousness, if not of all Christians,

then certainly of a large number. For many the Church is suffo-
catingly 'churchy', an escape to the unreal, a 'funk-hole' for the
cultivation of private or group illusions, while God is primarily
to be found in real everyday life. *There* he is to be met, *there* to
be adored. Worship in church is inevitable, but must be open to
the world, and take its cue from it.

And so we come to John Robinson's little book *Honest to
God*. The sensation following its publication in 1963 brought to
light a state of affairs which had been developing for a very long
time, but had so far remained unacknowledged in the public
consciousness. It now became abundantly clear that Christianity
was riddled with a crisis of credibility. People found it difficult
to believe in God as he was traditionally conceived, and now a
bishop had said so, and it was like the lancing of a boil. A quarter of a million copies of the book were sold in the first month,
and it rapidly became a sell-out in the many languages into
which it was translated. *Honest to God* is not an easy read, and
the vast response to it is something of a puzzle. People's grati-
tude seems often to have been more for the fact that a bishop of
the Church had voiced radical doubts in public, than for what he
had actually said. Robinson became a symbol for new-found
honesty in doubt and faith. Things which had troubled people
had hitherto been swept under the carpet, but a bishop of all
people was now publicly endorsing their unease. Robinson
attacked the Church for being out of touch with real life. The
faith he had grown up with had become unreal: he could no
longer believe in a God 'out there', but had come to realize, he
said, that what we call God is in fact the 'depth' in everyday life.
God is not imprisoned in a sanctuary set apart from society. The
churchiness and religiosity of the Church, he claimed, make it
blind to the place where God is really present, in daily life.

> Worship, liturgy, on this ['churchy'] understanding, is not
> meeting the holy in the common . . . The sphere of the reli-
> gious constitutes the holy of holies, and we are back at the
> Jewish priestly conception of the relation of the sacred to the
> secular which was shattered by the Incarnation when God
> declared all things holy and the veil of the Temple was rent
> from top to bottom.[11]

It has long been recognized that Robinson's book is in some
ways muddled and incoherent, but whatever its failings, the fact
of great significance is the spontaneous response it provoked.

People felt it spoke to them, that it put a finger directly on a sore point. The British public had long been able to see that there was a crisis of credibility in Christianity: churchgoers had, after all, become a minority of the population; but now doubt was shown to be couching not at the door but in the very heart of the Church itself. For many, the traditional ways now became more difficult to take seriously, people began to ask whether those ways were built on sand, not rock, and many of the claims of the Church no longer seemed so sustainable. The cultural revolution of the 1960s felt like the falling of a veil from people's eyes, as hallowed institutions one after another came under attack. Church attendance and vocations to the priesthood dropped dramatically. A (by comparison) quiet, staid, conservative and ordered world melted away, to make room for the Permissive Society. For some, the sense of excitement was tremendous. There was relief at the new honesty, and great hope that the Church would be released from its ghetto, to become credible and 'relevant' to the modern world.

### God becomes shrouded in mist

Thirty years later, we can see that these events have affected the Church in more ways than we might care to acknowledge. Our unconscious mental furniture has undergone a far-reaching shift: if there are such things as the absolute demands of God, they seem much less accessible by the direct transcendent route, and more easy to find in the concerns of the world we live in. This shift was overdue: too much religion had been a 'flight from the world', even though often accompanied by philanthropy of the highest order. The benefits brought to the Church by this revolution have been immense. The shift marked by the Second Vatican Council was a sign of it, part of a larger seismic movement in the human spirit, desiring to break through the walls which separated the Church from the life and experience of twentieth-century people. Most Christians are aware of the benefits, and probably are grateful for them. We have seen a massive reorientation towards the world by the Western Church, a reorientation of the mind and the spirit which affects all of us, so that most mainstream forms of Christianity today take seriously the question of relating the faith to the modern world. However, there are different ways of holding the elements in balance, and this has become a source of quite deep division. While all Christians aim to make the gospel their priority, some put their major emphasis on the Church, and some on the world. David Jenkins, as Bishop of Durham, wrote in the *Church Times* on 9 March 1990: 'Mission and witness are important – not pampering a few in church . . . My task is to be clear about theology, faith and practice. I have to face reality and point to a living faith and lively gospel to do with God. The basis of all that I stand for as a Christian is that God is in reality as we experience it every day.'[12]

When compared with the religion we have inherited, life emerges as more real. A reviewer in the *Church Times* is therefore able to write: 'The word "prayer" in a book's title makes me jumpy. I'm on my guard, wondering how much the contents will really engage with people in the thick of experience'.[13] People can still remain committed to Christian tradition, to the importance of prayer to God in his transcendence, and the efficacy of grace and providence as supernatural realities; but also today to one degree or another they often see that God *is* in his world, that the Church has been too churchy, and that a vital connection has to be made between gospel and life. Often daily life seems the place where God's grace is most abundant, while the Church has a secondary role; and because it has usurped too much to itself in the past, it has to be put in its place. This is found even in Christians who would call themselves Catholic, and who therefore hold a high view of Church and sacraments. Richard Holloway (at present Bishop of Edinburgh) is a case in point. He has written in an article in the *Church Times*:

> Jesus belongs to the world, not to the Church. He died for all, not for a few . . . He was closer to my father, running endless bales of cloth through steaming red dye in a freezing and dilapidated factory, than he was to me in my spiritual exaltation in Kelham chapel . . . Our tragedy is that the Church contradicts the liberality of God, by trying to get the world to pay a religious duty on what has been so freely given. The Church is not the gospel, but it ought to be its news agency, here to announce what another has won. I am glad now I did not succeed in converting my father in 1954, but I am sorry I did not find a way of sharing with him the joy of our liberation in Christ, though I suspect he already knew it. When he died a few years ago we did not bring his body into church for the funeral. We left him in the hearse outside the church, where he was more comfortable – outside with Jesus.[14]

13

(Notice, incidentally, how much of our conversation turns around Christ's *presence*. We shall find ourselves returning to it frequently.) Holloway's words echo those of a student approvingly quoted by John Robinson: 'We must try to be at one and the same time for the Church and against the Church. They alone serve her faithfully whose consciences are continually exercised as to whether they ought not, for Christ's sake, to leave her'.[15] This raises the question of the designation of the Church in the Creed as 'holy', something to which we shall give our attention later.

We have all been affected by the reorientation of Christianity to the world, a reorientation whose different emphases take many forms, often making it difficult to distinguish exactly where a particular person stands. And this desire to put daily life at the centre has under its own natural momentum continued to assert itself in ever stronger forms. The 'Sea of Faith' grouping, inspired by the writings of Don Cupitt and others, wants to abandon all talk of and attempt to communicate with an objective transcendent deity. A vociferous representative of this point of view is Hugh Dawes, who writes:

> The foundation of faith is always a human activity. Liberals reject the notion of a faith 'once delivered to the saints', the idea that theology is given to us from outside our limited, time-bound existence. There is that to which we give the name God . . . yet even that statement and the use of that name . . . is all the work of men and women as they seek to respond to that which has been given that name . . . We have played along with ideas of the miraculous or of prayers being answered from beyond, or of 'spiritual gifts' (which are more really a blend of chemical ecstasy, fortune-telling and witch-doctoring) for fear of hurting people . . .[16]

Daily life is so central to the way we are as human beings that it has gathered to itself a large degree of the authority which in former times we associated with the supernatural world. As a result, our roots in God have become more tenuous and uncertain.

We have spent most of this chapter walking about upon the earth, and it is now time to go up in our space shuttle – for if what I call 'humanitas' has moved into the centre stage of Christian living, it has by no means swept the board. There are many Christians who would want at least to qualify some of the utterances cited in this chapter by pointing firmly to the supernatural as the primary location for Christian living. To them we now turn.

# TWO

# *Eternal Things*

WE HAVE FOUND many advocates of the belief that God is present in ordinary life today – now we need some witnesses to the opposite, to the supernatural dimension, or, as I have called it, 'eternalism'. We could turn to appropriate 'parties' within the Church, or we could find some representative theologians from this point of view. However, the first run the risk of being too divisive for our purposes, and the second are probably too detached from the experiential level which we need. There is another group of people, however, who illustrate quite boldly the grip that the supernatural is still capable of exercising, and they are the religious orders; and while their view of the transcendence of God is strong enough for them to stake their lives on it, they tend also to stay close to the earthiness of life, avoiding suggestions of polarization. In the first chapter I attempted to give a potted history of 'humanitas', and it makes sense to give another potted history here for 'eternalism', and this time in terms of nuns and monks.

## THE NEW TESTAMENT BEGINNINGS

In the gospels we see Jesus calling people to leave everything and follow him, and he makes of those who respond a distinct group with a strong sense of community. The development of this community is erratic – there is at least one reference to disciples abandoning the attempt when the going gets tough (cf. John

6.66ff.). Those who survive the course, however, are caught up in events which will so transform them that nothing will ever be the same again. The Acts of the Apostles describes the primitive Church in perhaps idealized terms:

'They devoted themselves to the apostles' teaching and fellowship, to the breaking of bread and the prayers . . . and all who believed were together and had all things in common; and they sold their possessions and goods and distributed them to all, as any had need. And day by day, attending the Temple together and breaking bread in their homes, they partook of food with glad and generous hearts, praising God and having favour with all the people'. (Acts 2.42 and 44–47)

Whatever the veracity of this account, there is plenty of testimony to the fervour of the apostolic Church, something that can be demonstrated by the speed with which the gospel spread, and by the blood of the martyrs poured out in witness to it. However, evidence abounds as well to show, as we would expect, that the fervour varied from person to person. Some carried on living much as they had done before, while the fervour of others was so great that they left everything, giving themselves up wholly to the Church's life and worship and to the proclamation of the gospel.

## THE PATRISTIC PERIOD

By the time we reach the third and fourth centuries these trends are settling into strata: there is the local congregation, and within it there are three groups which particularly stand out; the baptized laity, the clergy, and those who might be called especially 'devout'. Around the year 384 the Western nun whose name is thought to have been Egeria describes these especially fervent believers at Jerusalem as *monazontes*.[1] They are a distinct group within the local congregation, attending daily public worship, but staying on afterwards to hold extra services of their own. This phenomenon we find across the Christian world, and by the fourth century such people were not only coming together from their individual homes to worship with the local congregation, but were also beginning to live a life in common in buildings put up for the purpose, and were coming to be known as *monastic,* that is, single (from the Greek word *monos*). Like Jesus or Paul, they were not given in marriage, but gave their

17

whole selves to God. Between the first century and the beginning of the third there is a 'tunnel period' when, as in many other aspects of church life, we know little about how they developed, but there is strong evidence to suggest that the movement which came to be known as 'monasticism' was simply the continuation of the old primitive fervour of the first generation of the Church, passed on among fervent circles as the wider Church began having to adapt itself to 'the world'. It can partly be interpreted as a protest against a more worldly Church, but also it was simply that these people could do no other than give all their life to the direct pursuit of God, and there needed to be some folk around who would continue to witness to these things on behalf of all.

Meanwhile, there were others for whom the element of protest was stronger, the increasing numbers of 'devout' in Egypt (but also in Palestine) who left the city and the public church in order to live severe lives of prayer and struggle with demons (as they understood it) in the wilderness. These started off as hermits – St Anthony (?251–356) was the great inspirer here – and later they came together in 'co-operatives' under a spiritual father or *Abba*. In their most extreme form, they represented an alternative society, not in rejection of secular society, but in witness to certain elements in the gospel which could not be given so free rein in normal life. Quite soon in Upper Egypt there emerged full-blown monasteries run on almost military lines.

These were one strong element within a wider spectrum. At the other end were the urban communities such as those described by Basil, who combined a 'monastic' life with indefatigable service of the local community. Basil's monks and nuns were an early form of social workers. Although Basil was keen on the contemplative life, he was also heard to say to one person planning to be a hermit, 'but whose feet will you wash?' The ingredients which went into the making of Christian monasticism were multifarious, and it has remained multifarious to this day. Some scholars see evidence that there was a direct inheritance from Jewish communities such as those at Qumran, and at least one order, the Carmelites, have claimed to trace their origins as far back as the prophet Elijah!

A great deal of space could be taken up in describing succeeding developments, but I have probably said enough to evoke that sense of the direct quest for the transcendent God which colours the whole history of monasticism. There is the danger of élitism in all of it, and in the Middle Ages the mistake was made of coming to describe it as the 'perfect life'. But the oldest and strongest tradition sees monks and nuns as the lowest of the low, the most unworthy of God's servants, and in order to complete the disclaimer, many religious brothers and sisters have found that predicament at the same time both serious and humorous.

## TERMINOLOGY

I use the word 'monastic' in a very broad sense here, and have to apologize to those many religious brothers and sisters who live active lives of service 'in the world', and would not at all want to be called monastic. First of all, then, a note on terminology is needed. Monasticism properly so called is a life lived under obedience in community, sealed by vows of obedience, stability and conversion of life. In the Middle Ages two of these vows came to be outshone by considerations which have always been taken for granted in the life, but which at that time became the preferred subjects of a vow: poverty and chastity. Modern services of monastic profession are now tending to return to the more ancient vows of obedience, stability and conversion of life.

A problem with terminology arises because from the Middle Ages onwards there have arisen variants on this life which could not be called totally monastic. The friars took monasticism on to the roads in their travelling life; later, Ignatius developed an even less communitarian form in his Jesuit order; and between then and now there have developed thousands of permutations of this kind of 'Religious Life', as it is called (I shall give these terms capital letters throughout this chapter to avoid confusion for readers unfamiliar with the terminology). There are millions of members of religious orders in the world, and hundreds of thousands in Europe. Only about ten per cent (say) of these could be called 'monastic'. The rest are 'Religious' – people who may do a full-time job of one kind or another, or live some form of community life while perhaps running an institution such as a school or hospital. There are all the variations under the sun, and all manner of combinations of asceticism and liberty, community and individuality, and of balance between prayer and work. It is a matter of debate how far the word 'monastic' is applicable to all of them, and many would deny that their life finds its origins in Christian monasticism at all, being, rather, a separate development. In Eastern Orthodoxy, meanwhile, the question of these two types does not arise, as there are no orders – there are simply monks and nuns, and in theory all live the same life, which is centred on monasteries, whether it be for men or women (and sometimes both together). The English language produces another problem here, as the words 'monastery' and 'convent' are traditionally interchangeable, and only English usage has distinguished the one from the other in terms of gender. There are many religious communities and orders in the Lutheran churches, and in the Anglican communion they knew a great flowering in the nineteenth century and some decline in more recent years. They are also to be found in the Methodist, Reformed and other churches.

In this chapter the word 'monastic' will be used for brevity's sake, while wishing to include all these types of people as appropriate.

## THE MONASTIC JOURNEY

Monasticism seems at first sight to contradict all we have been saying about daily life: it is a quest, the goal of which is God. The quest is enabled by the removal, to some degree or other, of ties and involvements in the ordinary everyday world. Many Jesuits are teachers, many nuns are nurses, but with all of them some of what other people regard as everyday necessities have been quietly put out of the way.

### Setting out

The contrast between the monastic vision and that, say, of David Jenkins in the previous chapter can be shown up quite well by tracing the kind of thing a person goes through when they first join a Religious Community. There is no standard process here, and the way it works out differs as widely as people themselves do, and what I describe is simply one very common type of experience.

The journey may well begin with an apparent withdrawal from a world of noise and bustle, withdrawal into the vibrant silence and solitude of the monastery, and the wisdom of the monastic tradition. The seeker may come to pity the world, just as newly-weds may pity every other mortal. The rich things of God, which point inwards into the soul, beckon and summon with great power. Yet it is not a transition which all find easy. Some come straight into the monastery with little ado, while others follow a long meandering path: some are attracted from in front, others feel pushed from behind. What they find when they come is a tent in the wilderness, a space cleared in a turbulent world, where God is invited to reign. The law in this tent is the gospel, and the wisdom of the tradition. The setting for the divine presence is communion – that is, the love of the brothers and sisters, and the common quest for the will of God. It is exceedingly difficult to evoke what a monastery can be for people, but it can very often be something like this, an Eden, a new Jerusalem, filled with light.

## Beyond the romance

That is the first layer, that 'whiff' of the things of God, the magic of solitude and silence, the beauty of worship. Below it is a second layer, which we take a little time to reach: ordinariness. The monastic life, when lived properly, is not one of ease and retirement. It makes commonplace demands which are also relentless, and stay with us to old age. A monastery will take a great deal of running, and much of the life simply involves getting ordinary tasks done. These, however, are an integral part of the quest for God. Rather than finding ways of making the best of an unfortunate necessity, or seeing the chores as taking you away from prayer and study, they are as closely involved with the journey as is the liturgy. God is found in the commonplace things just as much as in prayer. While this may sound a shade domestic, it hides a formidable set of teeth. It excavates the interior of the individual, and proves and tests the *koinonia* (the New Testament word for communion) of the community. It can be easy to do inspiring things for the guests and visitors, easy to preach and to pray, but in the other members of the community with whom we live eyeball to eyeball we find the real test of the claim to be serving God. It can be relatively straightforward and satisfying to be of service to people at one remove from us, but community is an unfailing test of what all of that means. There, the things that we fail to be or to do are paid for by everybody else. The monastic tradition speaks in this way of the life being a mirror held up to us, in which, if we look, we can see the unadorned truth reflected.

## Getting down to business

Now we begin to come nearer to the heart of the matter: we reach the layer of the self. Exposed to ourselves by the solitude,

21

and exposed to the community by closeness of life, we embark on an inner journey which, God willing, will lead, not without much ado, to growing knowledge of self and others. Not only can we no longer get away with so much, but none of our companions, not even the most inspiring and impressive, turns out to be perfect. People, however good they might seem to be, and however inspiring their public reputation, are always at close quarters to some degree or other *difficult*. So we discover that some of the most abundant grist to the monastic mill is conflict and darkness, the depth and intractability of people's fallenness, the cussedness of human nature. Monks and nuns are *in via*, on the way, certainly not angels, and unlikely to become so in the short run. One thing they are doing, when their common life is in good order, is working at the coal-face of our darkness. The monastery explores and maps some of the polar regions of the human spirit (and the poles are lands of great light and great darkness). This is of course a process that takes place in other areas of life too, such as the family or the psychiatrist's couch. The aspect which is more or less unique to the religious life is the particular way in which these things are consistently and explicitly related to the quest for God, and serve as grist to that one central mill. Conflict, indeed, is never far from the presence of Christ in the gospels, and in a Religious Community, often contrary to appearances, it is never very far away either.

The unique nature of this exploration in communities of brothers and sisters is defined partly by the vows. By *stability* we are bidden to stay with the present moment, however difficult, rather than move away to things more congenial. Stability seeks to stay on the same spot, the reality of the present, and to drill for oil on such unpromising earth – as that is where some of the richest oil is to be found. Staying with things where and as they are, facing up to what is left when all possibilities for distraction are taken away, and finding God there, and ourselves there.

*Obedience* asks for mutual listening, in the expectation that we will hear the voice of Christ in the other; it coaxes us away from our immediate inclination to exercise our own will, and into the quest for the will of God. Christ's perfect obedience is the source for this, in which he and the Father were one, and it was his meat to do the Father's will.

*Conversion of life* shows that it takes a lifetime to make a monk or nun, and in the meantime a depraved beast is going through a process of daily conversion through engagement with the grace of God. So a very unlikely group of people manage to be a place where the *Shekinah* of God, his holy and glorious presence, hovers above the roof, as it were, apparently despite the occupants of the building below. A Religious Community can be a most unlikely group of people, who purely as people have apparently nothing very much at all to offer to humanity. They are like an organ: the individual pipes will never produce any glory, however hard they are blown. All the glory comes from God, who is both organist and composer. Without him this Community is a mere box of whistles. The transcendent God stands at the centre to such a degree that it is very difficult, if not impossible, to talk in terms of goals or objectives.

### Providence

Of all the things which particularly make the monastic life stand out today, one must be its attitude to Providence as a live reality. Everything that happens, whether negative or positive, all that life brings, becomes a manifestation of the Providence of God. Christ speaks in every situation that presents itself, and this puts the sister or brother somewhat on the spot – we find ourselves in the awkward situation of having to expand our openness to what life brings. A brother may have a very cherished plan, but his community may have other plans. And the astringency of Providence inside applies equally to outsiders – as pushy television companies, or institutions of the wider Church indeed, can sometimes find when attempting to deal with a monastic community. This should not imply any absence of doubt or uncertainty in respect of Providence in the life of a Religious Community – what it does mean is that Providence is objectively enshrined in the external running of the community's life, and individually internalized as a foundation of personal life.

### This-worldly and other-worldly

Monastic communities are only one example of Christians who place a high value on the supernatural and on what could be called the specifically religious. However, they are a sufficiently strong example of it for certain contrasts with the this-worldly Christianity of Chapter 1 to become apparent. While for David Jenkins Christianity is not about pampering a few in church, here we have largely private communities 'pampering themselves' several times a day in church. While for Richard Holloway Christ was out on the street, Religious Communities exist whose members rarely see the street! While for many Christians the Church is seen as too churchy, these people appear to revel in being in church. While the people of Chapter 1 can look for God in life as it is lived in all its humanity, Religious brothers and sisters always retain a fundamental commitment to the 'things of God': the Scriptures, the Church as holy, the sacraments; and they can in some cases devote almost their entire life to them. To be sure, I am depending on great generalizations in order to make these distinctions, but there is enough reality in the difference between Thomas Merton and David Jenkins to justify it.

## No monopoly

There is a paradox about this, however, for there is in fact nothing in the monastic life that is not also found outside it: celibacy, sacrificial service of neighbour, fervent prayer, obedience, simplicity of life, can all be found in ordinary life, and while many have attempted to identify single elements in monasticism which are unique to it, no one has convincingly succeeded. There is a danger that communities of Religious brothers and sisters fall for a temptation to set themselves up as 'something special'. It is good in any calling to be proud of it and to think that other people do not know what they are missing. Members of communities, however, have a particular temptation here which has to be recognized and rejected. In his early years in the monastery Thomas Merton revelled so much in his monastic withdrawal that he tended to look on the ordinary world with pity. He was going through the sort of stages that I have just been outlining. At some point the individual has to rediscover daily life and its vital relationship to the monastic calling. So one day an errand took Merton into town:

> In Louisville, at the corner of Fourth and Walnut, in the centre of the shopping district, I was suddenly overwhelmed with the realization that I loved all those people, that they were mine and I was theirs, that we could not be alien to one another even though we were total strangers. It was like waking from a dream of separateness, of spurious self-isolation in a special world . . . This sense of liberation from an illusory difference was such a relief that I almost laughed out loud . . . It is a glorious destiny to be a member of the human race, though it is a race dedicated to many absurdities and

24

one which makes many terrible mistakes; yet, with all that, God himself gloried in becoming a member of the human race.[2]

Later on Merton was horrified to receive a request from Pope Paul VI that he, together with other contemplatives, should issue a message to the world. It was preposterous for Merton that contemplative life should try and teach other people how to live. As far as he could see, 'myself and my brothers in the world we are just two men who have fallen among thieves and we do our best to get each other out of the ditch'.[3]

The apparent contrasts between 'this-worldly' Christianity and 'other-wordly' Christianity seem increasingly difficult to pin down the closer we look at them. Monasticism is concerned with a pulling-away of masks, and with facing the unadorned truth about ourselves and other people. If it is healthy, it is thoroughly earthy, avoiding many comforts and props, and throwing itself into good, old-fashioned work in close contact with the material world. It is totally anti-romantic – no one could survive long in a Religious Community on romantic rations. It has, in fact, an exceedingly uncomfortable propensity to uncover everything, to look into people and know what is in them, and to have little time for nonsense. In this there is no monastic monopoly – it simply reveals that, on examination, the apparent contrasts between these two types of Christian seem to mask an underlying unity. There is sufficient in it to encourage us to think that the best kind of *via media* is not carefully distanced from the fervent humanist and the fervent pray-er, but seeks instead to stretch in order to put a hand on the shoulder of each.

In all of this discussion there is a constant danger of falling into over-generalization. Few 'this-worldly' Christians totally reject the quest for the transcendent God, and few 'other-worldly' Christians are completely out of touch with everyday life in the modern world. There can be great benefit, however, in sharpening up the distinction for the purposes of discussion, because it can help us see the degree of misunderstanding and projection that is going on when Christians who incline one way react strongly against Christians who incline the other way.

# THREE

# How Did We Get Down Here?

WE HAVE COME down to earth. This striking fact is true about all of us. Even among monks and nuns it is much more difficult to find a God-centred awe unseasoned by the wisdom of the world, and a faith unmarked by that questioning uncertainty and reserve which is innate in a world which is post-Darwin, Freud and all the rest. If it is true that we have come down to earth, how did it happen? The story is as complex as veins in marble, but I will take a strand in it which throws especially clear light on this shift in our centre of gravity. It is the strand of the development of the sense of 'self' traced with striking vividness in Charles Taylor's book *Sources of the Self*.[1]

## ANTIQUITY

For ancient peoples, the sense of who we are was firmly bound up with the human community and the external order of the universe. Plato (427–347 BCE) is a good representative of the ancient view. For him the universe presents us with a wonderful order: our task is to attune ourselves to that order. That is how truth and goodness are to be found, by attuning ourselves to the inherent order of the external universe. We are, if you like, aligning our 'grain' with the grain of the cosmos. This order of the universe, according to Plato, is higher than us, and outside us: it is something we were called to aspire to, and its source is God. The way to attune ourselves to this order is through contemplation. In the process of this 'tuning', the disparity within us becomes unified. We become attuned, at equilibrium, at peace with ourselves and the universe. Our attention is directed outwards.

## AUGUSTINE RE-ROUTES THE PROCESS THROUGH THE HUMAN PERSON

When Christianity appeared on this scene it introduced something new: it has the same understanding, but now the God who is higher than us is also at work within us. That was new. Christianity speaks in terms of grace, and in terms of the Holy Spirit speaking within (Galatians 4.6). Our attention now begins to be directed inwards, into the person, in addition to the basic outward orientation to the beautiful order of the universe. This receives a particular twist through Augustine, who draws attention to the individual character of each person. Augustine in this way puts a new emphasis on the inward working of God: he takes the New Testament doctrine of the Holy Spirit working within us and brings it under the spotlight. An important part of Augustine's turning of the attention inward concerns our individual responsibility for sin. Our sinfulness is in fact grist to the mill of this inward journey. We are drawn to attend to the sin which is within us, and our sense of guilt helps to compel us on this inward journey.

For Augustine, however, this quest for the God within is simply a stage in the quest towards the old ideal: being attuned to the divinely appointed order of the universe. The picture we have found in Plato, which is typical of the ancient understanding as a whole, is still in place with Augustine. It now takes a route, however, via self-reflection and the working of God within us. Augustine, furthermore, pushes this to a conclusion which shows his spiritual genius, for God is not only the goal of our inward quest, but he becomes also the principle behind the very quest itself. If I know, it is because God is enabling the knowing in me. The very process itself *is* God at work. God's activity in me enables me to know him. So the only way to be able to know what is good and true is through allowing God to empower my journey inwards, where God is waiting to be recognized. Indeed the attention is now drawn to the very process itself of coming-to-know. Augustine shifts the focus partly from the objects we seek to know and towards the activity of knowing.[2] The relation to the outer reality has to start with a journey inwards. Reading Augustine's autobiographical work, the *Confessions*, we are struck by how like a modern autobiography it is – we are surprised by its modernity. In contrast with most other authors of his time is the way he pays attention to himself as an individual, speaking from the heart as a flesh-and-blood human being. The result is a vision of humanity and divinity of a new grandeur.

Augustine's greatness as a human being, a theologian and an artist is beyond question: his utterances have a grandeur and clarity of insight which put him in a league with Michelangelo or Beethoven. And yet there is a dark side, more ambiguous, perhaps best represented in his attitude to sin, which many now feel had some unhelpful consequences for the development of the Western Church, for Augustine encouraged distortions of our understanding of creation which have only begun to be restored to healthy proportion in our own day, for instance in his teaching that unbaptized infants could not go to heaven.

As we have seen, Plato's understanding of how we attain to the good still holds – it is a process of becoming attuned to a higher order which is outside and above us. But it receives this new twist of having to pass via introspection. For Plato (and for ancient humanity as a whole), the process is simple – mankind seeks to respond to the order of the cosmos. For Augustine this changes: 'Do not go outside of yourself, but go into yourself; the truth dwells in the interior man'.[3]

It is Augustine's awareness of sin which brings him to examine with a new attention the psychology of the human individual, and it is the encounter between God's grace and the imperfect, distorted glory of humanity which is one of the most gripping insights in Augustine's theology. Our very wickedness is an essential part of the mix and of the process: it is in facing the darknesses of our soul that redemption is to be found. The spiritual journey has started to come down to earth.

Augustine leaves us with several matters of account in our investigation: humanity's understanding of the universe starts coming down to earth, a major step forward is made in the value placed on each individual person, and yet this still assumes Plato's distinction between a harmonious, 'spiritual' heaven and a lower, transitory order of the physical.

## THE MIDDLE AGES

Momentous developments gradually took place through the long period we call the 'Middle Ages', and it lies beyond the scope of this book to trace through that long and significant era in human history. Two things need a brief mention, however. One is the discovery of the importance of the human mind and discursive reasoning (a 'scientific' approach, in other words) for making sense of the relation between heaven and earth, between divine revelation and our life in the physical order of things. So there emerged a new confidence in the possibility of using earthly reasoning to work towards greater comprehension of the ineffable.

The other major development in terms of our investigation was the recognition of nature as a basic good which is capable of being transformed by grace. All tendency to see the creation as basically alien from God was shown to be false: the world is 'very good', and is capable of being perfected by grace. While for Plato sanctification involves ascent to heaven, the Christian complement of heaven descending to earth receives ever stronger affirmation. In all of this the towering figure is Thomas Aquinas (c. 1225–74).

## MONTAIGNE

We are not tracing a history – such history is much better provided elsewhere – we are bounding over stepping-stones, and our next leap takes us to the sixteenth century. Here we encounter signs of a shift which brings us down to earth in a major way: at that period there first appears an interest in our personality for its own sake. With the French essayist Michel de Montaigne (1533–92) we meet something which was to have a long future before it. For Montaigne, each person is unique, a puzzling array of contradictory and sometimes even chaotic behavioural characteristics. For him there is a whole world to be investigated here, a world of which we need to be able to make sense, 'Everyone looks in front of himself;' he wrote, 'me, I look inside myself'.[4] And the quest seems now to be more for self-understanding as the terminus of the journey, rather than for passing through it to the vision of God who is beyond. In our own time we can easily recognize the fruits of this development

29

in a strong and at times obsessive interest in self-examination, self-knowledge and self-fulfilment.

## PROTESTANTISM

Meanwhile, something very important was happening on the other side of the Reformation divide. Protestantism rejected much of the medieval notion of the sacred, and in particular anything that might be thought to come between the believer and God. The church building was emptied of its saints and sacraments, its liturgy and priesthood. Some of the terminology survived, but its meaning was drastically revised, reducing the places where God was thought to be encountered to a new minimum: the individual believer's inner disposition. Under the old dispensation, life was full of holy things with a power to impart grace: the church building and its holy contents, the liturgy which went on within it, and the holy things which came out through its doors to sanctify daily life. The parish clerk toured the parish blessing things and people with holy water, and all manner of festivals and ceremonies turned up the divine volume-control, revealing the presence of God and his saving power in all manner of places, events and things. Now most of it was gone, and the new arena for the operation of the holy were the family and the individual believer. This holiness became expressed not in lighting candles, paying for masses, or taking part in processions, but in living a righteous life in daily work and in the family. Protestantism in fact gave a powerful, and perhaps decisive impetus to something which had always been there in Christianity: the gospel was about fishermen and carpenters' families, sickness, weddings, human conflict. This now came into its own. The old world had thought in terms of higher and lower: some aspects of life were lofty, exalted, special, and were to be looked upon with deference. The other, ordinary things were of a lesser order from which it was important to escape, if possible, to attain to the higher, the lofty. Blacksmiths' forges were an unfortunate necessity, while art, literature, gentility, and all that might be represented by italiate ceiling paintings and the like were incomparably higher. Protestantism gave free reign to a spirit which saw all this as fatuous, and simply transferred these significances to daily life itself. Reverence was now directed towards a godly living of the ordinary things of daily life. Tragically, most of the old order was tarred with one brush, and the baby went out with the bathwater, as most churches in the Reformation tradition would now agree. A positive result of the change, however, was that perhaps for the first time in history the ordinary and the everyday had stepped into the limelight on the centre stage of the cosmic order.

## *DESCARTES*

The seventeenth century now produces real signs of the ushering-in of modern times. The towering figure is René Descartes (1596–1650). Plato had thought of the person becoming attuned to the order of an exterior cosmos which was good and divine. Augustine relocated the journey so that it passed through the person's interior, and in the process was empowered by God's power within. Now with Descartes in effect the power within becomes human. God moves to a back seat in the proceedings. Human reason is equipped with all that should be necessary for proper perception. In addition to this, the external order of the universe is demoted from its throne of distant perfection and holiness to the position of an inert object waiting to be analysed. Descartes abandons any notion of our needing to look outside ourselves for understanding. The understanding is generated within, by the procedures of reason. Plato's cosmic order is no more – what we have in its place is the universe seen as a mindless mechanism. The role of God involves setting everything up and sustaining it in being. But now we are able to stand apart even from God in order to examine him too – he becomes 'a theorem in *my* system of perfect science'.[5] Thus the human being becomes an autonomous, disengaged subject, able to stand back from all that is around and examine it scientifically and dispassionately. Descartes stands back even from his body, now separated categorically from his mind. The mind-body divide takes a new turn, no longer simply a matter of higher and lower, but rather of what is human and what is merely ancillary to the human. This disengaged subject of Descartes marches on to the stage to stay – he is in all of us. Even the writing of this book and these very sentences employ his method. What we are tracing is incontrovertibly a process of gain, but it is the accompanying loss which we have failed to notice so that we now begin to wonder whether it was necessary to lose so much.

The modern self as we picture it today has been formed by a motley array of characters apart from Augustine, Montaigne, and Descartes. More thinkers still were to march on to join the throng in the succeeding centuries, and they make an ill-assorted company. Descartes and Montaigne in essence flatly contradict each other, yet both their attitudes are inside me, and you, the reader, as we shall see.

## LOCKE

We shall turn to the heirs of Montaigne shortly. Before that we need to see what happened next among those of the Descartes brigade. We can see by now a historical pattern of frontiers falling, like dominoes, one after the other. John Locke (1632–1704) attracts our attention next. He further expands the disengaged subject and her powers of reason into parts Descartes did not dare to reach – now for Locke our reason can stand back and analyse our very own person. We can stand apart from ourselves to examine our passions, inclinations and intuitions, and so gain the power, where necessary, to remake ourselves according to the results of our reasoning. This gives a radically mechanistic understanding of the whole of life, a questioning approach whose main moving force is, as Locke put it, an 'uneasiness' with regard to the life around us. Everything now has to justify itself according to the canons of reason before we can commit ourselves to it. Many traditions in society, says Locke, claim a status which they have no entitlement to – he speaks like the boy in the fable of the king with no clothes – people claim authority who have no title to it, whether they be in the State, in the Church, in the family, or in whatever field of human life we care to name. The credentials of these 'authorities' often prove to be worthless, and where this is so they should be demolished and replaced.[6] It is not hard to see how, in a climate such as that in which the theories of Locke had currency, Christian faith and practice might seem to be following an irreversible trend towards centring everything on the human mind, on humanity in general, and on this 'earthly' life.

## DEISM

From Locke's world-view yet others branch out, yet more radical again. One of these was Deism. Deist thinkers saw God to be a benign Creator who set the world in motion and then in effect withdrew. He desires the best for human beings, and is happy for us to rework gospel standards in contemporary human terms. So the *love* (*agape*) of the gospels is transformed by the eighteenth-century Deist into *benevolence*. God is benevolent, and everything that happens is intended ultimately for the good. This good, however, is of purely human dimensions. Nothing of the ranting, raving, jealous God of the Old Testament survives the Deist transformation, nor the bloodied God of the crucifixion. The Lord of the universe is now more positive – he affirms humanity on its own terms. All of this is set within a vision of the cosmos as a wonderful interlocking order where everything makes complete sense.

It did not take long to discredit Deism as a formal creed, but much of it came to stay in the popular imagination. The majority of non-practising Christians who profess 'belief in God' today seem little different from Deists – God is there as a great help to humanity, full stop. Any notion of Judgement, of the need for the Holy Spirit to work within us, or of participation in God, seem to be entirely absent or reduced to such puny proportions as to be hardly recognizable. Such believers might well be close to the life of God in their love and service of others and in their upright living. But the God at the centre of it all can seem uncomfortably close to the puny, comfortable God of Deism.

I have tried to trace the emergence of the 'rational' mind, and its stepping back from a formerly enchanted universe, placing its feet instead firmly on the earth. We know well enough how this developed in the next two centuries in the triumph of the scientific world-view, without needing to catalogue it any further. We have traced sufficient to see how the wonderful external universe of the ancient world and Middle Ages was gradually 'disenchanted', and how Augustine's passionate engagement with God was transformed into cold observation.

## ALL OF THIS IS IN ALL OF US

These many attitudes live together in a not always easy tension. They can coexist in an unlikely manner in the same one individual, and to a certain degree they are all indiscriminately present in all of us, so much part of our make-up that we cannot distinguish them for what they are. A measure of the contradiction can be gained from reflecting that bits and pieces from most of the authors I have examined, from Plato through Augustine to Montaigne, Descartes and beyond, coexist in me and in you. This chapter has been written with a considerable degree (I hope) of Descartes' detached reason. But with this goes a strong dose of Plato's response to the external Other, strongly routed through Augustine's sinful 'I', while at the same time throughout this book Descartes' approach will find itself in paradoxical relationship with an appeal to personal experience and examination of our personal psychology and feelings. Each person is a living demonstration of a strange fact: however we might wish to wave a flag for any particular outlook and to dub the others foolish, we are still stamped in differing but inescapable degrees by all the ones we are denying. They exist in tension in us, sometimes sliding into muddle; but this tension has the capacity to rise to a surprising fruitfulness.

## CAN OUR PICTURE OF GOD SURVIVE THESE CHANGES?

So far we have tried to articulate some things of which we are perfectly aware and others which we can quite easily recognize once they are pointed out. In particular we have remarked on the increasing normativity accorded to everyday life in recent centuries. A problem is now shown up by all of this: the place of God. His position in relation to ourselves has changed so radically that it is difficult to see how we can have very much in common with Christians who lived before this process was fully under way. If the gospels were written by people who without any difficulty and without any question found their identity rooted in the God above, how can we, for whom such a framework is fundamentally altered, practise the same faith and celebrate the same liturgy that was alive and real for them? The problem might be stated like this: for most ancient peoples human life was a common life, and people found a large part of their identity in the tribe, the city, the ethnic group. This was intimately bound up with the supernatural world (in whatever way it was conceived) and was somehow reflected in the cosmos. Our sense of self was bound up with being right with the heavens and with the gods. In simple terms this can be taken to hold until the seventeenth century in Europe: there was strong, confident, two-way communication, which could be represented by a conduit:

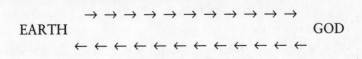

$\rightarrow \rightarrow \rightarrow \rightarrow \rightarrow \rightarrow \rightarrow \rightarrow \rightarrow \rightarrow \rightarrow$

EARTH                              GOD

$\leftarrow \leftarrow \leftarrow \leftarrow \leftarrow \leftarrow \leftarrow \leftarrow \leftarrow \leftarrow \leftarrow \leftarrow$

Naturally, this is a very simplified picture. It ignores that element of doubt and faltering faith to be met throughout the history of the Church. 'Lord, I believe: help my unbelief' (Mark 9.24). But the conduit is true enough for our purposes here, where we want not to describe in detail, but to show up a contrast.

Since the seventeenth century such a relationship with the divine has been increasingly difficult to sustain. We live in a Church which has put the Scriptures under the microscope. They have undergone the indignity (as it might at first seem) of scientific scrutiny, and we are no longer able to treat them in the literal way which was still possible in the seventeenth century or even the eighteenth. The masses of biblical commentaries that have appeared in modern times have taken the Scriptures minutely apart and shown the degree to which they have been determined by local culture, authorial prejudice and accident. Our interpretation of the Scriptures, and the place we accord them in the life of the Church, now seem to depend very much on a human 'by-your-leave'. Then there is Christian doctrine, which has all come under rigorous question. Even the most central doctrines of the faith such as the incarnation and the resurrection have been minutely examined, and in all manner of ways apparently found wanting. The world of systematic theology is now characterized by a multiplicity of points of view, even within a body like the Roman Catholic Church. Most of those who today would count themselves orthodox believers would admit of a degree to which a question-mark hangs over details of Christian doctrine. Our age naturally questions anything before it can decide what kind of assent to give, and such questioning is naturally taken to be healthy. It is also realized that scientific study of the object of belief makes use of a gift that has been given us by God. If this gift is there, presumably we are expected to use it, and a refusal to use it would be a denial of the reality of who we are, and of a gift God has given us. Therefore we are bound to use our capacity for scientific investigation.

## NO BELIEF TODAY WITHOUT
## QUESTIONS FIRST

For many Christians today a consequence of all this is that the Christian tradition can only be embraced piecemeal, after passing it first through a filter of questions. A privileged position is very widely given to the individual's enquiring mind, informed by the shared climate of questioning characteristic of our culture. What is certain is our questioning. We can only attain to faith insofar as our questions can come to reasonable conclusions about the object of faith. It is a situation that might be represented by the ladder of a fire-engine. The ladder, when extended, is long. It is attempting to reach a cloud in which, we have been told, God lives. The further we go up the ladder, the more unsteady it becomes, and the more we are exposed to the destabilizing effect of the wind and our poor head for heights. In addition, we have the use of a personal telephone. We have been told God has one too, but we are never completely sure we have made contact, as the signal is faint and the interference so great.

Here is one of the crucial differences between the conduit and the fire engine. In the conduit there is two-way movement, and what is more, it passes through us. The fire-engine's ladder, however, is only fixed at one end, and the movement is only in one direction. For users of the conduit the entire cosmos was a manifestation of God, and God's values were enshrined and vibrating in it, calling us to be enlarged to their dimension, and to become as beautiful as they. Today, however, we almost automatically assume that in order to relate to God we have to start from where we are, reaching out as best we might into a cold silence, hoping for an invisible helping hand on the way, but not very sure of it. Even what we *do* believe only derives its solidity from the starting-point of human reasoning and intuition. It is based at ground level, and the other end of the ladder has little, if anything at all, to lean on. Meanwhile, our many doubts and questions contribute to the undermining of our confidence, as we go further up the fire-engine ladder. So worship continually falters for us, constantly threatens to mean nothing, and often it only seems to hold on by its fingertips.

## THE QUEST FOR THE ETERNAL WILL NOT GO AWAY

Despite all of this, large numbers of people today yearn for a recovered sense of unity with the cosmos, whether it is through the ecological movement, through the strange mystic yearnings of the New Age, or the much more widespread interest in retreats, 'spirituality' (whatever that is), prayer, holy places and pilgrimages, not to mention the great attention now paid to the liturgy and our participation in it. Many want to find a way of re-establishing the intimate relationship with the cosmos of God which a Plato or an Augustine took for granted. We cannot *make* ourselves believe in it, but somewhere down in our psychological layers it is innate in us. The difficulties are greater for some than for others, and we should not forget that many people continue to have strong faith in the supernatural dimension, and the hidden economy of God, and they are not always among those branded as conservatives.

## THE CHANGES CANNOT BE UNDONE

Even monks and nuns, however, or evangelical charismatics, live this reality in a way Augustine could never have done, for whether they recognize it or not, Descartes, Montaigne, Locke and countless other genies are in their bloodstream and determine their sense of who they are and the way they respond to the world. We therefore have to say that there can be no journey back to the past, no simple return from the fire-engine to the conduit. We cannot undo what has been done. We cannot pretend that the Enlightenment never existed. Unless we expunge all evidence about it, and burn all its books, we cannot avoid knowing about the Enlightenment; and to know what it knew is to be rendered incapable of returning to a pre-existing worldview. Insofar as the baby has been thrown out with the bathwater, however, there has to be a return or restoration of some sort, as the baby comes back through the window. Babies, furthermore, never cease to grow, and any thought of archaeological restorations must be doomed to failure.

A much more interesting possibility is that depicted by Alasdair MacIntyre,[7] when he speaks of picking up threads which have gradually been dropped since the sixteenth century, in order to enable them once more to continue their natural growth and development. In such a process, we cannot throw Descartes and the others out of the window in exchange. They are in us for good. Our identity, in which they lurk, is composed of a motley array of perceptions and presuppositions, often living together in an unlikely and tense partnership. Problems arise when we try to exalt one of these insights and presuppostitions further than it can be exalted, for this can only be done by failing to recognize how deeply we are influenced by the very ones we oppose. A radical theologian may think it important to maintain the maximum detachment in analysing matters of Christian doctrine, but would not find it so easy to exercise the same detachment in his love life. He is Locke for the one, and Montaigne for the other. And when he listens to music or goes to a play and is taken 'outside of himself' we can without too much difficulty see a touch of attunement to the grandeur of the cosmos going on. If disparate attitudes are capable of being held within us in positive tension, then it might seem that a more sane approach would be to find ways of regulating the balance between these attitudes. This would have to be done, however, without falling for the pluralist mistake of treating all opinions as equal across the board. Some of the strands in our make-up, consumerism, for instance, are warped or even potentially evil. Our quest is, rather, for a vigorous *via media*.

We have seen that it has generally been true throughout history, in Graeco-Roman culture at least, that people have looked outward to the mystery of the cosmos for an understanding of who they are and how they are to live. This larger reality in which we are set has most often been seen as divine – behind it stands a God or gods. The question which now invites our attention is this – what sense can we make of the 'up-thereness' in this story?

# FOUR
# *Transcendence and Immanence*

THIS CENTURY HAS seen a massive move away from the transcendent God and towards a God who is 'immanent' in his creation. The transcendent God of Augustine and the wonderful order of the cosmos, reflecting his glory and beckoning us out towards him, no longer prevail in the world-view of Western society. So if we are to make any sense of the notion of a true and beautiful divine order of things, then we need to take a glance at the question of transcendence, to see what it can possibly mean for modern people.

In ancient times the universe was thought to have three levels. Human life was lived on earth, while above it hung the blue dome of the sky where God dwelt, while the third level, the earth descending beneath our feet, solid, dark, airless and paralysing, is the realm of death. Relating with God was therefore easily thought of as a communication between earth and sky. In most European languages the word 'heaven' also means 'sky' and even for modern people the physical heavens are a natural image for the divine. However, the Hebrew and Christian traditions also see that God works in human events, and can be known in people, in relationships, and in all the works of his hands. The incarnation then comes along and enacts this, so that a human being appears who is able to say that in seeing him (on earth) we see the Father (in heaven). However, the image of God-in-the-sky came first, and conceiving God as 'above the earth' has remained a primary Christian image until very recent times. This aspect of God is often referred to by using the word 'transcendent', a word more difficult to pin down than might at first seem.

## TRANSCENDENCE

The notion of God's transcendence can be said to speak of God as wholly 'other', and wholly beyond us; and yet God communicates to us, and receives our communication, in a relationship that we see as a personal one. We are dealing here with something beyond description. How can we find adequate words? All we have to hand are things we are familiar with: therefore our talk about God has to be limited to human-sized images, but they carry with them a danger of misleading us. So we cannot talk of God as 'a person', for our picture of what a person is is less than what God is. By using picture-language with circumspection, however, we are unavoidably brought to say that amongst other things God is indeed 'person'. Yet he is not like any person we know – he is out of sight, beyond our reach, infinite; with God we have to use special forms of communication – worship, prayer, Scripture and the rational processes of theology. Such a picture of the transcendent God poses many difficulties for modern Christians, and some reject it altogether. Partly this is an objection to the images our mind's eye summons up when we think of God. As physical beings we inevitably localize him, either 'out there', beyond the stars, or perhaps in a very involuntary way just in front of and above our foreheads when our eyes are shut. The difficulties are in fact with the way our mind automatically oversimplifies when it images things. As Meister Eckhart took great pains to tell us, our tendency to conjure up images of the ineffable God has to be resisted, because at one level all such images are idols, leading us astray. If I have a picture of God in my mind (and I will have one) it will automatically be a misleading one. So John Robinson warned in *Honest to God* against imaging God 'out there'; God is not simply 'outside' the universe: he is another dimension, whose spatial relationship to the universe is beyond our conceiving. 'Out' and 'in' are inadequate. The difficulty is one of not knowing how we are to conceive of transcendence if it is not in physical terms of being 'beyond'. But God cannot be beyond his creation, because that would confer on it an independent status in a place apart from him: and that is to diminish God. So transcendence itself is a difficult word. Its limitation, as well as its great advantage, is that it springs out of human experience, and this is where we need to go if we would begin to understand it.

*Self-transcendence*

Transcendence has several layers to it in human experience. Closest to home, there are occasions when we seem to pass out of ourselves, we are opened up, and feel ourselves to be enlarged, almost as if our interior selves were taking flight. Sometimes we can use a word like 'ecstasy', which means to 'stand outside ourselves'. This may feel like being opened up towards an infinity of immense richness, an infinity within which we seem to receive the invitation to soar further, and where we feel we have an experience of being profoundly human, living life to the full. It can happen when hearing music, or reading a novel, or taking a walk, or participating in a tragedy, or playing cricket. The experience may be joyful, it may be painful.

Self-transcendence for most people most of the time is triggered off by something, and the things which have the capacity to do this can be said, for the sake of clarity, to fall into two categories. First, there are all the ordinary things of everyday life as they fortuitously happen, be it the sound of a barking dog late at night in the deserted city, or the death of someone we love. The seventeenth century mystic Jacob Boehme had a transcendental experience triggered off in this way as he turned and noticed the light of the sun reflected on a kettle. It was triggered quite unexpectedly.

Second, there are areas in which we actually *expect* to encounter self-transcendence. The arts more often than not function like this, and sex, in all its ambiguity, seems to belong here too. So do the many kinds of social ritual such as marriages, the songs of rugby teams, parties and outings. Some may be trivial, others so exalted as to be beyond the experience of most people.

Self-transcendence ranges from the trivial to the earth-shattering. Whether triggered off in the first way or the second, it can be modest or grandiose. It can be almost indistinguishable from the ordinary, a slight tinge passing briefly across our consciousness, as may be the case, say, when seeing a bird in flight. A 'grand' experience of self-transcendence on the other hand may not be part of common everyday living (although enough research has been done to show that a surprising proportion of the population do claim to have experiences which they describe in this way).

Self-transcendence is an expansion of our 'self-ness', to such an extent that we seem, it is sometimes said, to gain a sense of the unity of all creation. There is another layer to the question, however, which complements it. This is our encounter with the 'otherness' of things, and especially of people. In one sense all my fellow human beings are entirely 'other'. I cannot encompass their personalities or control them, I can never adequately comprehend them. They stand over against me in sovereign otherness. Often it is because of their sheer otherness that people force us to change, to transcend ourselves. That happened to the disciples when they met Jesus, and it happened to many people when they met St Francis. As far as we are concerned, other people are transcendent to us, surprisingly 'other'. It need not involve specially gifted personages – married couples find it stays with them throughout their life – the partner, however close, always retains the quality of otherness. We meet in them a transcendent dimension which is in front of us but separate: people are totally outside us, and are 'other'. Beyond the boundary of our selves (as we imagine it) there is a gap – and then some long way further on there begins the territory of the transcendent other.

Now we discover a strange thing which is at the same time very obvious: the first and perhaps the only bridge we can make to the other is through the material world. Speech, looks, hands, gifts, activities, are the means for knowing one another. Via the things and events of every day we make contact across the gap of otherness. It may be accompanied by no experience that we could call transcendence – no ecstasy, no lifting of the spirits. In an ordinary and mundane way we transcend ourselves in the ordinary communication that takes place between human beings. In getting on with the ordinary round of life, we truly meet each other in a very matter-of-fact way, in the physical dimension. How am I to find a bridge across to that other person who is so *other*? Only words, gestures, objects, actions, can help me. Transcendence and its overcoming are deeply implicated in the physical, practical nature of things. Words, music, dance, common work, chit-chat, meals, evenings out at the pictures. With these bricks slender bridges are built, while deep things nip across on their underside. And still our companion remains right to the end a mysterious other.

## Meeting the God who is Other

It is in such terms too that we meet God; experience of people introduces us to God's own 'otherness'. As with them, the only way that most communication can take place is through material things. This may sound a surprising statement, and yet (as we shall see) it is true. Just as in our daily come-and-go with people around us, so too with God; there may be no extraordinary self-transcendence in our encounter with him, no purple patches of exaltation, and yet we can know we have made contact. It may all be ordinary. Here we meet the odd fact that people can be fervent Christians all their lives and have what they would call an intimate relationship with God, and know his love, and yet say that they have never had a religious experience. I think for example of someone whose faith is transparently built on a rock, leading a loving and caring life given to God in worship and service, and who said, after first participating in the Maundy Thursday Vigil at the altar of repose, that for the first time she thought she knew what people were talking about when they spoke of having a religious experience. The term 'religious experience' can have a wide reference, and it is not clear exactly what people are trying to say when they use the term, or what value can be put upon it, and it needs to be taken with a generous pinch of salt. But there can be little doubting that in using it people are attempting to describe some transcendent experience. Most of the time most Christians' contact with God manages without this, and remains at the same ordinary level as their contact with each other.

Transcendence, then, is all around us. If we want to understand what this word is trying to say about God, then a good place to start is by looking at transcendence in human relationships. If 'person' is an earthly image applied to God, then so is 'transcendence'. We ought not to be afraid of the word by thinking that it has little to do with real life. Similarly, if we have problems in thinking of an eternal transcendent order overarching our ordinary everyday life, then one reason for that will be that our picture of it is divorced from personal relationships. It is not an 'it', but it is 'thou'. Transcendence only makes sense as an attribute of persons, not of things.

43

## IMMANENCE

It is sometimes thought that the direct opposite of God's transcendence is his immanence, or presence, within creation. This
could seem quite probable standing by the sea on a balmy,
sunny day; less so when we are frostbitten in a blizzard; more
evident in a fellow human being; less evident in a brick. The
term immanence (literally: 'remaining in') is often used today
to refer to the fact that God is in the things of daily life. The
enthusiasm with which it can now be used is part of a reaction
against the old distinction between the holy Church and the
profane world. On the rebound from this distortion we are
anxious to emphasize the incarnation. God is not 'out there'
but 'in the midst', we want to say. There is a danger here,
however, that we take immanence to mean that God is *behind*
what we can see in everyday life, an invisible presence behind
the appearances. This is a valid understanding, certainly, but
on its own it is simply transcendence in another guise. There
is a second aspect to immanence which is central to it. This
refers to God's presence in things simply as we see them, not
behind them nor beneath them, not in their 'depth', as if we
have to pass beyond the things we see to a reality which they
veil. God, rather, is present in the simple 'is-ness' of things and
people and events as they are. When a woman gets off a bus,
God is simply present in that event as we see and hear it. In
seeing the event, what our eyes physically see is a manifestation of God. God's immanence is concrete, not abstract. It is
not simply to be sensed with our intuition, but seen with our
eyes, touched with our hands.

We seem to have two uses of the word 'immanence' here. The
first keeps God's transcendence, but brings it nearer, closer to
hand. The other brings it closer still, so that it is encompassed in
an earthly span. I suppose that is what the incarnation is about.
God the Word is not *behind* the child on Mary's knee, but *is* the
child. Christ is not merely represented by the hungry whom we
feed – he *is* the hungry person. Perhaps we could call the two
types 'deepdown immanence' and 'visible immanence'. This
distinction will become important later on, when we look
more closely at how Christ is present in the world and in worship.

44

## Transcendent immanence

The modern proponents of immanence often seem to think in terms of 'deep-down immanence'. John Robinson found it difficult in *Honest to God* to be clear on the point – he said he did wish to speak of God's transcendence, but that it is within the immanence,[1] and elsewhere he says that God is 'the beyond in the midst'. He is convinced God is most near to us in everyday life. Within everyday encounters, and in the varied experiences of our lives, there is a 'depth' and a 'ground' to our being. Here God is to be found. Daily life is thus seen to have a transcendent dimension. Robinson's immanence is a 'deep-down' one. Jürgen Moltmann has the same insight, and chooses to speak of 'immanent transcendence',[2] while Ross Thompson has coined the word 'inscendence'.[3] This deep-down presence of God in the world is really, in fact, another form of transcendence. What is really interesting is to compare it with that on-the-surface presence I have called 'visible immanence'.

## Visible immanence

This refers to the presence of God in the form of what we hear, see and touch. Encounter with them is an encounter with God – he is not *behind* them, but there in, or indeed *as* them. This appears at first sight an extravagant and even shocking claim to make. It is so crucial to the contemporary Church that a good deal of attention will be given to investigating it in Part Two, and I will confine myself here to introducing the issues. Once again, it is with human relationships that we need to start, for visible immanence is in fact all around us in our life. Take, for instance, the story of the prodigal son (Luke 15.11–32). The son returns home after leading the life of a rake, expecting to be punished. Instead his father, seeing him far off, rushes out and throws his arms around him. When the father did this, was he thinking to himself, 'by this embrace I am meaning this, this and this'? Such a thought is absurd. The significance of the embrace is not *behind* it, nor in its depths (though that might be said too). The meaning is one with the embrace itself. The two things cannot be separated without fundamental loss. The 'depth' is present and visible and feelable in the thing itself as it happens to us. That is visible immanence at the human level, in which our person itself, with its feelings, desires, affections, thoughts and so on, becomes so united with an action in the physical world that it is impossible fully to separate all these various elements. What I call visible immanence is attracting increasing attention nowadays in the study of ritual.

## RITUAL

The word 'ritual' carries slightly negative connotations in English, and the anthropologists and others who have in recent years begun to study it speak often of an ingrained Western prejudice against the word. Much patient work is therefore going on in 'defumigating' it.[4] Ritual is in fact one of the most important constituents of our daily life together. Anthropology and psychology now tell us that humanity cannot live without rite, ceremony and communal symbol. 'What goes on in churches, temples, state ceremonies, weddings, feasts, funerals . . . is built upon an urge to ritualize that we share with other animals and that has been part of our make-up since long before we evolved into our present form . . . Human beings share with other animals a communicative world that depends upon gestural routines.'[5] Rituals, ceremonies and paraphernalia borne along by a lively tradition are essential to a healthy life and include many everyday things which it would never occur to us to see as rituals. Making a cup of tea for a neighbour who calls by is a very powerful ritual. If you doubt that, try welcoming them in but offering nothing.

Our distorted understanding of ritual has been examined by many modern writers, but the Methodist theologian W. D. Stacey puts it as well as any:

> The study of primitive ritual has been beggared by simple-minded observers who have taken the ritual at its 'Aladdin-and-the-lamp face value' . . . Both Lienhardt and Douglas [however] assert that ritual . . . is a symbolic activity that moves parallel to experience. It evokes common experience, represents it, deepens it, refashions it where it has gone awry, and, within certain limits, controls it . . .
>
> There is plenty of spontaneous behaviour at the Cup Final, but there is much ritual behaviour too. Before the match there is the wearing of colours, the chanting of slogans, the bellicose gestures performed in concert. After the match there is the public display, the lap of honour, the tour on the open-topped bus. The central phenomenon is a game of football,

but the surrounding ritual attracts an extraordinary amount of attention. The Sunday papers lead, not with a photograph from the game itself, but of the winning captain holding the trophy aloft – the ritual, not the reality![6]

As we are physical and ritual animals, the means we use to engage with each other are predominantly physical and ritual-ized. As every person to us is a transcendent other, there is a need to bridge the gap, and this takes place almost entirely by means of our senses: sight, sound, touch, and smell. We can manage without one of our senses, and there are people who can still communicate even though most of their senses are not func-tioning, but their achievement only serves to highlight the degree to which communication depends on sight, on words, on ges-tures. When these become developed to a sophisticated degree, as they can be in a married couple, then the slightest nuance of movement or expression can speak volumes to the other partner; no other person, however, can pick it up.

### Ritual and God

The situation is not so very different when we turn to engage-ment with the transcendent God. If he is 'person', then we must be able to know him personally, and the only way we know of bridging the gap is that which employs our senses and the phe-nomena of the physical world. The rituals which correspond to the neighbour's cup of tea and the Prodigal's embrace are prayer and worship. There is no other way. If some Christians with 'humanitas' leanings might say that God can be worshipped in enjoying a summer's day or in enjoying our neighbour's com-pany, then we need to be clear about a very important distinc-tion. While God may be encountered in all things, there is no substitute for the kind of encounter that takes place in worship. If the humanitas and eternalism dimensions need each other, that cannot be clearer than in this particular matter. We cannot know God adequately without that specific activity called wor-ship, and this can be relatively easily shown. For even though Elizabeth is John's wife, I cannot communicate with him very well by talking to her. Relationships at second hand are not eas-ily personal. They have to be direct. If not, what does the word 'person' mean? People met Jesus and had physical come-and-go with him. Then he was taken away. But the incarnation was not withdrawn, the principle was not abandoned. The incarnate

Christ makes himself practically and physically known to us as he was known in Galilee. The disciples would not have thought that talking to their neighbour was as good as going out to Galilee to see Christ face to face. What form this Galilee-like encounter takes, it will be our task to discover in the following chapters, but in basic terms it involves what we call worship and prayer.

God may certainly make his presence felt to us in our neighbour, but the centre of our attention must stay with our neighbour. In worship, however, we are enabled to put the emphasis on the other side, on God himself, without being ungracious to our neighbour. The liturgy enables us to aim our attention directly at God, something not possible while we are socializing with our neighbour: such behaviour would make contact with God impossible anyway, for we would simply be using our neighbour as a means for experiencing God. We cannot do that, but we do need some means for direct focus on God, and because we are human this will have a strong physical element. In other words, we use the created world as a means to attend to God, and we call that activity worship, or the liturgy. During worship, our physical involvement leads us to attend to the transcendent, while in 'the world' our brush with the transcendent within it leads our attention back to rest on the physical, and especially our fellow human beings.

In worship we are together as people and community, but our attention has to remain primarily directed to God. Conversely, in daily life we find God, but our direct attention at the moment of our finding has to remain on people. God dwells in his creation because it is good, and he communicates with us via his creation in a way which will naturally keep us *in* the created and not take us out of it. So this on its own cannot work as a way to God. Simone Weil wrote about these two aspects in one of her letters: 'Just as there are times when we must think of God and forget all creatures without exception, so there are also times when, as we look at creatures, we do not have to think explicitly of God . . . There are times when thinking of God separates us from him'.[7]

## EXPLICIT AND IMPLICIT PRESENCE

There is a paradox which needs to be pointed out at this stage: the presence of God in the liturgy is explicit, while in daily life it is implicit. In ordinary life we have to be told about God's presence – it is not self-evident; in worship, however, God is named for what he is, and all the decor, ritual and texts proclaim it. The Divine Liturgy of the Orthodox churches of the East puts a major emphasis in one sense on God's transcendence. It is possible to be critical of many aspects of Orthodoxy, and yet to see that in a curious way their approach is very attractive. We Westerners are attracted, and yet at the same time we want to say, 'this is too transcendent'. There is one particular reason why we are attracted: it is that the screen is physical; the altar and candles, and all the other paraphernalia with which the church is full are objectively physical, and they are explicitly related to God. It is all profoundly immanent. It will also be very prayerful and recollected, but what particularly strikes us is its *material* nature. There is no doubt here that the centre of attention is the God of Jesus Christ. It is explicitly stated in all that we can see and hear.

Now let us go to daily life. George Herbert's *The Priest to the Temple* gives us a fine example of the Christian vision of God's presence in daily life. Herbert writes of the country parson: '[N]either disdaineth he to enter into the poorest cottage, though he even creep into it, and though it smell never so loathsomely; for both God is there also and those for whom God died.'[8]

Notice this striking fact – the reader needs to be told God is in the cottage – the thought would not come naturally to all people, either then or today. Herbert has to point out the transcendent dimension in a scene many readers would assume to be anything but holy. Herbert, and his twentieth-century counterparts, are concerned with the holiness of life, but this can only be seen by a transcendental method, by going beyond appearances. The liturgy operates in the reverse direction. It is concerned with the holiness of the transcendent God, but this can only be entered into by employing immanental methods, whereby God is seen to be at one with what is seen and heard. This is visible immanence at its most obvious.

The odd thing here is that under these terms a solemn eucharist avowedly proclaims an immanent God, while a Christian's attempts to see him in a factory require a transcendental effort! Liturgy, at least in this way, comes down firmly on the side of God's immanence, while for daily life we need a transcendental faith.

Life and liturgy are distinctive and complementary, and we

need to purge our heads of present-day muddles in order to see that complementarity. There are several ways of putting it. One would be to say that there are two ways of relating to God, each is necessary, and each is mediated: (1) attending more directly to God and less directly to people; this is mediated through a living tradition in special rituals, postures, things and roles grounded in the story of Christ; (2) attending more directly to our neighbour and less directly to God; this works through the normal human relationships of everyday life. Both have about them in different ways the immanent and the transcendent.

If the reader is reeling from this switchback ride, we now have to add a further twist again: each dimension seeks to impel us towards the other. The world in the end sends us looking for God; worship on the other hand wants to open us to attend to the world. 'World' and 'Church' are in a continual conversation, a game of divine ping-pong. When we engage in the liturgy with desire, and also engage in the world out of the same desire, there we gain a unique glimpse into the nature of things, and a unique participation in them. If we find God by transcending ourselves through the physical events of everyday life, the same thing happens in religious rites, with the same God and by the same means.

## PRAYER

It is all very well to say that we communicate with God in worship, but is it credible? If modern discomfort with the transcendence of God is partly occasioned by the ways we image him, as an old man in the clouds or a king on a throne, a crisis is brought about even more by the difficulty we have in accepting that between ourselves and this transcendent God there is the possibility of direct communication. Part of our problem arises out of the peculiar presuppositions we have inherited from our forebears. We need to be pulled up short, to have these odd presuppositions pointed out to us, and to be shown what is wrong with them. Anthropology tells us, and Christian history confirms it, that communication with God is rooted in community and in the physical. The West, however, has developed the God of the Gas Board. He is a kind of gas we can sniff, or he is like radio waves which can be picked up by some internal radio station. God is way beyond, behind a cloud, and we perch uncertainly on our ladder, trying to tune in with our very inefficient walkie-talkie. If we shut our eyes tight and concentrate hard we may succeed in tuning in to this abstract being. The God of the Bible, however, is a God of community, and of the physical phenomena of planet Earth. The place where that community and that physicality come into their own is in Christian worship. My prayer, whether done alone or with others, is the community's liturgy in action. We need a course of therapy in order to be able to seize upon this stunning fact with our whole being.

John Robinson saw the problem, but because of our Western presuppositions his response was to reject what he called 'out-there' transcendence because communication with it did not work. Of course it did not work. Tuning in to the invisible, private God of the airwaves simply produced a deafening silence. It was like telephoning somebody who never answered. In David Hare's play *Racing Demon* there is a moment like this when the hero, the Revd Lionel Espy, shouts up 'to heaven' (as the stage directions revealingly say):

> What can you do, Lord? You tell me.
> You show me the way. Go on.[9]

There is a deafening silence in the auditorium. Nothing happens. The implication is obvious: God does not respond, so how can he be there? The kind of clergyman represented by the hero of this play is now a standard character in modern life: the compassionate priest committed to serving others, while having ceased, in effect, to believe. The deafening silence of God, however, is a product of the ingrained and mistaken assumption in the Western mind that our primary contact with God is through the airwaves – the hermit in the head talking to the hermit in the sky. The physical, so necessary to our human communication, has been side-stepped. It is not even considered in this telling scene: all is cold and abstract – there is no whiff of a suggestion of the father's embrace of the prodigal son. Our communication with God is assumed to be fundamentally 'personal', and yet it relies solely on an inbuilt spiritual radio, a method which has little or no connection with how we normally communicate as human beings. We have been left with damaged goods – the God of the airwaves.

This should not be taken to imply a rejection of private prayer and the contemplative life – quite the reverse. They are essential. But if the Church and its liturgy are bypassed then private prayer is seriously, perhaps fatally undermined. It cannot exist without living, active incorporation in the Body of Christ and its worship. This may sound a preposterous thing to say. Was not Simone Weil outside the Christian Church for the whole of her life, and yet is she not recognized as an outstanding woman of prayer? The point is that had the Church not been around, and had Simone Weil not engaged with it at many levels, there is no way she could have witnessed to prayer in the way she did. The prayer of other religions, in addition, has much to teach us. But it still cannot be called Christian prayer, springing from and explicitly referring to the crucified and risen Christ.

The English way of prayer – 'you are nearer to God in a garden . . .' – can only be called sub-Christian. Once, however, the full life of the Body of Christ is entered into, the way is open to that inner journey to which we are all called to some degree or other.


The aim of these first four chapters has been one of setting the scene. We now have in front of us the task of identifying how all the issues raised may fit together in a coherent theological vision through which many disparate elements in the contemporary Church can find the common focus we believe is possible. There is likely to be a bracing price for this, however – the expanding of our horizons.

*Part II*

# FIVE

# *The Mystery of Casel*

I HAVE COINED the terms 'eternalism' and 'humanitas' to refer to two elements in Christian consciousness: the one looks to eternal things, to the Church and to the sacraments for insight and strength, and for the primary locus of God's engagement with us; humanitas on the other hand takes its cue from the nitty-gritty of daily life, convinced that God asks us to look there for insight and for the object of our attention. Both exist in all of us: what varies is the balance and the emphasis. There are people in whom the one dwarfs the other, but those in whom one entirely supplants the other are few. We are talking not of parties, nor of clearly marked-out lines of battle, but of elements existing side by side. If we try and take both seriously, we run the risk of mediocrity, of toning down each in favour of a moderate balance. We need to find a different way, by which we can embrace both in their full vigour. To admit that there is a problem is to say that something has gone wrong; and if that is the case, then how did things look before they went wrong? In the preceding chapters I have traced several paths through history to give an idea of how human attitudes have developed. There is another path now to be followed, which seems to offer some answer to our question. It takes us back to the New Testament and then onwards through the Fathers and into the Middle Ages; and in the Fathers in particular we find the development of a New Testament insight which can help us in our difficulty. The person who did most to bring this to light was the German theologian

Odo Casel (1886–1948). What he produced in his lifetime's writing turns out to be an all-embracing theology, a gospel. I shall rely heavily on him in all that follows, to such a degree that the rest of this book will also function as an introduction to Casel and his theology.

In this chapter most of our attention will be devoted to 'eternalism'. Then as we go along we shall be brought to draw consequences for 'humanitas', which in their turn then bring consequences back the other way.

## CASEL'S MYSTERY-THEOLOGY

Early on in his career Casel (pronounced 'Carzle') had come to a realization about worship which fired him for the rest of his life. It centres on the question of what actually takes place in worship. In his day the Catholic eucharist was understood from the attender's point of view to be a means for receiving grace. Grace became available in worship and was poured on the worshipper. Grace was almost a substance that could be cut up in lengths. Amongst Protestants the picture was not as dissimilar as might be thought. The believer went to church to be edified and instructed, and hopefully to be blessed through personal communion in prayer. Casel came to see that things were not always thus, and he discovered this through his reading of the Fathers, who hardly speak of worship in these terms at all – for them, what happens in worship is an encounter: an encounter with events. The gospel is about unique events through which the human situation has been changed. These events are not dead but alive. Basically, Casel says that Christian worship has a unique character which operates on the principle of the incarnation. It is sacramental. In it the events of Christ's life, death and rising become truly present. He grounded this on a key word in the New Testament, the word 'mystery'. The Fathers pointed out the connection between this and the saving events and Christian worship, showing that all were one thing, a phenomenon which is sacramental. Christ is not simply a human person present in our worship, he is the particular person of those events, and he is not simply present in our heads or in our feelings, but sacramentally present.

This enables us to take a key step in making sense of the relation between eternalism and humanitas. For both the Bible and subsequent Christian tradition speak of Christ's presence in two significant modes: in worship, and in the ordinary things of everyday life. The relationship between these two presences gives us a key to our quest for the vigorous *via media*. It helps us to heal the rift between creation and redemption which has distorted Christianity for many centuries, to bridge the gap between heaven and Charing Cross, between the altar and the paint-spraying shop. As we now trace in more detail the theology of Casel and its implications, it is necessary to bear in mind that the saving events were no ordinary events: they were sacramental. Christian worship has the same sacramentality, and the role of Christ himself in all of it is sacramental. All of those things belong together as a whole; but they are also intimately related to 'secular' life as we live it, revealing its sacramental nature. This whole scheme is grounded in the New Testament, and its heart is the resurrection.

## THE NEW TESTAMENT AND THE RESURRECTION

It is a commonplace to say that the apostles were, as it were, inebriated with the resurrection of Christ. So real was it for them that Paul could speak of dying and rising with Christ in baptism, and of showing forth Christ's death in the eucharist. The first Christians were so gripped by the resurrection that nothing else in life was as real as this. They walked in a new light, the radiance of the Lord's *Pascha*. There is no word in English which can adequately translate *Pascha*. The nearest word is Easter. The *Pascha,* however, is the whole story of the Lord's passion and death on the cross, his resurrection from the dead and his exaltation in glory. This it was which filled their every waking hour.

There was at first no church calendar as we later came to know it, but every Sunday was a little Easter. According to the New Testament this was the most common day of the week for the risen Christ's appearances to his disciples (Matthew 28.9; Luke 24.13ff., 36; John 20.19ff.). Sunday 'stood out in the minds of the early Christians as "the day which the Lord has made" (Psalm 118.24)'.[1] After the period of the New Testament, Ignatius of Antioch says that Christians 'live in observance of the Lord's Day on which our life dawned through him and his death',[2] and from the time of Tertullian we hear of Sunday commonly being called 'Resurrection day'.[3] Initially the only major feast in the year for Christians seems to have been the Passover, now treated not as a Jewish festival, but as the celebration of the Lord's resurrection; and every Sunday of the year was an Easter in its own right. As we read the epistles and other writings of the New Testament we cannot but be struck by the power of the Easter experience animating them all.

## 'MYSTERY'

The Christians of the post-resurrection Church were filled with an energy which impelled them with extraordinary force. Sometimes this is referred to the Holy Spirit, sometimes to Christ himself, and sometimes to his resurrection. Often another word is used, particularly in the Pauline writings: the Greek word *mysterion*. The significance of this word in the New Testament is often obscured by the translation used – in the RSV it is frequently translated 'secret', for instance. *Mysterion,* however, means more than that, and ought always to be rendered by the word 'mystery'. In English the word conjures up detective stories, exotic tales, puzzles, and unknown entities which might instil a sense of awe. We have to go beyond these associations if we are to understand its meaning for the New Testament authors.

### The Mystery is Christ himself

The Mystery of the New Testament is in fact God himself, and by derivation it is Christ. In Colossians, Paul (or whoever the author is) makes his great efforts on their behalf that they might have 'the knowledge of God's mystery, of Christ, in whom are hid all the treasures of wisdom and knowledge' (Colossians 2.2f.). Through our baptism Christ is in us – 'this mystery . . . is Christ in you, the hope of glory' (Colossians 1.27).

### First hidden and then revealed

The Mystery is hidden, and in due time will be made manifest. It has always been present in the world through all the ages, hidden like a seed, but with Christ's coming it was in the end made manifest. It is 'the mystery hidden for ages and generations but now made manifest to his saints' (Colossians 1.26). Again, 'we speak God's wisdom in a mystery which was kept hidden, which God decreed before the ages for our glorification' (1 Corinthians 2.7); it is the 'mystery which was kept silent about for long ages' (Romans 16.25).

58

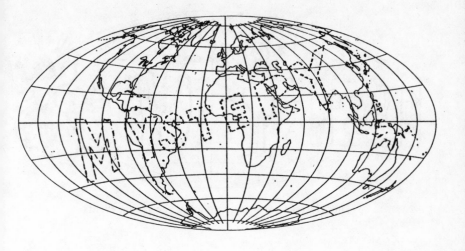

It is also God's great plan for creation. God has 'made known to us in all wisdom and insight the mystery of his will, according to his purpose which he set forth in Christ as a *plan* for the fullness of time, to unite all things in him, things in heaven and things on earth' (Ephesians 1.9f.). That plan is not a thing but a person, the person of Christ.

The theme of the Mystery being hidden and in process of being made manifest among those who believe connects with Mark's characteristic language about the kingdom. In Mark's gospel the kingdom is depicted as pressing upon us, neither completely present nor entirely in the future; and yet at the same time it is a kingdom which is to come. This state of affairs can only be seen by those who have eyes to see, and Jesus has to explain to the disciples why there are those who cannot see it: 'To you has been given the *mystery* of the kingdom of God. But for those outside, all is in parables' (Mark 4.11).

### The Mystery is the saving events

This leads us to a key aspect of this notion: the Mystery burst forth from its hiddenness in the saving events. It is all the stupendous events of the saving story, at whose centre is Christ.

The Mystery becomes manifest in the saving events

Great indeed, we confess, is the mystery of our religion:

> He was manifested in the flesh,
> vindicated in the Spirit,
> seen by angels,
> proclaimed among the nations,
> believed in in the world,
> taken up in glory (1 Timothy 3.16).

We see in the passages quoted above an attempt to put into words something which is alive, and because of its liveliness it eludes description. Its vitality is Christ's story, it is Christ himself, it is that life which was released at the bursting of the grave, coursing through the veins of the first Christians, impelling them out to take the message to the peoples of the earth. The deep· root of this, piercing down to the centre of their being, is the memory of being *with* Christ; and this being-with-Christ continues undiminished since his death; in fact it is heightened, in the times when they are together for worship.

## The Mystery becomes present in worship

The 'Mystery hidden through the ages' is time and again present to the primitive Church in its worship. In the Mystery we are coacting with Christ, reliving the events. Here there are two key texts: Galatians 6, where Paul speaks of the death of Christ being present

The Mystery is made manifest in worship

in baptism – in the waters we die with him, so he is in that moment dying and rising with us; and 1 Corinthians 11, where Paul says that 'so often as you eat this bread and drink this cup you show forth the Lord's death until he comes again'. The primitive Church could not think of the crucifixion in isolation from the other saving deeds of Christ – so the references to his crucifixion and death have to be understood as references to the whole *Pascha,* all the events which make up the acts of our redemption. So to show forth his death is to show forth the whole Easter Mystery.

To sum up so far, the New Testament speaks of a Mystery which until now has been present in the world, yet hidden and unrecognized: (a) it is the divine presence, (b) it is Christ, (c) Christ is God's hidden plan for his creation, (d) now no longer hidden but made manifest in the saving events, (e) this manifesting of the Mystery at the time of those events now lives on in the sacramental life of Christ's Body the Church. Here is the connection between the Mystery-language in Scripture and the Christian sacraments. At this point we need to stop for a moment and take a careful look at what exactly we mean in using the word 'sacrament': for our use of this word traces its origins back to the word 'Mystery'.

## MYSTERIES AND SACRAMENTS

It is no coincidence that Christian worship, and especially certain kinds of worship, came to be known as 'mysteries'. Worship is 'celebrating the mysteries': this language grew automatically out of an understanding of worship as engagement with the Mystery. Then came another development: out of the word 'mystery' grew the word 'sacrament'. 'Sacrament' is the Latin word which was used to translate the Greek *mysterion*. The sacraments are the 'mysteries' (as they are still called in the Orthodox churches – the 'seven mysteries'), and they are called that because the New Testament Mystery of salvation becomes present in them. In baptism that mystery which was 'kept secret for long ages' is made manifest. The same is true of the eucharist, and of many other things, as we shall see. Jesus said to Zacchaeus, 'Today has salvation come to this house' (Luke 19.9). In the Christian mysteries salvation comes under our roof. When the Fathers, and the Orthodox churches in unison with them, speak of baptism, eucharist, marriage, and so on, as mysteries, this is because they are actions in which we become involved in the Mystery, the *Pascha* of Christ which filled the apostles with burning zeal.

In the early Church after the New Testament period the word 'mystery' is used frequently, and in a variety of senses, principally referring to the saving work of God in Christ. It includes the whole of salvation history, and the re-presentation of it in worship. And it is used to refer to the liturgy, and all that came to be called the sacramental order. As Günther Bornkamm puts it, the 'relation between the saving acts and their cultic representation is brought out particularly well by the fact that both are called *mysterion*'.[4] That was the understanding of the early Church, whose heartland was in the East.

### Translation problems

When this terminology moved over to the West it ran into translation problems. The word *mysterion* was foreign to Latins and smacked of the exotic and pagan, calling to mind the mystery-cults which were then prevalent. The Romans therefore opted for a military word, *sacramentum,* the oath a soldier made on joining the army. In this way the word 'sacrament' appeared, carrying the same meaning as 'mystery', but retaining some of its own military flavour. Both words were used interchangeably, but the use of *mystery* gradually fell into the background, partly perhaps because of its pagan associations for Romans. The result was a damaging of the link between the sacraments and the Mystery of the New Testament. 'Mystery' is a New Testament word, 'sacrament' is not. For Leo the Great (d. 461), the word 'sacrament' still has the broader meaning: for him too it refers to the saving deeds of Christ. In the other Latin Fathers, and in liturgical books up to the early Middle Ages, the two words 'sacrament' and 'mystery' are more or less interchangeable. Sometimes 'mystery' has the broader sense, with 'sacrament' referring rather to the actual rites themselves,[5] but more often than not the two words become interchangeable, and this survives even today in some turns of phrase. The Book of Common Prayer continued the medieval custom of referring to the eucharist as the 'holy mysteries'. In baptism also it speaks of the 'mystical washing away of sin'. The original breadth of associations of this vocabulary, however, had by this time been obscured.

*Many sacraments*

Not only was the word 'mystery' broad in its meaning, but in its sense of 'sacrament' (as we would say) it was applied more widely. There was as yet with Leo, and for a long time afterwards, no notion of 'seven sacraments'. As Salvatore Marsili puts it, 'for Leo there is no distinction . . . the sacrament is a rite which makes present a saving reality, and this can happen in a thousand different ways'.[6] Only later were the sacraments limited to seven.

However, while the word 'mystery' continued to be used in the East, retaining its original polyvalence, in the West the word 'sacrament' went through successive narrowings, until it was finally used simply to refer to precise moments or *loci* of divine action through effective signs, the power of these precise moments being heightened in direct proportion as the other 'sacraments' (such as the calendar or the divine office) lose this sacramental understanding; and the refining process goes even further, so that there arises an order of 'second-class' sacraments, called *sacramentals*. In the Orthodox churches, however, the word 'sacrament' does not exist (except as a borrowing from the West for the purposes of theological teaching): the word used, as we have seen, is 'mystery'. Under Western influence a similar seven were eventually identified by the Orthodox from the seventeenth century onwards, but because these seven are called 'mysteries', the breadth of the term mitigates the over-precision of the word 'sacrament'.

If it was only in the Middle Ages that the concept of 'sacrament' came to be narrowed down to the familiar seven (or two by the Reformation), the mysteries, the sacraments, would therefore seem rightly to include baptism, the eucharist, the pastoral offices, but also the calendar, monasticism, funerals (frequently described as mysteries by the Eastern Fathers) and other rites and paraphernalia. This may seem surprising, and may appear to imply a devaluing of the notion of a sacrament. In actual fact it means the reverse – recovery of this history makes us realize how much of the Church's life and practice we have been underestimating.

## THE 'MYSTERY' IN THE FATHERS

So we come to the heart of Odo Casel's discovery: the sacraments, the 'mysteries', are called by that name because they are the Mystery. When the people of God gather in worship they enter into engagement with the risen Christ whose presence was so vivid for the apostles – the saving Mystery. For Casel it is to be understood in terms of the saving events. They become present, are made manifest, in the mysteries. To demonstrate this he points to a host of patristic texts, among which his favourite was a saying of Leo the Great: 'What was present in the Lord has passed into the mysteries'.[7] In other words, what people experienced in first-century Palestine when Christ passed through, we encounter now in the mysteries of the liturgy. Theodore of Mopsuestia says of the eucharist that, 'In contemplating with our eyes, through faith, the facts that are now being re-enacted – that he is again dying, rising and ascending into heaven – we shall be led to the vision of the things that took place beforehand on our behalf.'[8] He even adds at one point concerning the eucharistic celebration, that 'it is necessary, therefore, that our Lord should now rise from the dead by the power of the things which are taking place'.[9] Elsewhere he says that 'we sacramentally perform the events that took place in connection with our Lord'.[10] Gregory the Great says that 'In a completely unique manner this sacrifice . . . makes present for us, in Mystery, that which has already happened: the death of

In the Mysteries we become involved in the Mystery

the Lord'.[11] Leo, again, says, 'As often as the remembrance of the sacrifice which is well-pleasing to you is celebrated, the work of our redemption is made present'.[12] Ambrose puts it in this way: 'we are now no longer in the shadow, nor in the figure, nor in the type, but in the reality; O God, not by mirrors and enigmas, but face to face have you revealed yourself to me, and I find you in your mysteries'.[13]

Casel was profoundly struck by the way the language of the 'Mystery' repeatedly bounced up at him from the pages of the Fathers, and it eventually became clear that a problem which was taxing liturgical reformers, and whose answer they 'knew in their bones' but could not formulate, was in fact being touched on in this language – and so a breach was being made in a blocked channel.

There was, however, one problem with the Fathers: as we can find so often in their writings, and indeed in Scripture itself, when we think we have nailed them down to a nice tidy formula, we discover they say in another place something which seems ever so slightly to go against it. Not only that, but they rarely go as far as is required by our needs, so that what they were very passionate about is nevertheless often painted in pastel colours and shifting shapes. Ancient writers are, for example, habitually imprecise and woolly in describing the texts and actions of worship (and so they make frustrating reading for liturgical scholars) and they are often as elusive when dealing with abstract concepts. In this way while Casel amassed scores of quotations from the Fathers on this theme of the 'Mystery', few of them quite say enough to elucidate it for those who are meeting it for the first time. He therefore had to be more bold than they in stating their doctrine with greater precision. The result, like great scientific discoveries which are clinched by a small intuition, was a picture which for many has proved so breathtaking and fascinating that it has contributed to a revolution in our understanding of the Church and the liturgy which has yet to receive the full recognition it deserves. As far as we are concerned in our own investigation, Casel opens up for us a way of seeing how heaven and earth stand in relation, and of discerning the connection between the liturgy and daily life. This will become clearer as we proceed.

## THE PRESENCE OF THE SAVING EVENTS

Odo Casel assumes, along with mainstream tradition, that the liturgy lies at the heart of the Church's life. He then goes on to say that the Mystery becomes uniquely present in the liturgy. This is especially true of the eucharist, where, according to Casel, the saving mysteries of Christ, with the cross and resurrection at their heart, come into the midst. The gathered worshippers are at Golgotha and at the empty tomb, and are enveloped in their saving and converting power. This presence of the 'Mystery' comes about in the liturgy and in the liturgical symbols. Christian worship is *action,* he was fond of saying, and this worship-action is a memorial of the Mystery, a re-presenting of it. Casel liked to repeat a formula which for him summed it up in a nutshell: 'The Mystery is a holy cultic action in which a reality of our salvation becomes present: by carrying out this rite the worshipping community becomes involved in this saving deed, and so salvation comes upon them'.[14]

The phenomenon has many aspects to it. Sometimes it can be most vivid in the calendar, which, Casel says, is in this way a sacrament in its own right. At Christmas we really are at the crib, in the presence of the mystery of the incarnation. In Holy Week we really do kneel before the cross on Golgotha, and are truly present in the paschal vigil at the bursting of the gates of

66

hell and the rising of Christ from the dead. If you are familiar with the liturgy at these times you may already have some sense of what Casel means. (It cannot be emphasized strongly enough, however, that we are not talking about personal experiences in the first instance, but objective realities.) In *baptism* Casel says that the cross and resurrection must inevitably be present if the candidates are really to die and rise with Christ (how we can say this without it seeming to be make-believe will emerge as we proceed). There is a real presence of Christ here – it is not confined to the eucharist. Various authors (not least Pope Paul VI) speak of 'real presences' which are distributed through the Church's life. There is a real presence of Christ in ordination, in anointing of the sick, in the daily office: the saving Mystery becomes real in varied and analogous ways in all the sacraments and sacramentals, and is closely related to the physical characteristics of these things. The Mystery is physical, not simply abstract – the gospel is the gospel of the incarnation. This may seem obvious in the eucharist, if you hold a high doctrine of the real presence, but Christian practice has made the mistake in the past of concentrating this presence so exclusively in the bread and the wine that it has lost sight of the other real presences distributed through the eucharist itself, in the people, the proclamation of the Word, the prayers and the peace, the preparation of the gifts, eucharistic prayer, fraction and communion, and in the total action. All of these things and others too go to make up the physical phenomenon of the presence of the Mystery, that paschal glory which gripped the apostles with its wonder and filled them with faith. C. H. Dodd, in elucidating the word *anamnesis,* puts this in strong terms:

> In the eucharist . . . the Church perpetually reconstitutes the crisis in which the Kingdom of God came in history. It never gets beyond this. At each eucharist we are *there* – we are in the night in which he was betrayed, at Golgotha, before the empty tomb on Easter day, and in the upper room where he appeared; *and* we are at the moment of his coming, with angels and archangels and all the company of heaven, in the twinkling of an eye at the last trump. Sacramental communion is not purely a mystical experience, to which history . . . would be in the last resort irrelevant; it is bound up with a corporate memory of real events.[15]

If the above interpretation of the word 'Mystery' is correct, and it is the one assumed from very early on by Christian writers, and endlessly repeated by the Fathers and in Christian tradition, then it forces us to ask several .questions about the way we understand a whole range of things, such as the person of Christ in prayer, belief, salvation, the Church, and all the content of the Creeds and Christian thought and tradition. We tend to divide them into tidy compartments: God, Jesus, belief, the Scriptures, the events of Christ's life, and so on – but this will not do. We might say we go to church to 'meet Jesus', but that is not good enough. We want to get to know God – but that is an inadequate way of putting things. I may believe in the salvific effect for me of Christ's life and death and rising, but that on its own is a diminishment. It is not enough to talk of these things in this way. Odo Casel reminds us of something which the Church has half forgotten, even if it has never lost it completely: that we are dealing with a living presence encompassing all of these things – not a row of separate light bulbs, each working off its own current, but a noonday sun whose sure strong rays pierce to the bones of creation. Casel points to age-long tradition which says that in worship something of a totally extraordinary nature happens: we engage with the Mystery, we are taken into it – we are taken into him. The Mystery becomes *present*.

## Physically present

The Christian gospel is first of all a physical phenomenon. Incarnation, ministry, passion, death and resurrection are all described as physical events. William Temple once said that 'Christianity is the most materialistic of all the great religions'.[16] Perhaps he might have thought also of Berkeley's dictum that physical matter is 'one of the languages of God'. In our human development we express ourselves through physical ritual long before we do so through language, an established fact for anthropologists, but perhaps a surprise to those of us who have not before considered it. The baby learns to ritualize before it learns to speak, and it depends for a large part on received traditions of ritual. Tom Driver writes:

> The brain of the newborn human is not suited for interaction with nature alone. It requires a *cultural* milieu . . . This dependence of the human brain upon a cultural environment indicates that culture became a significant part of human development *before* the physical evolution of the brain was

68

complete. Otherwise, the brain would have evolved, like that
of other mammals, with much less dependence on cultural
factors . . .

Consider a child as she finds out how to exchange smiles, to
crawl, to walk, and to dance. She learns a lot by experiment
but she is immensely aided by her society's pathways – that is,
examples for her to follow.[17]

The West in particular has a hard lesson to relearn: that nothing
can be understood without the participation of our bodies.
Words, thoughts, 'inner experiences', are all illusion if they have
no physical dimension. Nothing can be said about a walk on a
mountainside that can come anywhere near the effect of doing
it. Nothing much can be said about any abstract concepts at all
were it not that our eyes and ears and hands and limbs had for
many years continually engaged with the physical world. Yet
our physicality is so much second nature that we cease to notice
it and happily entertain illusions of pure thought and abstract
belief. The Mystery is 'sacrament', however: physical, visible,
part of the material world.

One reason why Casel was so fired by the physical dimension
of the Mystery as it is mediated by Scripture and the Fathers was
that this revealed in a clear light the poverty of the understanding of the eucharist current among Roman Catholics at the time.
The mass, as we saw, had come to be seen as a means for dis-
pensing grace. Casel insisted that this was bad theology. Nor
was it good enough to speak of the 'presence of God' – nor even
the 'presence of Jesus' – those terms on their own could cover a
multitude of sins, and any convenient Jesus of our imaginings
could be the result. In order to gain the fullness of salvation,
humanity must *take part itself* in the saving work of the
redeemer. Neither the 'person' of Christ who accomplished the
work of salvation, nor the 'divine life' which was active in him,
nor the body and blood of the Lord which were offered in the
most important saving act, are enough for this. We cannot really
participate in the redeeming work unless it is present here and
now.[18] However important they may be, simple ideas about
'worshipping God' or 'receiving grace' are secondary compared
with this. Through the liturgy of the Church, we become simul-
taneous with the 'charter events', and we share in the primordial
experience of the apostles, in a manner which is both spiritual
and physical.

*A higher gift than grace*

As a result of all this, grace is now seen in a more satisfactory perspective. It remains of fundamental importance, not only to the liturgy but to the whole of Christian living. Augustine was quite right to point to Paul's high doctrine of grace; but our sight has to be trained beyond that grace to its source. In Newman's words, there is a higher gift than grace: 'God's presence and his very self'.[19] Grace abounding continues to stand at the heart of the good news, but now we can look back behind medieval diminishments to recover the primitive vision of grace imparted through engagement with the God of salvation history.

## DIFFICULTIES

The theology of the Mystery has great power and fascination, but how can things conceivably be so? To some of Casel's contemporaries it was far from congenial. He met strong opposition for instance from those who saw the faith as a logical system capable of being encapsulated in rational categories, a breed represented by scholastic theology which since has largely disappeared from the main stage in the Roman Catholic Church. That kind of scholastic was easily shot down, although at the time they found some vulnerable chinks in Casel's armour. One was the fact that he failed to demonstrate his teaching from sufficiently categorical statements in Scripture and the Fathers. The cumulative evidence, however, combined with immemorial Church tradition, made his position very difficult to assail. Another weak point was the parallel Casel drew with the so-called 'mystery religions' of late antiquity. While he remained content to point out the parallel, he was mistaken to do it so repeatedly as almost to imply that there was a direct Christian inheritance from them (something which he denied). There was a relatively superficial connection in, for instance, the kind of ceremonies which came to be incorporated into the baptismal rite under the influence of the mystery religions later on, but there was little or no connection at foundation level. Raymond Brown has shown that the term 'mystery' (*raz*) was used abundantly in Jewish literature, and the New Testament authors had no need to look beyond it to the mystery religions for its interpretation.[20] Because of the particular kind of information available to him, Casel had in fact chosen a side-path in seeking the context for the emergence of the Christian Mystery, a path which was only of incidental relevance, putting more weight on it than it could take. His pointing to the mystery religions as 'preparing the way' was not entirely invalid, in that it revealed fundamental truths at an anthropological level, and in that sense his observations on the mystery religions continue to have force. But had the necessary scholarship been available to him at that time, he could have pointed to stronger precedents in the Jewish notion of *zikkaron*.

*Zikkaron* denotes an understanding of making remembrance, particularly in connection with sacrifice, where the thing commemorated becomes truly present. It is familiar to many nowadays in the term *anamnesis*, which appears in the New Testament accounts of the last supper, and which in English is usually translated 'remembrance'. This Jewish type of realistic remembrance differs from the Christian in that it thinks more in terms of travelling back to the saving events rather than their being summoned into the community's presence. Hence the traditional words at the Passover: 'it is you who are passing through the Red Sea'. A rabbinic saying runs: 'It was a night of vigil for the Lord. In that night they were set free, and in the same night in the future too they will be set free, because it is said, "It is the same night for the Lord" (Exodus 12.42)'.[21] So far the reader might be asking whether there is anything so very unusual in what is being said here. The response is at least twofold: (a) this thinking was so effectively propagated by Casel that it has become familiar to many people. We need think only of the documents of the Second Vatican Council, or the WCC Lima Document (*Baptism, Eucharist and Ministry*).[22] The origin of these ideas in Odo Casel's theology has been largely overlooked in the English-speaking world, while the theology itself has become common currency; (b) because we fail to go back to Casel's writings, we fail to grasp the full force of what he is saying and its revolutionary nature.

There is continuing debate regarding the extent to which the terms *anamnesis* and *zikkaron* can be understood in the way set out by Casel, but it is enough to say here that, had he been writing later, he would have done better to follow that road in doing his archaeological digs, than to follow that of the mystery religions. Towards the end of his life he began to recognize this, and he made appropriate alterations to a late edition of at least one of his works.[23]

## Is it subjective?

Casel easily survived all these onslaughts, only to come under more serious attack from his own supporters. In attempting to answer the question, 'how?', various theories were put forward to explain it in a subjective sense: the saving events were really present, so far as the individual could perceive them; or the mystery within the saving acts was present, but not the acts themselves, and this is only identifiable in the heart of the believer. Not content with routing his adversaries, Casel here dropped a rain of depth-charges on his supporters. He thundered that they were denying the incarnation and relaxing the connection between our salvation and its historical basis (we could add that in fact they were preaching a form of receptionism). He insists time and again that the presence is not abstract, it is physical. We are dealing here not with something that can be 'read into' a liturgical mime: we are dealing with the physical presence of the cross and the empty tomb. In other words, the liturgical action, its participants, its paraphernalia, the whole way it is enfleshed, is a sacrament in which saving deeds are made visible, tangible, smellable and hearable.

These words are enough to make any of us stop in our tracks. The notion of the physical will receive our attention in due course, but for the present it may be sufficient to express it in this way: in the Church we engage with God; the physical actions and phenomena of this worship are so intimately part of the engagement that we find ourselves speaking of it in terms of the physical – not only that, but certainly that.

Casel clearly holds a very high doctrine of the liturgy, but one entirely consonant with the New Testament and the Fathers. The liturgy as a physical phenomenon is shown to be central to what the gospel is about. Saving history is not dead and gone, it is alive and forward-pressing. It is a living entity in our midst, the saving deeds of Jesus, carrying on their work. The liturgy of the Church as a result is nothing less than the manifestation of Christ's developing saving work, here and now, the latest stage in the work of our redemption.

'The liturgy', says Casel, 'is nothing other than the God-man Jesus carrying forth his work on the earth'.[24]

*How?*

If, founding himself on such texts as the baptismal charter in Romans 6.1–11, and Paul's saying that as often as we eat the bread and drink the cup we show forth the Lord's death (1 Corinthians 11.26), not to mention countless texts in the Fathers, Casel felt able to assert that the saving events were present in the celebration of the liturgy, we still legitimately have to ask: 'how?'. How does this become credible and proclaimable? To Casel it was not granted to be able to answer that question in more than the most general terms. Philosophically and theologically he was not equipped to analyse further the vision which had been vouchsafed to him by the tradition. He was content to say that the Mystery was beyond our comprehension.

Since Casel's death in 1948 his teaching has gained an established place in Western theology, and has been profoundly influential both on the Second Vatican Council and on Roman Catholic liturgy since then, not to mention that of the other churches (cf. for example its affirmation at the Faith and Order conferences at Lund, 1952, and Montreal, 1963, and especially the Lima Document *Baptism, Eucharist and Ministry*).[25] It has always been regarded, however, as unfinished business. Much work remains to be done in teasing it out, and in establishing the connection between this theory and actual experience. In particular, certain questions are immediately raised, which puzzle even the most sympathetic hearers:

(a) How can we realistically speak of the presence of the *saving events*?

(b) If something so unusual happens in our worship, then what *counts* as Christian liturgy, and who counts as celebrating it? Hence: is the Church special?

(c) How can the Mystery be *physically* present?

(d) Does it square with our actual experience of worship?

(e) If this understanding of the Mystery is so central, why did it appear to be forgotten for a thousand years or more? What happened to it in the long interval?

(f) What relevance does all this have to daily life, and is such teaching accessible to ordinary Christians in the parish?

If Casel's message is to be taken seriously, a credible response has to be made to questions such as these. A response can indeed be made, and this will be our aim in what follows, and in the process we shall begin to see heaven and earth from a changed perspective.

# SIX

# How? – Presence, Scripture and Disclosure

THROUGHOUT THIS BOOK we rely heavily on Casel's theology of the Mystery. There are two reasons why he has such a high profile: one is that he is unique among modern theologians in filtering through to us the outlook of the early Church and the Fathers regarding the Mystery; secondly, while it would be impossible to write on the Mystery without reference to Casel, there is no basic introduction in English that readers can be referred to. This book, therefore, ventures a double task, pursuing the quest of the Mystery, and providing an introduction to its greatest modern exponent as we go along.

The Mystery-theology of Casel begins with the perspective of *eternalism;* from there we are led to conclusions about its sister perspective of *humanitas.* We now turn to the first question posed at the end of Chapter 5: how does the Mystery become present in Christian worship?

## PRESENCE

In Christian mission we proclaim the living Christ of real historical events: the person at the centre of events through which we were saved. So when we talk of the presence of Christ in worship we are talking also of the presence of those events. In order to make sense of this, we need first of all to look at 'presence' itself.

The notion of presence is not foreign to the Bible. Where two or three are gathered in his name, the Lord will be present in their midst (Matthew 18.20). If we open when he knocks he will come in to us (Revelation 3.20). 'Behold', he says, 'I am with you always, until the end of the world' (Matthew 28.20). By the time John's gospel came to be written the Word was spoken of as *pros ton Theon* – before, or in the presence of, God (John 1.1). In the resurrection appearances the miracle is that Christ is there, and is seen to be there. However, the fact of a person's presence is something we normally take for granted in talking to them. We do not make a song and dance about the fact of their presence, and so we have to ask, why this need to talk in terms of 'presence'?

One way of using the notion of 'presence' is to say someone is simply there, in the same place as ourselves. We use it of people, but not usually of things. 'The sideboard is present' suggests it has walked into the room and presented itself, which is impossible. When we speak of presence we are thinking of something alive, an animal or a person, and this is one reason why we have difficulties with the phrase, 'the saving events are present', for events are things. If we are to use such words, then, we are not to think of the events as things, but as persons: persons-in-action. The presence is that of Christ, dynamic and active. Casel calls him the Spirit-filled Christ (another term he uses may startle the unforewarned reader: he speaks repeatedly of the 'pneumatic' Christ, from the Greek word *pneuma*, which means Spirit).[1] But while presence is normally applied to persons, this needs further qualification. A person can be physically present, but their mind totally elsewhere. I can say I was present at the meeting of a committee, but if I was absorbed in a daydream my presence was not of much account. We find it possible, on the other hand, to conceive of spirits (or God) being present when apparently they have nothing physical to show for it. Humanity has always been able to imagine invisible presences, ghosts, spirits, gods, without having any problem with the complete absence of sensory data. Here we can see clearly that 'presence' is normally used of people, not things, for we can have a sense of the invisible presence of Napoleon, but not of an invisible sideboard. If we said of a haunted house that there was a presence of a death, it would be the *persons* involved in that death that would be present, rather than the weapons involved, or the abstract notion of death itself. Whenever we use the word 'presence', then, we expect it to refer to persons.

## THE ABSENCE OF GOD

George Steiner points out that for modern people God is absent, not present. He has not yet completely disappeared, however – there is a backwash, an echo left behind by his departure, something which is reflected in many works of art and literature which worry over the absence of God; but soon even this echo will disappear:

> It is like the recession from us of one whom we have loved or sought to love or of one before whom we have dwelt in fear. The distancing is, then, charged with the pressures of a nearness out of reach, of a remembrance torn at the edges. It is this absent 'thereness', in the death-camps, in the laying waste of a grimed planet, which is articulated in the master-texts of our age. It lies in Kafka's parables, in the namings of Golgotha in Beckett's Endgame, in the Psalms to No-one of Paul Celan. It is, to reverse Kierkegaard's phrase, where the helper is no longer the help, but one still resonant with recent receding.[2]

There is a venerable Christian tradition which suggests that such experiences of the absence of God can be in fact *our* absence from him, whom we cannot see because our eyes are out of focus. Our society finds it hard to sense God's presence, partly because we have ceased to revere and to worship. In worship God's presence calls us towards his present-ness, so that we become more present to him, more present to ourselves, more present to our neighbours, and to the entire physical order in which we are set. It is we who grow in the quality of presence. To speak of presence is thus also to speak of attention. The degree to which I attend to a Mozart opera is the degree to which I am able to make myself present to it, the fullest presence being a balance of physical, cognitive, emotional and other modes of attention. Growth in attention to God is part and parcel of our growth in attention to others and to ourselves. Our sense of the absence of God, therefore, is a way of saying that we find it difficult to attend to him.

## DYNAMIC PRESENCE

In Mircea Eliade's novel *The Forbidden Forest* there appears a character named Anisie who seems to have advanced far along the road of being present.

> 'He's discovered a great secret,' Stefan whispered, leaning over the table. 'This man has learned how to live. He lives as a man, as a total being. He doesn't let himself live by his tissues, his glands, his reflexes, the way all the rest of us do.'
>
> 'But how do you know he lives in a different way?' Biris enquired, beginning to search for his cigarettes.
>
> 'I've seen how he cleans the trees in his orchard,' began Stefan with a mysterious smile. 'I sat on the porch and watched him. Then I understood. I was convinced that his work is of a different quality from ours. Besides, I was prepared for this because I had known something of the same bliss too when I was painting. Only in my case it's not a matter of serious work with a definite object as it is with him. He cleans the trees of the caterpillars. I watched carefully and I felt that he was present in every motion. He wasn't thinking of anything else when he was working on a tree. His mind didn't wander. I perceived that the tree revealed itself to him in its totality. For him it wasn't a simple object, one among thousands of others of its kind, as it would appear to us, to the majority of men. To him at that particular moment, the tree that he was cleaning revealed the entire Universe. He saw it in its totality, roots, branches, leaves, parasites . . .'[3]

If the modern age has a vivid sense of the absence of God, then one way of expressing this is in terms of our incapacity to be present ourselves, even to the creation which is all around us. We regard it as an object to be manipulated for our purposes, and are unable to see it as having a mysterious life of its own inviting us to attend to it. We have located what counts as 'real' so firmly within the individual, that it has become difficult for us to see the natural world as making demands upon us from a life of its own. Only now are we beginning to regain a sense of that, with the increasing attention given to 'green' issues. God in his turn is difficult for us to be present to, because in our minds he has become a thing, an entity to be used for our own ends. God is not static, however, but alive: all times are his and all the ages, all things are present to him. The events

of Christ's earthly life are part of his presence, which is not a
'something' but a 'someone', and someone not just sitting
there, but engaged in action. To such a one it is entirely possible for us to seek to be 'present', to attend with the whole of
ourselves. But we are absent, because we find it difficult to
believe God is alive.

We are dealing both with action and at the same time with
stillness. A still presence can be full of life – this is a common
experience both in ordinary life and in prayer: to be absolutely
still in the presence of another who is also absolutely still,
whether sitting quietly by the fire with another, or praying alone
in God's presence in church. Such a stillness can be wooden, a
mere absence of activity, or it can be a living stillness. It is the
living stillness with which we are concerned. It is a stillness of
action. This is one reason why some people express dissatisfac-
tion with the term 'presence' – it can simply imply being there,
without any sign of life. And it is one of the problems people can
have with doctrines of the real presence in the eucharist, for this
is sometimes expressed in terms which make the presence a
static thing: it has become reified. There is also another problem
with the word 'presence': not only is God's presence full of life,
but also our own relating to God often involves real action, the
saying of words mentally or aloud, the performance of liturgical
actions, and singing. Here is a paradox: there is both stillness
and action, but even the stillness of which we are talking is one
that is active.

Action comes before knowledge, as Wittgenstein insistently
tried to show; our first experience of learning comes not by sitting still and being told something, but by *doing*. 'Language did
not emerge from some kind of ratiocination . . . Children do not
learn that books exist, that armchairs exist, etc. – they learn to
fetch books, sit in armchairs.'[4] There are problems with Casel's
use of the word 'presence' because although it refers to a key
aspect of the Mystery, it can fail to do justice to it, and is in danger of implying something quite the opposite to the real Mystery
– a dead presence.

This takes us again to the New Testament, which speaks of
the presence of the Lord, but of more too. The gospels would be
strange books if they spoke solely of Christ's presence. They
speak of his action. He is active, in addition to being 'present'
like another person on the bus. In his ministry he calls others to

be with him by *following* him. In the synoptic gospels he proclaims another presence bearing down on his hearers: 'The kingdom of God is at hand' (cf. Matthew 3.2, 4.17, 12.28, etc.). At the last supper he seems to proclaim the continuing presence of his body, in the bread and the wine, and the operative verb is *do*: do this in my remembrance. Even in the post-resurrection appearances he speaks with the disciples, eats with them, breathes on them the Holy Spirit, allows them to touch him. We talk of the saving *acts* which are to be remembered: Christ was incarnate, he taught, healed and witnessed, he loved and attracted love, he died and rose again. A static notion of presence does not begin to say all that must be said, and interpreters of Casel have therefore searched for other words, such as encounter, engagement, involvement, commerce, exchange, participation. None of these on its own seems sufficient. In Christian worship the events described in the Scriptures are happening. And they are not things but persons: Christ, that is, and the Holy Trinity, and the kingdom, and humanity, and us. The Christ of the events of our salvation and we ourselves are, together, *happening*.

## CASEL'S USE OF THE TERM 'PRESENCE'

Because Casel's preference, and the preference of many official pronouncements in the ecumenical domain, is to speak in terms of 'presence', this is surely one of the reasons why there are not a few who find his vision difficult to embrace without reservation. There are many passages where Casel emphasizes the dynamic nature of this presence, and this is most evident in the importance he assigns to the Holy Spirit. The Holy Spirit is dynamic power: 'The Spirit of God is something disturbing, driving', he says, '. . . for he desires to turf us out of our everydayness'.[5] Casel uses a primitive model which associates the Spirit very closely with Christ himself. It is reflected in Paul's saying in 2 Corinthians 3.17, 'The Lord is the Spirit'. So Casel speaks frequently of the 'Spirit-filled Lord' as the essence of the Christian Mystery. It makes us perhaps think of the majestic fresco at the church of Kora, where Christ strides above the deep of Limbo.

While Casel's vision is thus not so static as might be implied, it is nonetheless true that his picture of the 'presence of the saving events' leaves some people uneasy if not unconvinced. It does

not immediately ring the powerful bells that such a grand statement might presuppose. Once it has been heard a number of
times, it can acquire the quality of a cardboard cut-out, while
behind it lies a haunting question asked time and again by writers on Casel: '*How?*' How are the saving events present? There
are many layers to the response that needs to be made, and these
layers turn out to line up with our questions about the relation
between heaven and earth, between the 'self' and the great truth
outside us, between human beings and God. So how is the Mystery present?

## THE LIVING 'KERYGMA'

First of all the Mystery is there in the *kerygma,* the living message of the good news. The first Christians in their proclamation
of the gospel had a simple core-message which they continually
repeated. It is referred to by the technical term *kerygma* (which
is Greek for 'preaching'). The *kerygma* as it appears in the books
of the New Testament takes a variety of forms, all approximat-
ing to the following sequence:

1   The prophecies are fulfilled and the New Age inaugur-
     ated by the coming of Christ
2   who was born of the seed of David,
3   who died for us according to the Scriptures, to deliver
     us from the present evil age,
4   was buried,
5   rose on the third day according to the Scriptures,
6   is exalted on the right hand of God as Son of God, and
     Lord of living and dead;
7   this has been confirmed by the gift of the Holy Spirit.
8   He will come again as judge and saviour of humanity;
9   therefore repent and be baptized into the name of Jesus
     the Christ for salvation and remission of sins, and the
     gift of the Holy Spirit.[6]

For the first Christians the *kerygma* has power: it is more than
information, it is a living presence with the power to transform
those it meets, either converting them to repentance or harden-
ing their hearts. 'The Word of God is living and active, sharper
than any two-edged sword, piercing to the division of soul and
spirit, of joints and marrow, and discerning the thoughts and
intentions of the heart. And before him no creature is hidden,

but all are open and laid bare to the eyes of him with whom we have to do' (Hebrews 4.12). The author of Colossians says that 'I became a minister . . . to make the word of God fully known, the mystery hidden for ages . . .' (Colossians 1.25f.). The message of salvation, the *kerygma,* is a living entity, Christ himself. Christ is the Word, the Logos, the Word become flesh who has dwelt among us in order that we might behold his glory. He is the one 'who is able to strengthen you . . . according to the revelation of the mystery which was kept secret for long ages but is now disclosed and through the prophetic writings is made known to all nations . . .' (Romans 16.25f.). The proclamation of the gospel in the reading of Scripture and in the preaching of the good news is something living, which comes upon its hearers as the living presence of Christ. It may not always seem like that in our parish churches, but it is certainly how it is understood in the New Testament; and when the Church is living faithfully, this life comes through, despite all our inadequacies. 'Faith comes by what is heard, and what is heard comes by the proclaiming of Christ' (Romans 10.17). For Odo Casel, 'with the reading of the Scripture we return to the first age; we place ourselves into the primaeval act which is made present; from it we learn to understand what our own very being is . . . This reading is alive and takes possession of us . . . By the solemn reading, the deed of the first age is made immediate presence; so then the readings in the mass are in a sense a *sacramentum*'.[7] It may cause surprise to hear the proclamation of the Word described as a sacrament. In another place Casel lays his picture out more fully, speaking of this 'kick' in the *kerygma* as being no mere mental experience, but objective, and we might almost say physical:

Paschasius Radbertus (c. 790–865) has summed up the attitude of the early Church in the words: 'The holy scriptures are also a sacrament, wherein the Holy Spirit brings something about through effective speech' . . . in [holy scripture] too the hidden power of the Holy Spirit is revealed for the sanctifying of the Church. It too contains objective divine power under the symbolic veil of human words. From this we understand the great reverence with which the early Church treated the book of the Gospels; even greater reverence was shown at the actual reading of God's word. In fact the liturgical reading in the Church was understood as an epiphany of the divine Logos [Word] to the Christian community. What is read there is pneumatically (that is, through the Holy Spirit, *pneuma)* present, and so becomes the Mystery . . . The Fathers speak repeatedly of this, as they experienced it daily in the liturgy . . . they are not teaching a purely subjective presence of the *concepts* of holy scripture in the heads of the listeners, but an objective presence of the Spirit of God in the words . . .

Let us hear some texts. Leo the Great says: 'the Mystery of the Lord's suffering . . . has been so clearly and luminously disclosed by the gospel text that for godfearing and devout hearts it means the same to have heard the text read as to have seen the events' . . . the exalted events themselves are expressed in this way, by the returning cycle of holy days and by the pages of the gospel, so that the *Pascha* of the Lord becomes less the repetition of a past event, and more the celebration of something present . . . So Christians, according to Leo, can say: 'what [the apostles and evangelists] saw we also have seen; and what they learned, we also have learned; what they touched we have also touched' . . . A sermon attributed to Leo . . . but [now] attributed to Proclus of Constantinople, says: '. . . Now is the miracle of the past presented before our eyes, as the divine readings hold forth to us the events of old time year by year . . .'[8]

This passage not only provides fine examples of Mystery-language from patristic texts – it also shows the degree to which the reading of the Scriptures in the liturgy was understood as an encounter with the living events themselves.

This very brief sketch shows us one of the first ways in which we encounter the Mystery – in the proclamation of the good news recorded in the Scriptures. Because of its accessibility it is a good place to start, but we have a lot of ground yet to cover if we are to introduce ourselves to all the ramifications of the presence of the Mystery.

## DISCLOSURE SITUATIONS

Ian Ramsey's coining of the phrase 'disclosure situations' can help us start on the next stage. In his book *Models for Divine Activity*, Ramsey quotes a passage from the writer Joseph Conrad which describes the experience of a sailor in danger of being thrown overboard in a violent storm, hanging on for life and mercilessly battered by the water. An awesome sense of the sheer sovereign power of the storm comes over him – here is a vast, self-assured reality towering over him, terrifyingly other, and seeming to have a personality and will of its own. It is a terrifying experience of the beyond, of things greater than himself. Then he hears another voice, and through the turbulent chaos a few words are exchanged. After Conrad's thrilling description of the violence of the storm and a dark and heaving sea, Ramsey comments:

> A gale – awesome indeed; and my claim is that in and around the gale occurred a cosmic disclosure . . . a situation where I am confronted in principle with the whole universe, a situation where God reveals himself . . . Conrad . . . wrote in *A Personal Record* some six or seven years later [comparing] his literary struggles with those of sailors who face the 'sombre stress of the westward winter passage round Cape Horn', and characterizes both as 'the wrestling of men with the might of their Creator, in a great isolation from the world, without the amenities and consolations of life, a lonely struggle under a sense of over-matched littleness, for no reward that could be adequate, but for the mere winning of a longitude . . .'
>
> Here were Captain MacWhirr and Jukes finding in the gale a loneliness, an isolation, a helplessness, and then finding in human dialogue an infinity of peace, resolution and purpose coming from some remote spot beyond . . . Here is a situation leading to a disclosure of God, and then to discourse about God developed in the context of a gale, wind, and so providing us with specimen discourse about Spirit . . . But when the biblical writers spoke of Spirit, it was no doubt the winds of their own land which they took as models. There were winds which, in their destructive discord, may be somewhat compared with Conrad's typhoon. These were the winds of which the term SherKiyeh, or Sirocco, was used. They are, we are told, hot winds, coming 'with a mist of fire sand, veiling the sun, scorching vegetation, and bringing languor and fever to men. They are most painful airs, and if the divine economy were only for our physical benefit, inexplicable, for they neither carry rain nor help at harvest'.[9]

Ramsey then goes on to describe the kindlier and more welcome winds from the west which brought benefits to all. In this experience of the wind, something was disclosed to people not just about the wind, but about the very nature of life. The wind was what he calls a 'disclosure situation'. People found a close association between this experience of the wind and their experience of God as Spirit. In Greek (and in the Aramaic which Jesus spoke) the same one word is used for wind and spirit (in Greek this word is *pneuma*). In English we use two words, 'wind' and 'spirit', which confuses matters. We have to remember that when the Scriptures speak of the Spirit, they use the same word they use for wind, they identify the Spirit with the wind. In other words, the physical experience of wind itself is no mere symbol or allegory of God's Spirit – our experience of the wind actually tells us something about God, and it tells us through our senses: it gives us physical experience of him. As Ramsey puts it, 'discourse about the Spirit is a way of being articulate about God's initiating activity and our responsive activity, and it is a way which is licensed by, as it originates in, situations where God discloses himself by wind and gales . . . whenever we can speak of Jesus in terms of Spirit it is because the situations in which men found themselves with him had echoes of the situations in which they have known the revitalizing, powerful effects of the wind. Jesus situations and wind situations were isomorphous' (that is, they match).[10]

The saving events of the Bible take their meaning from experience of the world in which we live. For example, the exodus of the children of Israel from Egypt echoes ordinary-life experiences of struggle, escape and freedom. The exodus was 'isomorphous' with such experiences – it matched. The annual celebration of the Passover in its turn becomes isomorphous both with the ordinary-life experiences of escape and with the exodus.

Ramsey's notion of a 'disclosure situation' helps us to understand the connection between three levels of life: (a) certain things in daily life, such as death, escape, wind, water, put us in touch at the 'gut' level with truth about the universe, and about God; (b) the events of salvation history as recounted in the Old and New Testaments work in the same way but take it further – so the gales of Palestine revealed something about the Holy Spirit, and Pentecost then came and clinched it; (c) the Church and its liturgy renew the encounter yet again: the eucharist is an encounter with the crucifixion, and so with the disclosure situation of human death; death in its turn is an encounter with the crucifixion. All three levels, life, salvation history, and the liturgy, are isomorphous – they match.

Here we begin to see why talk of the 'saving events becoming present' can be unsatisfactory. First, an event cannot be *present* - it *happens*. Second, what is important is *involvement* in the event. Third, for those originally involved, this was *disclosure*. This means that in Galilee and Golgotha the disclosure situations of Jesus' ministry, suffering and death in daily life were notched up to another level as salvation-events. It also means that the same process continues in Christian life and worship, in the same Galilee-way and Golgotha-way. If that is not true, then the events will be less for us than they were for the characters in the gospels, and the gospels are about the *fullness* of salvation, not its diminishment. If we have less of an encounter with Galilee and with Golgotha and the empty tomb than the disciples did, then our salvation is less than theirs. That cannot be so.

Here is one preliminary response to the many questions stirred up by Odo Casel's teaching: it is not simply that the saving events are made present, but also that original disclosures are happening again. We are dealing with a disclosure of the Mystery in creation 'which was hidden for ages but is now made manifest'. And note that disclosure takes place *in* the world, in the things of daily life: when the body of Christ gathers to worship God it lives again the disclosure which took place in that daily life amongst which Christ moved, and the form the disclosure takes in the liturgy matches daily-life events – baptism, eucharist, anointing, singing of hymns, all have correspondences in daily life.

## THE CHRISTIAN TEMPLE

We are beginning here to see a connection between the Mystery and daily life, between human experience and God. To take this further we now turn to a pupil of Casel, Salvatore Marsili. If Ian Ramsey has shown us a striking way of recognizing disclosures of God in the life around us, Marsili sets us on a similar road but from a different starting-point. We begin with the image of the temple in the New Testament. The temple is Jesus' body, raised after three days. The stone thrown out of the vineyard has become the chief cornerstone. Christians are joined with him as living stones, to make a spiritual house, the temple of the wider

Body of Christ, the Church (1 Peter 2.4–10). Then each individual Christian is in turn the temple of the Holy Spirit (1 Corinthians 6.19). Our own bodies become like Christ's human body, risen from the dead as the new temple. Realities which were separate in paganism now in Christianity become fused: the Christian is temple, priest and sacrifice, following in the footsteps of the Lord. His or her physical body is not only the temple, it is also the sacrifice – 'present your bodies as a living sacrifice' (Romans 12.1) – and in both physical and spiritual terms the Christian is also the priest (consecrated by bodily immersion and the gift of the Spirit, and constituting the Body of Christ when all converge on one place to celebrate the mysteries).

Given all of this, Marsili concludes that 'there is an act of worship which every single Christian, consecrated by baptism, offers daily to God in his or her holiness of life; by means of this he or she enters into the inner essence of the Church, as a stone in that building which is the temple of the Lord, founded on the cornerstone which is Christ'.[11] This daily sacrifice of Christians is a life lived after the model of Christ.

Marsili was here enlarging on something which had been said before by the French writer L. Cerfaux: 'The most definite text is Romans 12.1 . . . All Christian action devoted to good, to what is acceptable to God and is perfect (Romans 12.2) constitutes the matter of the sacrifice [i.e. the material which is sacrificed]; and all Christians thus "offer" this spiritual sacrifice to God. Christians, says Paul in Philippians 3.3, are the true circumcision, "consecrated to liturgical service in the spirit of God"'.[12] This liturgical service is a life lived in God's service, the offering of our daily life. In Romans 15.16 Paul is 'a minister of Christ Jesus to the Gentiles in the priestly service of the Gospel of God, so that the offering of the Gentiles may be acceptable, sanctified by the Holy Spirit'; and in Philippians 2.17 we read: 'Even if I am to be poured as a libation upon the sacrificial offering of your faith'. In all of this language in fact we are seeing another facet of the 'how?' of the Mystery. The Mystery is present in the life of each believer as a priestly offering, in unison with Christ, of his sacrifice. Our participation in the liturgy therefore leads us to take our experience of Christ's Mystery with us into our daily life, a point made frequently by Casel. He often remarks that one fruit of Christian worship is the going-forth of believers to a life of love and service. This is because 'At the centre of life stands the liturgy; [Christians] are conscious that their life hangs on its celebration; it can never become for them mere tiresome routine. This is so because the life of every day draws its meaning from it, and is continually stimulated by the presence of the primaeval event'.[13]

This way of formulating ancient truth introduces a line of thought which it is surprising Marsili did not choose to follow up: the cross and the empty tomb are themes of all our lives, realities of every day – Christians have no monopoly of the universal experience of death and of life; the whole of saving history in fact, through Moses and the Prophets to Jesus and the life of the Church, is made up of things which have always been found everywhere: struggle, suffering, despair, hope, battles, reconciliations, loss and gain, death and new life: it is on the bus and in the living-room, and in the whole of human living. We see the crucifixion re-enacted time and again, among our family, our acquaintances, and, more widely, on our television screens. All around us too is the resurrection (usually taken more for granted). The stuff of which the saving Mystery is made is present in the whole of creation, and the crosses and resurrections of every day, and of all people everywhere, are real presences of the Mystery of Jesus Christ. We may on occasion even have a profound sense of their cosmic significance, though we may have no means of formally recognizing it. Everywhere there are folk who would not immediately describe these things in terms of God, and yet they know them for something of what they are: a presence of the Mystery.

## GOD'S PRESENCE IN CREATION

It is nothing new to believe in the presence of God in his world. The Old Testament sees God as vigorously active in the world, in the exodus, for instance, or in nature, or in the prophets. God sustains the world in being, and its life-breath comes from him. In Christianity too God's involvement with the world is blazoned forth through his presence *within* it. This is naturally spoken of in terms of the Holy Spirit, but also as the presence and activity of the Son, so that Irenaeus could speak of both as the two hands of God, working complementarily and co-operatively, but in distinctive ways. Christ speaks of his presence in the poor and naked (in the parable of the sheep and goats in Matthew 25.31–46), and Paul speaks of the Spirit praying with our spirit (Galatians 4.6), and so on.

More controversial is the notion of God *suffering* with his people. The doctrine of divine impassivity upholds the truth that God cannot be affected by anything we do, and is without passions in the broad sense, meaning, among other things, that he cannot be a passive object of our actions. However, there is a thread running through Christian history which finds itself compelled to speak in terms of God sharing in the sufferings of his people. Obviously this is the case in the incarnation and the suffering of Christ. But we want to say more, that this sharing in the suffering of the world continues – the Godhead himself does not protect himself from it. Traditional theology would say that Christ continues to suffer in his humanity, and in this way God is intimately close to our suffering. In the Jewish tradition we find those who speak of the *Shekinah* (a word used by Jews to describe God's holy presence) enduring suffering with the people of Israel, and travelling with them wherever they go. Some of this language comes very close to Christian language about the persons of the Trinity, granting the *Shekinah* a certain separateness from the Godhead: God, as it were, standing apart slightly from himself.[14] In the New Testament there are hints at a sharing by the Holy Spirit in the sufferings of God's people (the Spirit himself intercedes for us with sighs too deep for words – Romans 8.26). All of this language seeks to hold together the sovereignty of God with a deep conviction that God is with us in all we undergo.

## THE MYSTERY HIDDEN IN CREATION

Here we naturally come to the New Testament's picture of the Mystery hidden in creation. The Mystery, let us remember, is that paschal glory which was all that Christ was and is in the acts of our redemption. This had always been hidden in the world God created, waiting to be fully manifested and fully recognized. The Mystery of our worship is also there in the marketplace, and always has been, and in a sense people have always intuitively known it, in glimpses and snatches, wherever the goodness and love of God shines through in ordinary human life.

This knowledge which is simply there, but never expressed in anything like our Christian Creeds, is a part of people's experience of life, and has no need of the Church's formulations for that to be so. The Church's role is that of Christ in his Palestinian ministry: to make manifest what is under the surface. The Church's vocation is to enable the implicit to become explicit. This happens not through the simple pulling away of a veil, but through conversion of heart. Those who come to see the Mystery for what it is have their life changed from top to bottom. Through baptism they become priests who celebrate in their daily lives the liturgy of the saving mystery, as living stones of the temple of Christ's Body. The Body of Christ is then the midwife, bringing to birth in all people that which was hidden in them since the world began, the Mystery hidden in creation, the plan which now is made manifest. The world to which we belong has to be born again through the waters of baptism. We are a servant Church, at the service of God's creation, so that he may summon forth from all of us who are born with veiled eyes the recognition of truths only tacitly and stumblingly known, and which none of us shall ever know perfectly until we are made new in the kingdom of heaven. But to touch upon these truths is to become a different people.

The book of Revelation describes how the praises of creation rise up to the throne of God (Revelation 5.13f.). The beauties of nature, and ordinary lives of ordinary people everywhere, are a joy to God, who delights in his creation, and says it is 'very good'. Maximus the Confessor goes so far as to speak of the whole of humanity and the cosmos as a kind of hidden church. Dumitru Stăniloae sums it up like this: 'It can be said that the cosmic and human creation . . . have not only a similarity with the Church, but participate to a certain degree in her . . . In this sense we could say that creation is a Church with a different form, and undeveloped, incompletely realized, and having the Church within her as a ferment which can help her to evolve until she may become Church in a fully developed sense'.[15] Stăniloae is not talking here of the institutional church – we can see how laughable that would be if we added 'of England' to the word 'church' every time it occurs in this quotation. He is speaking of that perfect Body of Christ which is only imperfectly realized here on earth. What Stăniloae means in practical terms is that all the good things in life (and the bad) come into their own once we recognize Christ in them. The sacrificial dedication of the person who nurses for many years a dependent relative, the young couple celebrating the joy of life, the many who slog away at their work week in and week out, the many who suffer illness, debility, sadness and sorrow, the gifted teacher, the shop assistant who has verve, commitment and interest in people, and so on, and so on. All of life, good and bad, pleasure and pain, is not perhaps explained or made sense of, nor made easier nor more satisfying, but it is 'taken home', we see it in the context of God, and so we see it with different eyes. It must be in this kind of sense that the Vatican II document *Lumen Gentium* says that the Church includes 'all the just since Adam, from Abel the just to the last of the elect'.[16] The priestly role of the baptized consists in part, therefore, in so conducting the sacrifice of Christ's mystery in their bodies and souls that around them the hidden 'Church' in all humanity gains the freedom to become explicitly the Church. The Body of Christ in this way performs a service of midwife to the world.

## THE LORD WHO IS NEVER ALONE

The notion of Christ's presence in the world has various take-off points. One is the Holy Spirit, who breathes life into all things. The life with which the plants reach upwards to the sun, the life of animals and humans, all comes from the driving force of the Spirit who animates all things. Life in its surging growth, creativity and action is the Spirit at work. Then close to the Spirit is the Son – Christ the Spirit-filled Lord, present in all creation.

This life derives from the Godhead. The Trinity is no group of individualists each doing their own thing – God is Trinity, and here there is no solitude. As the Spirit is close to the Son, so the Son and the Spirit are close to the Father. So when the tradition speaks of the divine presence in the world, it is not the static presence of an individual God. The world is caught up into the circle of life, where in the Spirit we come to the Father through the Son. Even if it serves no other purpose at all, such a theological riddle debunks a picture of Christ that is standard in the modern West: an isolated individual with a beard and long hair, the lonely bachelor Christ of Western European Christianity. The Christ of revelation is a family man, and cannot be conceived (or known) on his own. His family first of all is the Trinity. Then second it is his people, the Body of which he is the head. Then third he is the Christ of a historical drama which involved large numbers of real people who lived and died, and through and with whom he changed the world for ever. That drama we call salvation history. Finally he is the Christ of all humanity, who are his sisters and brothers, fathers, mothers and children. When we speak of Christ being present in our neighbour, and in daily life, we therefore miss the point utterly if we see him as 'a wonderful person' who is just that – a kind face in a picture-frame. Christ is family – he is persons and events. It follows that we are mistaken to look for a lonely Palestinian bachelor in our daily lives. We are to look for Christ, who is no isolated individual, but part and parcel with the women and the men who are his people, and one with the Spirit, and with the Father. He is not Christ the Palestinian bachelor – he is in the truest sense the cosmic Christ – all times belong to him, and all the ages. All people are part of a growing coinherence in him, growing towards that oneness in Christ which reflects Christ's oneness with the Father. 'As thou, Father, art in me, and I in thee, that they also may be in us . . . I in them and thou in me' (John 17.21 and 23). To do justice to our full humanity, and to the feminine which is in Christ, as it is in all of us, we speak at the same time of a oneness in her which reflects her oneness with God our Mother. This Christ united with people and with God, the Christ of the cross and the resurrection, 'fills the whole creation' (Ephesians 1.23).

## GOD'S DISCLOSURES IN DAILY LIFE

If we go so far as to say that this Mystery is knowable in daily life, then that means Christ in his saving events has always been there in life's 'disclosure situations'. It would be a help to be more specific – what kind of situation in daily life are we actually talking about? Salvation history in its fullest sense encompasses all that is told in both Testaments, Old and New. That is too much to deal with, but to test our hypothesis we could construct a shortlist of saving events and see how they match up with experience of daily life by taking one example to correspond to each.

*Incarnation.* Even if we have in our bones the worst Western notions of a disembodied 'soul' which can live without the body, our own experience tells us something that is also abundantly clear in the Scriptures – our body and soul are inseparable. At death both come to an end, and the resurrection will be a conferring of new life on both. We have a deep temptation to separate bodily and spiritual, and this has over the centuries emerged in various forms of gnosticism, docetism, materialism and the like; but any serious account of what it is to be human has to regard the body as fundamental. Incarnation is basic to being human. It is not difficult to look for examples, as our whole life is full of them. The German Evangelical theologian Wilhelm Stählin chooses to take our sexuality as an example of the presence of the Mystery in our body. After pointing out that the body is integral to what we are, he says '. . . our bodily nature is bound up with the Mystery in its narrower sense, the Mystery of salvation . . . the incarnation . . .'.[17] Then he develops this in relation to sexuality:

> 'If we reflect that every sexual relation is a mystery, then we are brought to accept that something takes place here which transcends the purely physiological and physical experience of those involved. The superficial comment that there's nothing to it has to be gainsaid, precisely because there is something to it, even if the person cannot begin to comprehend the thing over which he or she has no power whatsoever . . . The Mystery of Christ is the Mystery of God's love, the mystery of self-giving love; it is not one and the same thing as Eros, love which desires to demand and to possess; but how perverse it would be to say that . . . erotic, sexual love must be left behind and be displaced by Christ's love!'.[18]

Stählin points out rather that sexual love is a disclosure of the divine love, and even that 'everything which characterizes the essence of the Mystery can be found in the enduring life together of man and wife'. What is true of the sexual relation is true also where it is denied to us, whether out of choice or due to circumstances. There are many roads, and many ways, in which our physical nature is part of our life and experience. The Christian tradition of asceticism and of celibacy paradoxically expresses the same thing (even if it has sometimes been tempted to deny the physical, or assign to it a lower place) because it too recognizes that the body has an active and determining role in our totality as a person. Our sexuality is but one example: the whole of our life in this created world is full of disclosure situations out of which the incarnation emerges, and to which it naturally relates.

*Christ's ministry.* If anything can be said of the stories of Jesus' ministry in Galilee and further afield it is that here is *life!* 'On with the motley', as many a parish priest must often say.

Where do we start in drawing our parallels here? There is too much of it. What stands out most is the *person* of Jesus. A disclosure situation behind this is our unending experience of other people: either we like them or we do not, or we are mystified, or attracted, but always we find ourselves up against a living entity difficult to assess and full of potential for many things. It is not difficult at all to see in the life around us the gospel stories of Christ going amongst people in Palestine and ministering to them.

*Passion, death and resurrection.* There is a long-standing tradition in Christianity of seeing the little deaths of life as preparing us for death itself, the tradition referred to by the Latin tag, *memento mori*, reminders of death. Every failure and disappointment, every time we lose something on which we had set our heart, from the most trivial to the most cherished, is a disclosure of death, and from it we can learn each time something more about the Mystery to which our life is leading. It must also have been in part the little resurrections of life that led people in ancient times to sense death not to be the end, even if the result was not a full-blown belief in resurrection. At the psychological level the 'little deaths and resurrections' have been shown to have far-reaching consequences for us as persons. The German psychologist and former Evangelical minister Peter Schellenbaum believes that

'Down at the very foundation of our being is the dimension of death, which sometimes in passing moments we can be aware of. The need to die in the course of life shows the psychological significance of that creative void which is the deepest level of the unconscious mind. If we fail to get down there, we are in danger of ending up with an up-tight soul. If we come right up against it, however, fear of death is transformed into creativity, a caged mentality becomes one of relationship . . . Access to this level of ourselves is nothing less than essential'.[19]

This seems to put in psychological terms one way in which Christ's death and resurrection are present in life, whether we have heard of Christ or not. We have to face death in order to live. That death may be the facing of a deep-seated fear and discovering the truth about it; the fear, for instance, of a tyrannical father. The pain of discovering such a truth is the first step on the way to greater freedom and self-acceptance.

Lest we should think of resurrection too much in abstract

terms, it would be good to add an example of a more practical kind. Here is a story from the First World War:

> It was a wet, cold morning, about 6 a.m. in winter, on the Somme. I saw half a dozen of my boys taking charge of two infantrymen at their last gasp from wet, mud, fatigue, and exposure. The poor fellows had actually lain down to die on the roadside by our battery. My men gave them their breakfast (we were short of rations in those days), their socks (we were short of these), shirts and everything; and rubbed them and lit fires all around them and sweated over them, and got them to hospital. Now they would be utterly surprised to hear that any of this had got to do with morality or religion.[20]

*Pentecost.* Here we meet the wind again, and not only the wind, but community born of a shattering transition. This again is an experience known the world over in marriage, in housemoving, in starting a new job, in the rebuilding of a nation after war. New life, a new start; we even have phrases, such as 'wind of change', 'getting a second wind', 'a breath of fresh air', being 'carried away' with enthusiasm. The earthly disclosures are seen even in our language.

Much more could obviously be said in seeking connections between people's experience of life and the events recounted in salvation history – we would find ourselves speaking about art, gardening, work, entertainment, enjoyment, friendship, scientific investigation – the whole of life in one way and another. There is enough here at least to remind us how we fail to acknowledge the Mystery of Christ is present in everything around us.


## SOME CONSEQUENCES

Several consequences follow from all that we have said so far in this chapter. First of all, the whole ordinary life of the Christian is an act of worship. Not merely morality or dedication: our every single act and our every thought is the liturgy of a priestly people.

Second, the Paschal Mystery is real in our lives.

Third, we will tend to such a love of our neighbour as the gospels proclaim, for our relation with our neighbour has to be marked by reverence for the deeds of Christ in them. 'What you did to the least of these you did to me' – and one of the acid tests of our faith is physical: food, drink, clothes.

Fourth, the Christian is not a lonely priest, but part of a priestly people. Life in community means that the first things which have call upon your attention may not be those you want to do, but those that need to be done; ninety-nine times out of a hundred they will be totally ordinary. In Dr Pusey's words, the heart of the matter consists 'not in doing extraordinary things, but in doing extraordinarily well the ordinary things of every day'.[21] This too is of the essence of the Christian liturgy of daily life: to be content with its ordinariness, and to do it extraordinarily well. We are conscious of the quality because we are conscious of our part in a common enterprise.

Fifth, the whole drift is towards becoming the Church. That means two things: on the one hand taking seriously the holiness of the world, and the Mystery hidden (and occasionally bursting forth) within it; and on the other hand taking seriously the act of coming together to celebrate the mysteries of worship, within which is hidden the future hope of a redeemed creation. 'The sacrifice of Christians', says Augustine, 'consists in being all one body in Christ'.[22]

Finally, when we ask what is distinctive about salvation history as recounted in the Bible, we can say that on the one hand it is all found in life as we experience it, and on the other that 'the presence of the saving events' in liturgy or in life means the living presence of the Scriptures themselves. It is the content of the Scriptures which becomes present, and in which we participate. Life, liturgy and Scriptures are one.

## ENCOUNTER OF WORLD AND CHURCH

We are now ready to come back to Christian worship and suggest a tentative drawing together of threads. Our business is the Mystery of Christ's incarnation, life, death and resurrection, his glory with the Father and his coming again. This is hidden in all of daily life, and the Church co-operates with God there so that it may cease to be hidden and become fully recognized.

This is complemented by the same formula turned topsy-turvy. Human life in all its 'real-ness' is anything but hidden – it is obvious. In the liturgy, however, daily life is hidden, and constantly waiting to be manifested there. Here there is a complementarity which will deserve closer attention. In both cases we are dealing with things which are both physical and spiritual: in the 'world' they are vivid in one way, in the Church vivid in another. One answer to our question, 'how do we encounter the saving events of Christ in church?' is: through their real presence in us, in our lives, in the lives of our neighbours, and in the daily 'liturgy' of living in, through and among them. We bring the saving events with us into church. They are present because we have brought them in with us. There are those who are shielded from life's crucifixions, but many others have no need at all to be told what it is to be crucified. It is not necessary to understand the word *Pascha* to have experienced what it is talking about. We bring our lives with us when we come to church, and they are presented and offered as the sacrifices that they are. The Mystery hidden in all creation is made manifest in those present, and the lives they have brought with them. The eternal drama of life reaches out, wanting to transcend itself (this is God himself within creation, his Spirit within us, crying, 'Abba!'). On the other hand, God in his transcendence meets us in the liturgy. God reaches out towards himself in both directions, and the two movements join to produce the hymn of God's people, where our music becomes a part of God's.

Two dimensions merge in this scenario. One is Christ in our neighbour: pursued on its own this leads to exhaustion of the vision. The other is Christ in worship: cultivated on its own this makes God decamp and leave us with an empty shell. We could think of two electrodes with a gap between them: the space is filled with electricity and moving light, but with only one electrode there is nothing. The calvaries of Coronation Street and the calvary of the altar mark out the space within which the drama of redemption is revealed and continues its working. They cast light upon each other, each brings a living presence into the other; each in its own way, the altar and the six o'clock news, is a Mount Tabor. But when we are in one, we need light from the other in order to see.

# SEVEN

# How? – The Liturgy of the World

IF YOU SHOW the tea-leaves at the bottom of a cup to a beekeeper, she may say, 'there's a bee'. You look, and there it is – a bee. You had not seen it before, but quite obviously it looks like a bee. Now show the same tea-leaves undisturbed to a car mechanic. He sees the same shape and says, 'there is a spanner'. You look, and to your surprise it is a spanner, but you are seeing it for the first time. Ross Thompson in his book *Holy Ground* coins a word for this kind of recognition: 'interillumination'.[1] Certain things are at the forefront of the experience of the person concerned. The scattered tea-leaves *interilluminate* with those patterns in our mind. Our particular 'mind-set' latches onto a corresponding pattern which is not immediately seen by those with a different mind-set.

This is very useful in trying to understand the relation between liturgy and life. Just as mechanic or beekeeper see in a particular way, so Christians can come to see in a particular way, so that the liturgy and daily life interilluminate with each other. Encountering the Mystery at the eucharist, we begin to see him in the high street. Then in reverse, when we are in touch with human life as it is, then we are able to perceive the uniqueness of the liturgy. Rowan Williams uses the happy notion of 'surprise'. He wonders of the great nineteenth-century incarnationalists 'if their constructive engagement in society would have been deeper and harder if they had let themselves be more surprised at the incarnate God. Christology, after all, like thought itself, should begin (and end) in wonder.'[2]

Coming from the street, we are surprised by what we find in the Church, which is the Body of Christ at worship. It shows us things we had not considered. Or it is simply strange and different in a way which enlarges our sight. Michael Ramsey had such a surprise when as a young man he wandered into St Giles's church in Cambridge as the Solemn Eucharist was being celebrated. His description could have been written by Casel: 'The sense of mystery, and awe, and of another world at once far and near . . . a sense that we were vividly in the presence of the passion of Jesus and also vividly near heaven, to which the passion mysteriously belonged, so as to be brought from the past to the present'.[3] Coming from the Church, on the other hand, we are further surprised at how this squares up with the 'nitty-gritty' of daily life. A new light is thrown – we see with different eyes.

The Church, if it is faithful to its task, is a body of people who through their worship grow in sensitivity to daily life *as such*. Worship opens our eyes. Then the movement is back again. As John MacQuarrie has said:

> The holy belongs not just to specifically religious experiences, but to the entire experience of being a human person, that is to say, to the transcendental conditions of all experience. Yet I think we would be able to recognize the holy in this broad sense and to place a religious interpretation upon certain aspects of ordinary experience only if we had also known the holy in concentrated form in some distinctively religious experience. Even if we were grazed and haunted by some elusive sense of a mysterious holiness present in some ordinary experiences, we would then seek a clearer, more direct awareness of something so significant and fascinating.[4]

This is one reason why liturgy and life cannot often be brought very closely together. Then the vital surprise, the interillumination, is lost. It is not possible normally to import much of daily life into the liturgy or vice versa, because we are dealing with a chemistry which happens between them. The eucharist on the

kitchen table can only happen regularly if the sense of the otherness of the liturgy is already soundly rooted in the participants.
Otherwise it will only be distinguishable from other kitchen-table
activities in a superficial way. Such a celebration will be the exception rather than the rule, unless the circumstances impose it. This
need not astonish us, for we find the same thing in music – almost
nothing of daily life is apparent in its sounds, and yet it can at
times be more 'real' than anything else we could imagine. Truly
contemporary liturgy likewise is characterized by being unmistak-
ably contemporary in idiom, and undeniably of our own age, and
yet there will be little in ordinary life which quite corresponds to it.

## DANGERS IN MAKING DISTINCTIONS

If we are to make such a distinction between liturgy and life, the
dangers are obvious, and we have to bear in mind that this is
more nuanced than such a simple formula might imply. On the
one hand Christians, because of the distinctive elements of their
life in the Church, may fail to see important things which the
'secular' world sees better, while the secular world fails to see
things which are only visible through the lens of Christian life
and worship. It is about complementarity rather than distinc-
tiveness, and all the strong tendencies in Christians to dissociate
departments of their lives are to be resisted. Compartments there
are, but there are doorways and open windows, and winds
blowing through both ways. We are tempted to keep the devo-
tional separate from the moral, or the liturgical from daily life:
one person may be full of piety yet totally ignore or even despise
the needy; another may throw all their energy into loving service, but secretly be scornful of the Body of Christ. The proper
response to that is not a toning-down of the one dimension or
the other, but an organic relationship in which each throws light
on the other, each by turns 'surprises' us. The liturgy gives us
eyes to see God's shape in the tea-leaves of life. But the world
gives us eyes to see God's shape in the tea-leaves of the Church.
The way we live our lives has to be all of a piece with the way we
worship, or we are living in a world of fantasy.

## KARL RAHNER'S 'LITURGY OF THE WORLD'

Karl Rahner speaks of the relationship between worship and life in
similar terms: for him God is present in everything that is good. All

the good things in life and in human living are manifestations of the divine. In these good things human beings commune with God, even though they might not recognize his presence, and even though they may be atheists. God's grace is not set apart from life, but

> proceeds from the innermost heart and centre of the world and of humanity . . . it is quite simply the ultimate depths and the radical dimension of all that which the spiritual creature experiences, achieves and suffers in all those areas in which it achieves its own fullness, and so in its laughter and its tears, in its taking of responsibility, in its loving, living, and dying, whenever people keep faith with the truth, break through their own egoism in relationships with their fellows, whenever they hope against all hope, whenever they smile and refuse to be disquieted or embittered by the folly of everyday pursuits, whenever they are able to be silent, and whenever within this silence of the heart that evil which one person has nurtured against another in the heart does not develop any further into external actions, but rather dies within this heart as its grave – whenever, in a word, life is lived as we would seek to live it, in such a way as to overcome our own egoism and the despair of the heart which constantly assails us. There grace has the force of an event . . .[5]

Until recently Christians had tended to keep the Church in a separate compartment from a profane and corrupt world. Rahner now wants us to see the goodness of the creation which God loves, and to seek God's presence there. He speaks of ordinary life as 'the liturgy of the world':

> The world and its history are the terrible and sublime liturgy, breathing of death and sacrifice, which God celebrates and causes to be celebrated in and through human history in its freedom, this being something which he in turn sustains in grace by his sovereign ordering of things. In the entire length and breadth of this immense history of birth and death, superficiality, folly, inadequacy and hatred . . . on the one hand, and silent submission, responsibility even to death in dying and in joyfulness, in attaining the heights and plumbing the depths, on the other, the true liturgy of the world is present. It is present in such a way that the liturgy which the Son has brought to its absolute fullness on his Cross belongs

intrinsically to it and emerges from it, i.e. from the ultimate source of the grace of the world, and constitutes the supreme point of *this* liturgy from which all else draws its life . . . This liturgy of the world is as it were veiled to the darkened eyes and the dulled human heart, which fails to understand its own true nature. This liturgy therefore must, if the individual is really to share in the celebration of it in all freedom and self-commitment even to death, be interpreted, 'reflected upon', in its ultimate depths in the celebration of that which we are accustomed to call the liturgy in the more usual sense.[6]

God is with us all the time, but we are so close that we cannot see him. Therefore the liturgy of the Church is needed in order to show this for what it is. In a similar way, the whole of world history can be seen as salvation history, but we cannot see that without being exposed to the *particular* salvation history which is celebrated in the Church's Scriptures and liturgy. The saving story of Jesus is, as it were, a publicizing and fulfilment of God's hidden saving work throughout human history, and is a unique and 'real' (rather than 'mere') symbol of it. This symbol has the power to reveal human history for what it is – salvation history.

## PROBLEMS

Rahner's picture of the liturgy of the world comes very close to what we have been saying in the last two chapters. At first sight it seems like a perfect gift falling into our laps. It does, however, present some problems. The main one perhaps is that the scheme is too simple. Christian truth tends to be expressed by paradox: God is three yet one, Christ is human and divine, we are to love the world and hate the world, we are not to take thought for the morrow, and yet neither be like the man who started to build a tower without first doing his sums, and so on. In an area as central as this we would expect to find a powerful clash of images, where the truth flashes around and between the two, which operate like two electrodes with their jumping streak of light. Rahner's picture, however, is plain white light, rather than that shifty, palpitating white which is caused by shining red, green and blue lights on one space. The scheme seems too simple because it appears to be one-directional. Rahner often makes difficult reading, and it is easy to misunderstand what he is saying. Unless I have misunderstood him, he seems to be implying

that the Christian liturgy only makes sense if seen as an emanation from God's working in the life of the world. A bipolar
image ought to be expected in a matter such as this, however,
rather than something so straightforward. It fits too neatly with
*humanitas*: when we shine the light of *eternalism* across it, there
is a clash. Liturgy comes both from the life of the world and
from the life of God 'beyond the veil'. To be fair to Rahner, he
speaks of both these models when he examines our understanding of grace: the first model sees 'the operation of divine
grace . . . primarily as an intervention of God in the world at a
definite point in space and time. The world is regarded in the
first place as secular, both because of what we call "nature", and
because of the inherited sinful state of this history of the world
and humanity . . . the sacraments . . . produce something not
otherwise available';[7] the second model, on the other hand, sees
that 'This grace is always and everywhere present in the
world . . . The sacraments . . . are not really to be understood as
successive individual incursions of God into a secular world, but
as "outbursts" . . . of the innermost, ever present gracious
endowment of the world . . . into history'.[8] Grace is not added
to a graceless world, but is there all the time. 'Worship is important and significant, not because something happens in it that
does not happen elsewhere, but because there is present and
explicit in it that which makes the world important'.[9]

Rahner believes that both models are needed, but that for pastoral reasons (and by clear personal preference) the second
model must be given top priority in presenting Christian worship to people in the modern world. They cannot respond to the
first model at all, indeed are repelled by it, as by magic and
mumbo-jumbo and empty ritualizing. The second model speaks,
however, to their direct experience, and represents the only way
most people today are capable of responding to Christian truth.

Many, if not most, parish clergy will immediately see the force
of Rahner's arguments. It is pastoral reality. Yet we have to ask:
how can we avoid this leading to a canonizing of human life to
a degree which excludes the God-ness of God? Rahner is no
horizontalist (by that I mean that he acknowledges both the
'horizontal' relations we have with each other and the 'upward',
'vertical' relation we have with God): he firmly believes in the
absolute importance of the liturgy. He defines horizontalism as
'the view that that which constitutes the true essence of Christianity, the true heart and centre which alone is signified in all its

doctrines, the true task of the Church, consists in something which can simply be called "love of neighbour" or . . . "commitment at the level of social politics and criticism of society", "responsibility for the world"'.[10] He sees this as 'far more than heresy', indeed as 'apostasy'. So Rahner is no simple horizontalist. And yet his scheme threatens precisely to encourage horizontalism, for it proposes to confirm in us the already entrenched mind-set that all human phenomena, including the liturgy, find their root and origin in the horizontal, in the everyday. The gospel, on the other hand, seems repeatedly to want to insist on the power of paradox: the world is holy, but the world is also tainted with death; God is near, yet God is far; the truth is familiar, but it is also alien; it sets people free, but also drives them away. God affirms people's own language, but tells them from square one that they have to start learning another language. Rahner is quite aware of this, and is careful to say that it is important that the 'first' model is represented in any embracing of the 'second'. In other hands than Rahner's, however, such an elevating of the integrity of the world and of people leads often to the sort of sentimentalizing of the common man and woman and of daily life which is widely prevalent in modern Christian apologetic and practice. It is sentimental because it underestimates the sin in all of us, and our enduring capacity to turn things consciously or unconsciously to our own ends. By contrast we find underplayed that astringency towards the world which is such a strong element in the New Testament, sparring in a paradoxical shadow-play with reverence for the holiness of God's creation. 'My kingdom is not of this world'; 'Seek the things which are above'; the Son of Man was 'rejected by people', and so on. This astringency emerges particularly strongly in the form of conflict, and there is suspiciously too little conflict in Rahner's picture.

## PRESENCE AS CONFLICT

In the gospels we find a process of conflict and struggle leading to a victory which is only achieved through weakness. The nativity stories are filled with an air of conflict, the breathtaking condescension of God, putting himself into the hands of sinners, and the consequent opposition of the powers of this world, and of all that is warped and fallen. There can be no doubt about the conflict which preceded the resurrection, both during Jesus' ministry and in the seeming victory of evil on Golgotha. The conflict is three-cornered, between us, our neighbour and God, and it is only by passing together through the eye of the raging storm, through the punches and the kicks and the poison, that we find ourselves and him. The conflict is fundamental to the process of redemption. Jesus was to be 'a sign of contradiction' (Luke 2.34). It is a conflict between the holiness of God and the perversity and self-centredness of every human heart, and every human society. In this conflict the total human person and the total fabric of society come under judgement and are found wanting. 'The heart is deceitful above all things, and desperately corrupt' (Jeremiah 17.9). If, however, we are encouraged to understand that Christian liturgy emerges in a simple, direct line from our experience of daily life, then we will excuse ourselves from the thick of this conflict with a God who is loving and jealous. That is why the scheme we have identified (liturgy and life interilluminating with each other) has to be preferred to Rahner's pastoral option. To put this in Caselian terms, the Mystery is present in daily life in one way, and present in the worshipping Church in another. The liturgy does not simply emerge from life – it emerges also from God, 'direct'. It is so different that it changes us, if we will let it. Common worship with the people of God gradually turns us into different members of society.

On occasion the liturgy can indeed crash into life with stunning force. I remember spending a week visiting friends and acquaintances in a communist dictatorship, where people were forced to live in a twilight society pervaded by greyness, fear and suspicion. Oppressed by this tragic world and its intimidating atmosphere, we went on Sunday to the Divine Liturgy in the cathedral. It was already in full swing, and at a certain point deep, sonorous bells began to clang, the choir struck up with a Te Deum, and the Holy Synod appeared in procession, to stand before the altar. Through the open window came the stamping feet of soldiers changing the guard at the nearby parliament-house. My companion and I were profoundly moved by the event in a way which is impossible to describe. Despite the superficiality of the oppressive world around, despite the knowledge that the raw recruits outside keeping guard undoubtedly had equal hatred for the dictatorship, and no doubt included some churchgoers, and despite the knowledge of all the frailty and sin to be found inside that church building and the celebrating community, despite the sin of all the people involved, despite *all* of us, in fact, the Mystery of God was making his glory known in his own stunning way on this spot of earth. The presence of the Mystery in the liturgy is, amongst other things, a presence of the conflict which Christ has a tendency to arouse, so that we find we are in the midst of a battle. In worship the battle is always there, the conflict between the evil in us and the love that is God. We must expect an element of conflict in worship, a going against the grain, a process of 'un-selfing', of wriggling conversion, willing but unwilling, running-to and running-from. The conflict shows the continuing work of the plan of salvation. This experience of being in conflict is the encounter with the Presence – being amongst the crowd in a Palestinian village as Jesus passes through. The response is mixed. How can we respond on our own, out of our own emptiness? We need help. Hence the ancient cry at the beginning of the daily office in the West: 'O God, make speed to save us: O Lord, make haste to help us' (and its ultimate response at the end of the day in compline – 'our help is in the name of the Lord: who has made heaven and earth').

It may be because of this that worship can seem empty and tasteless for modern people. Under the surface *we* are empty and tasteless. We cannot submit, we want to be wooed and courted, not honed and ground with a flinty wheel. Silvano Maggiani goes so far as to say that the liturgy requires us to die. 'Religious rite in general, and the Christian form in particular, require of the participants a symbolic death (death to the immediate, to the old Adam) in order to be able to enter into communion with the Mystery. The modern hiding of death in all its forms carries with it the rejection of symbolic death, and as a consequence that which expresses such a death: in fact, rite.'[11]

## RAHNER'S PICTURE OF THE INDIVIDUAL AND OF GRACE

Karl Rahner's vision is noble and pastorally realistic, entrancing in its immediacy. And yet it has something about it which is uncomfortably cosy. Our reflections on Mystery-theology imply that it needs completion by its opposite, the holiness and otherness of God, and his hidden and effective working in his world, through Providence, and the workings of grace which apparently go against what is reasonable, predictable and explainable. Rahner is legislating for a humanity which can no longer see an order outside itself which is beautiful and true, calling to us with an imperative voice. Another way of putting this is to note how greatly Rahner's thought here relies on the incarnation as a principle, and how little mention it makes in these passages of the resurrection.

Two further problems with Rahner's account deserve brief mention. One is that it is highly individualistic: 'the individual goes to Mass' is the framework for his discussion, and so he fails to do justice to the way human beings are communal in their nature. This allows him all the more easily to idealize the individual who is going to Mass, rather than depict the self-centred and difficult persons we all are. Had he spoken more of the community, he would have seen that the goalposts change significantly, in that any idealization of humanity's better side has always to be held together with recognition of the depths of human depravity. Ironically, it is not 'all of human life' which goes to Rahner's Mass, but the pious individual. The other problem with this picture is that Rahner speaks principally in terms of *grace*, assuming the medieval understanding of the sacraments as 'means of grace', something we have already had cause to criticize. While Rahner is brought to speak of grace as being present everywhere and not imprisoned in the sacraments of the Christian Church (which is true), the theology of the Mystery seeks to return behind the medieval reduction of the sacraments which gives them the status of dispensers of this uniform substance, and to recover the patristic understanding of Mystery, whereby, yes, grace is given, but within the physical-historical spiritual particularities of the incarnation, cross and resurrection, and in terms not just of 'receiving' but of active encounter.

Christ is truly present and operative in life, wherever we find what is true and lovely and of good report both among religious people and non-religious people. He is there too where there is cruelty and suffering, and in people's embracing of suffering, in themselves, and in their care for their neighbour. He is there in all those things which are mirrored in his own story. Salvation history is hidden there, a foundation component of all human life, as it has evolved over millions of years. Wherever we find these things operative, *there* is celebrated the liturgy of the world. Out of this emerges the liturgy of the Church, where the presence of God in the world becomes at last explicit, no longer hidden. However, the Christian liturgy also comes to us from the other direction, for half of its building-blocks belong to the kingdom which is not of this world, but which is the coming kingdom. It is different and other, it is holy and beyond our comprehending. For this reason the kingdom-presence of Christ can reveal to us the holiness of the ordinary world, by throwing upon it a light we can find nowhere else, a light which challenges our world and shows us that we are nothing, and have nothing to bring. We are empty, we are unprofitable servants, and yet at the same time we have everything, and cannot see it; not at least until this uncreated light streams across the fabric of our lives.

Now we have to repeat the same all over again, but this time swapping the categories around. The Mystery which is active in the Church is mishandled and obscured by the sin of church people, while the world, for all its professed emptiness, is always the place where we always first learn what the Mystery is. Congregations often seem blissfully unaware of the dynamite they are handling, or that their picture of the lion they claim to represent looks more like a poodle, while the paint-sprayer in the garage down the road can see it all, and rejects it. When David Jenkins says that his job is not 'pampering a few in church' an initial reaction can be to say this is undervaluing the worship of Almighty God. On its own it is just that, and on its own it is no gospel. But many people who might say that will have experienced occasions when they have been, say, at a civic service, or in a suburban parish that seems very satisfied with itself, or at a dreadful church council meeting, and have wondered, 'but where is God in all of this?'

There is no doubt that the attempt to hold together eternalism and humanitas in all their strength can seem very contradictory. We have reached the point, therefore, where we need to say something about the nature of the Church *vis-à-vis* the world.

# EIGHT

# Is the Church Special?

## THE CHURCH, BOTH SINNING AND HOLY

SOME TRENCHANT WORDS of Hans Küng:

> We cannot honestly regard as inevitable all the lack of feeling
> the Church and its representatives have shown towards the
> needs of mankind, their failures to adapt to the new problems
> and the views of different eras, to understand the changing
> forms and values of the world, their blindness to the signs of
> the times and their habit of always being behind the times.
> There is nothing inevitable about all the worn-out apologetics
> and lazy excuses, designed to maintain the *status quo*, about
> the Church's identification with particular systems and par-
> ties, cultures or philosophical schools, about the exaggera-
> tions of its powers and claims on the world, the disguising or
> suppression of past failings and errors. We are deluding our-
> selves about reality if we try to ignore the personal failures
> and the personal guilt which lie behind and beneath all the
> wrong decisions and false developments in the history of the
> Church. Behind the imperfections, defects and deformities we
> can discern evil, sin and vice . . . The history of the Church is
> not only a very human history, but a deeply sinful history,
> and it has always been so.[1]

On a more anecdotal level there is the story of an Anglican being

109

instructed for reception into the Roman Catholic Church. He ventured to his instructor a description of the four marks of the Church: it is one, holy, catholic and apostolic. 'Nonsense!' replied the priest, 'The four marks of the Church are the ignorance of the laity, the affluence of the clergy, the arrogance of the religious orders, and the scandalous lives of the popes.'

How, in the face of its compromised history, is it possible to speak of the holiness of the Church? It will help to begin by seeing how religions in general deserve our reverence because they draw our attention to ultimate things which otherwise we ignore. Edward Schillebeeckx writes:

> [R]eligions and churches are not salvation, but a 'sacrament' of the salvation that God brings about in the world he has created . . . Religions and churches are of the order of 'the sign': a sacrament of salvation. They are the explicit identification of that salvation. Churches are the places where salvation from God is thematized or put into words, confessed explicitly, proclaimed prophetically and celebrated liturgically. So there is an unbreakable connection between the world and religion . . . Religions and churches are the *anamnesis,* i.e. the living recollection among us, of this universal, 'tacit' but effective will to salvation and the absolute saving presence of God in our world history. By their religious word, their sacrament or ritual and living praxis, religions – synagogues and pagodas, mosques and churches – prevent the universal presence of salvation from being forgotten. But . . . the churches understand themselves wrongly (a) if they do not see that they are related to the whole world process as it can be experienced, and (b) if they think that in their practical and also interpretative relationship to this world process they can dispense with specifically religious forms: confession, word and sacrament. The condition on which church talk about God becomes possible is thus the real appearance of God in the world process, and the veiling of this presence in our world makes religious and church talk necessary.[2]

Schillebeeckx proceeds to identify the uniqueness of Jesus and as a consequence the 'necessary (but sometimes alienating) mediation of faith in Jesus Christ by the Church. And [yet] in a pluralistic encounter of divergent cultures and religions there is above all the problem of the reconciliation of belief in the uniqueness and universality of Jesus Christ with a positive evaluation of other world religions . . .', and Schillebeeckx sees that it is important to be able to do this 'without falling into "religious indifferentism", suggesting that all religions are equal'.[3]

Religion, then, deserves our respect, and the Church, by embodying the Christian way, merits the same respect. However, this is only possible, if we are honest, in terms which include recognition that the Church is sinful and that its enthusiasm often leads to arrogance. The Church has no right to claim superiority for itself. It has too long a record of slipping back into unredeemed nature, while many 'worldly' people and believers of other religions can show truer marks of holiness, and can be patently 'close to the kingdom of heaven'. The Church can be over-preoccupied with internal matters, and with that tendency of all institutions to make self-perpetuation a major priority. Energies can become vested in hierarchy, system and legalism, and while people in the parishes may domesticate and blunt the gospel, those at the steering wheel can turn it into a machine, where communion is replaced by system, service by clerical rituals, and freedom by law. It is easy to find justification for wariness towards the Church as an institution, and the intractability and imperviousness of many of the folk who are responsible for its ills will mean that the language of challenge sometimes requires a sharp edge. The Church's failings will always need to be exposed by the light of Christian prophecy, and God's people need constantly to be recalled from domesticating the gospel.

However, our Creeds tell us that the Church is holy. What are we to make of this?

## WHAT IS THE CHURCH?

John is always speaking in this way: 'the Church has always worshipped God on Sundays'; 'the Church should always condemn oppression'; 'the Church worships God in many ways'. This language irritates Mary, who want to ask, 'what *is* the Church? *How* can you talk about it in this way?' Hereby lies a great confusion, which is difficult to disentangle. First of all we use the word 'Church' in five principal ways, and repeatedly tend to confuse them:

1   The Body of Christ, perfect in heaven, and overlapping

111

into this world. With deliberate reference to eternalism, we could call this the 'eternal Church'.

2 The public institution of the Church, consisting of all
baptized believers. In itself this will always be marred
by sin, and could be called the 'human Church'.

3 Local churches (as in the first two chapters of Revelation) and denominations.

4 The clergy – a debased meaning, but still very much
there in our utterances (e.g. 'the Church teaches her
children' – a tautology, as the children, the baptized,
are as much the Church as those claiming to do the
teaching). Knee-jerk reactions against the word
'Church' often assume this debased usage. There is no
way in which the clergy, or even the formal organiza-
tional structures, can by themselves constitute the
Church.

5 The Church building.

The only uses of the word which are important for Christian
theology and belief are the first three. Their relationship is very
complex. The human Church is a sinful organization like any
other. At the same time it has been commissioned as an instrument for our access to the eternal Church, the Body of Christ.
But there is more to be said, for this organization is more than
some merely entrepreneurial agency: it is commissioned by
Christ in a sacramental way, so that the eternal Church infects it
and affects it. It is an ingenious compromise along the lines of
the incarnation, in which Christ puts himself into the hands of
sinners. In their disagreement, both John and Mary put a finger
on part of the truth. John is in danger of confusing love of the
Body of Christ with love for a human institution. Mary is in
danger of thinking Christ cannot set things apart in the material
world, for fear of damaging his purity. How, then, can reverence
for 'the Church' go together with passionate reverence for the
dignity of human beings in their ordinary life?

## REVERENCE FOR THE CHURCH

We are told in the letter to the Ephesians that love for each other
should follow the model of Christ's love for the Church – this is
set so high as to be the model for our highest human loves: 'Hus-
bands, love your wives, as Christ loved the Church and gave

himself up for her, that he might sanctify her, having cleansed her by the washing of water with the word, that he might present the Church to himself in splendour . . . For no man hates his own flesh, but nourishes and cherishes it, as Christ does the Church' (Ephesians 5.25–7; 29). The New Testament is paradoxical: we are to judge the Church as all-too-human, and also to revere her in that she is holy and loved by Christ. In Ephesians we read: marriage is a 'great mystery, and I take it to mean Christ and the Church' (Ephesians 5.32). The parallel between our attitude to the Church and interpersonal dynamics in daily life is fascinating in this regard. Those whom we love we treat as being in some sense holy. The medieval nuptial vow 'with my body I thee worship' illustrates it for marriage. Those whom we love we treat as sacrosanct, inviolable, worthy of our total commitment. Yet we can be quite aware of faults and failings in them, we will take many things with a pinch of salt, we keep our distance on some things, and we sometimes take pleasure in teasing them, debunking their foibles. In life reverence and 'knowing-you-only-too-well' go together in a piquant mix. Then again there is that darker layer of love which does violence to the person loved – a disordered love can take many forms. In this way, simple 'love' of the Church on the one hand or simple criticism of it on the other are both wide of the mark. The mix is a complex one, expressed in a realization that while the Church is a very fallible human institution, it is also a 'sacrament' of the salvation which God offers to his creation – it is holy. When a husband criticizes his wife or his son to outsiders, this will normally be a sign, if the criticism becomes serious, of something badly wrong. Blood runs thicker than water. Family loyalty runs deep – lack of that kind of loyalty can easily be thought dishonourable, for it shows a lack of the reverence peculiar to the family relationship, even though a family may never talk in terms of loving each other. If marriage is truly a model of the Church, then it is difficult to see how the bonds of family relationships and their reverences and reticences do not also apply to the Church. What we might be justified in saying is that the word 'love' is bandied about too much without sufficient regard to its seriousness. It is not often mentioned in many families, even though it may be very fully lived. And if it is talked about in families, then the tensions and conflicts are likely to be talked about too. If the family is a model for the Church (and I recognize there are problems with that image in other ways), then simple unqualified talk of love of the Church is not enough.

We can easily see ways in which the Church merits criticism. We can also identify areas where few would deny that the Church deserves respect: for instance, the Scriptures, the sacraments, the members of the Church in their various roles, simply as human beings. Then there is a further complexity: these two approaches are not neatly distinct. Respect for the Scriptures, for instance, is increased, not lessened, by a properly critical and questioning approach. The same goes for the sacraments and the Church as a whole. Refraining from criticism, on the other hand, has its place too: turning the other cheek or going the extra mile holds before us an ideal of bearing with humility the apparent stupidity of others in their misuse of the Church and of people. Hand in hand with reverence for the Church goes a willingness to be chastened and enlarged through a sometimes painful acceptance of its follies. Here is a paradox: respect is increased by an honestly critical approach, while the things criticized can be borne loyally because of the depth of our respect for the Church and what it represents.

Odo Casel puts a finger on something here in his review of a book by the Protestant theologian Gustav Mensching.[4] Mensching was not particularly representative of Protestant attitudes at the time – he seems to be making generalizations about German Protestant worship which many of his co-religionists would not have recognized – and Casel's response has to be understood as applying to him rather than to Protestants in general. Whether in criticizing him Casel believes he is also vindicating them is difficult to say. Casel had many friends and admirers among Evangelical Christians, was influenced by Protestant theologians and anthropologists, and is known to have helped Evangelicals in some of their liturgical projects. The many testimonies which came from them after his death are an eloquent witness to their esteem for him. For us, however, Mensching is a good example of *one* strand in the modern Christian make up. Casel writes:

> If all worship consists of purely personal experience, then it is hardly to be wondered at that according to Mensching Protestant (*evangelischen)* worship 'always has the character of liturgical uneasiness (*Unruhe)*. In itself it offers no certainty of God's presence'. As a result it cannot lead us closer to God;

'it only confirms and strengthens the certainty of salvation', and so is subjective. Indeed this worship itself 'is always in danger of becoming unevangelical and lifeless', something Mensching puts more strongly elsewhere, where he candidly defines as the essence of worship that the form it takes is constantly put in question by its content. 'Were it possible to *exclude* the *risk* of holiness disappearing from life, then religious vitality and originality would be lost!'[5]

What Mensching says will strike many sympathetic chords today, and has something of the stuff of risk and questioning which is very much part of the modern spirit. Such questioning is particularly necessary in a time of religious decadence. Here is David Jenkins again in similar vein: 'Religion produces quite as much unpleasantness as glory, and so much of the practice of religion is clearly for the benefit of the practitioners . . . The human and functional purpose of religion is clearly to shield people from reality and produce an induced warmness which protects them from the cold of actual reality'.[6]

We need to have our illusions exposed, and the only problem we can have with that is the salutary discomfort it causes. There is a problem here, however, and it concerns not so much what these authors say as the things they fail to say. Christianity is like family life in often finding itself holding opposites in tension. And if we take the family as an example here, then the critical outlook needs to be held in tension with a passionate love of the Church and of its liturgy and life as holy and to be revered. It is no answer to say that the whole of humanity is our family, because that simply erases the distinctive separateness of each human home which is at the root of any notion of family. Alan Clark, Roman Catholic Bishop of East Anglia, gives a taste of the tension involved in an interview with an Italian magazine:

> My Anglican colleagues need to give profound thought to the question of the authority of the Church, because they do not love the Church as we Catholics do. The Church for them is a 'thing', a society, a great society. Make no mistake: we Catholics are sometimes critical of the Church, and of the Holy Father, but we continue to love the Church, and the Pope, even if we can see that things are not going well.[7]

The convolutions of this are endless, for it is not uncommon to find Roman Catholic clergy, in Germany say, or in the USA, who show as little sign of love for the Church as do the Anglicans whom the bishop criticizes. On the whole, however, there is in Roman Catholic allegiance to the Church a bond 'in the guts' which is much less easy to find in churches of the Reformation, the absence of which the latter may not normally notice. At the same time it needs to be recognized that each attitude is too simple. Roman Catholic love for the Church is very often of a kind where charity begins at home, an extraordinary parochialism to find in the greatest Church in the world. It can be seen clearly in such a book as Owen Chadwick's *Britain and the Vatican in the Second World War*,[8] or in any number of ways in which the priority seems to be to protect the Roman Catholic Church before all else, and to ensure sound Catholic teaching and the sacraments to its people. These, of course, are all simply logical consequences of the call to stewardship of the mysteries of God, and yet it can often be the case that love of the Church is as capable of diminishing it as of benefiting it, and many outside the Roman Church see a disturbing element of 'kith and kin' over against Christians of other traditions. Two articles by Donald Nicholl on the Catholics and the Nazis, originally published in *The Tablet* in 1978, paint with graphic clarity some of the more ambiguous fruits of such a tradition. Having shown the unique degree to which the Roman Catholic Church had the measure of Hitler, and lacked neither the insight nor the courage to stand up to him, he shows why this failed to be put into practice:

> The bishops, the clergy, the Centre Party, the Catholic Workers' Movement, the intellectuals, those sort of people nowadays described as 'activists' did, to a large extent, see the evil in Nazism well before it got a grip upon the country. Why, then, did the German Catholics prove to be so impotent to change the course of events? One reason, surely, is that it is not sufficient simply to see the evil that is approaching yourself and your family; you must also see that which is threatening to get its hooks into other people as well. And here one notices how very rarely any Catholic voice was raised to ward off the blows that were threatening those people who were not members of the Catholic Church.[9]

It also emerges quite clearly that love of the Church is particularly dangerous stuff in a body which fails adequately to realize itself as the Church – in other words, in the German Church the clergy spoke for the laity without consulting them, seeking to protect a flock which did not ask for that kind of protection:

> In 1935 representatives of . . . youth organizations, trade unionists, academic associations, and other [groups] met in Mainz . . . [and] issued a *cri du coeur* to the German hierarchy then gathering for their annual meeting at Fulda. This moving cry from the heart of the German laity in 1935 listed the sufferings of the German people under the new regime and asked that their pastors, the bishops, should draw up a clear directive of how the faithful were to behave in face of each of the threats now facing them. The message . . . ended with the haunting phrase that unless this were done then the faithful would have to endure 'martyrdom without mandate'.
>
> In reply, on 15 August, the bishops sent a message full of solicitude and warm feelings but totally inadequate to the near despair that had prompted the request; and it can be said not unfairly that the faithful were indeed left to endure 'martyrdom without mandate'.[10]

The bishops' understandable worry was a repeat of the disastrous harrying of the Catholic Church which had taken place under Bismarck in his *Kulturkampf*. But they failed to listen to the very laity they mistakenly thought they were protecting, so that, by seeking to protect the Church as a whole from head-on State harassment, they left parish priests, laity and religious to be picked off individually and sent to concentration camps or worse, for resisting the regime without the 'mandate', the public endorsement, of the bishops. If we are to talk in terms of love of the Church, then we have to be sure that the voice of the Church truly is the voice of the Church at all levels. It does not seem that the situation between then and now has changed greatly in the Roman Catholic Church, so that it is not encouraging to see the minimal involvement of the laity, and some of the results of Catholic 'kith-and-kin' attitudes at the moment in Eastern Europe, in the setting up of parallel bishoprics in Orthodox countries.

Among Anglicans reverence for the Church is found in a variety of ways: for some, love of the Anglican tradition and its peculiarities and gifts, for others, simple (sometimes dogged) attachment to the local parish church. What is more difficult to find is a sense of the Church universal. If the church building were to burn down, many Anglicans would tend to stay at home on the following Sunday, while Roman Catholics would gather for mass anywhere, even on the street if need be. Frequently in Anglicanism we also find a picture of the Church in which *institution* and *Holy Spirit* are to some degree set in opposition in a mistaken way (God of the airwaves again). The Holy Spirit wants things this way, but the Church impedes the Spirit by wanting something else. It is not so easy to find among Anglicans a clearly visible and articulated sense of the universal Church as a unity which is holy, nor a very strong sense of family loyalty such as we would expect to find in any normal human family.

Anglicans are indeed weak on this sense of the Church, even if they will doubtless protest that they are not. If we turn our attention to the Orthodox, who always throw an interesting light on our foibles, the scene changes yet again. They would not speak immediately in Bishop Alan Clark's terms – before it came to that, we might expect to hear from them about reverence for the tradition and the liturgy, which is not to say that the Orthodox do not have a very high doctrine of the Church.

The main moral of such a conversation as this is probably to point out the different ways of seeing the question, and the need to beware of attitudes which are too simple or one-sided. We may even have a hunch that the truth includes all of them, Mensching and Clark, the Anglicans and the Orthodox, and many others too, and that the whole is greater and stranger still than the sum of them all put together. Modern wariness of the Church, therefore, has to go together with reverence for it. This is recognized in the world of narrative theory, where Paul Ricoeur has coined the phrase 'hermeneutics of suspicion' (hermeneutics means, in simple terms, 'ways of interpreting things'): the hermeneutics of suspicion takes nothing for granted, and questions all human motives for revering things; it 'unmasks human wish-fulfilments and shatters idols'.[11] On its own, however, this is sterile, and has to go hand in hand with a 'hermeneutics of retrieval which listens to symbols and to symbolic narrative discourse'. Our attitude to the Church will include a proper 'hermeneutic of suspicion', but equally essential is a 'hermeneutic of retrieval', a reverence for the Church as holy. It is here that Bishop Clark has something to say to Anglicans, and something which Christians as a whole have to say to the world (although often enough the world seems to see it more clearly than Christians themselves). The Church is 'not a mere object of theological knowledge; it is something to be lived'.[12]

## THE CHURCH AS SACRAMENT

Odo Casel does not fail to be critical of the Church where he thinks it necessary, and nevertheless, not least in his brush with Mensching, he is very definite about the view of the Church as Mystery. He bases it not so much on the incarnation as on the risen and glorified Lord.[13] He goes so far as to say: 'When we say "Church", we are not talking about some new mediator *alongside* the Lord: the Church *is* the *visible* Lord, that is, Christ now becomes visible to us in the visible Church'.[14] This echoes Bonhoeffer's dictum that 'the Church is Christ existing as community'.[15] This identity of the Lord with the Church has to be held in conjunction with a slightly different image, that of Christ as the head to whom the body is subordinated.[16] In the Church salvation history continues its work, and is carried forward. It is Christ himself who is at its head as the all-encompassing sacrament/mystery, and therefore behind this language of the Church as mystery there stands an understanding of Christ as the original Mystery (*Ursakrament*). This strong doctrine of the Church, so long as it is held together with recognition of the sinfulness of the Church, is an inevitable consequence of embracing the patristic notion of mystery, and the language finds its origin there. It reminds us that the Church's life is sacramental by nature. The Church is physical-spiritual, a psychosomatic organism.

The collect after the second lesson in the old Roman Paschal Vigil asks God to 'look graciously on the wonderful sacrament of your Church'.[17] There are many places in the writings of the Fathers where the Church is spoken of as mystery or sacrament. Cyprian says that the Church is 'the sacrament of unity'.[18] In the document *Lumen Gentium* the Church is likewise spoken of as sacrament.[19] On this subject there is an abundant literature. In speaking of the Church as sacrament, however, we have to return to the root-word 'mystery'.

The Mystery is Christ. The incarnation did not end with his physical departure – had it done so, then Jesus' followers would perforce have had to go back to a 'spiritual', abstract religion, for lack of anything better – back to the heaven-bound God of the Old Testament. The inevitable result of the incarnation and resurrection, however, was the emergence of a sacramental 'way', a body of believers who constituted a sacramental Church, in which physical engagement with God would continue. This emerged as a distinct body which was understood as 'holy'.

## A SPLIT-LEVEL CHURCH?

The use of the word 'mystery' in connection with the Church is not without problems. Edward Schillebeeckx criticises misuse of the word 'mystery' by those who would take it to mean a dimension of the Church which is over and above its human manifestations, as if there were the human, sinful Church on the one hand, and the 'mystery of the Church' on the other, and as if it could be said that the Church itself is holy, while its members are sinful. It is, rather, an ingenious, sacramental combination. The holiness of the Church is found in the very sinful people who make it up:

> The church community as mystery cannot be found behind or above concrete, visible reality. The church community is to be found *in* this reality which can be demonstrated here and now. We too, along with everyone in the base communities, are part of this living mystery. What happens in these communities is at the same time part of what we call the mystery of the church. The experiments and explorations, the mistakes and perhaps even follies and the findings, are parts of the phenomenon of the one great Catholica, which is found precisely as Catholica, here and now, in greater or lesser degrees of density in many Christian communities of faith, more watered down or more strongly concentrated. It is to be found in the meetings of base communities, of some house communities, of men and women, who come together in the name of Jesus, confessed by them as the Christ. Among them are many people who suffer from and over the present-day world and their own church and oppose the suffering which God does not will. They too are part of the mystery of the church, they too celebrate and bear witness to that mystery, and they do not allow themselves to be banned from this mystery by a church government with a short-sighted policy.[20]

120

## THE CHURCH AND THE WORLD

In the daily life of the world and in the men, women and children who make it up, God is present. This means that the world deserves our reverence. This goes hand in hand, however, with a sharp Christian critique of the world. The world of human beings is both to be revered and to be criticized. The same kind of two-edged relationship is also due to the Church. All people are sinful and corrupt, and there is as great a danger of idealizing them in daily life, as of idealizing them in the Church. The Church is holy and daily life is holy because, in the final analysis, in both of them is found the Mystery. And the Church is not the clergy, but the whole people of God.

Casel's doctrine of the Church is a strong one. Modern Christianity has yet to succeed in uniting such a vision with a strong doctrine of daily life. The two approaches are there, but even where they are held by the same persons, we do not succeed in enabling them to be an organic vision: a strong sense of the holiness of the transcendent God and his Church, fused with a strong sense of the holiness of life. The existence of the two poles among us is illustrated in this plea by an Orthodox Christian:

> That is our Church. We have no other. Only the Liturgy and the sacraments. The Church can be destroyed on the outside, but not internally . . . [In the West] the Church is, rather, being destroyed from the inside. There are many Christians here who have no understanding of what the Church actually is. For us that is unimaginable. The word 'Church' arouses both joy and trembling, as is to be expected in an encounter with the holy. The Church is always holy . . . The West and the East must help each other. The West needs this awe, this devotion, this faith, this trust. And we need the West. For Christianity must also get involved in the world.[21]

## WHO CELEBRATES THE MYSTERY?

Having said something about the balance of holiness and sin in the Church, we now turn to a set of questions which naturally arise among those who encounter Mystery-theology for the first time. What *is* the liturgy? Who *counts* as celebrating it? If it is a unique place of union with Christ, where we encounter nothing less than the saving events themselves, then there must be some clear way of distinguishing the kinds of worship at which this happens. If a group of assorted lay Christians gather together informally for a prayer service at their place of work on Christmas Eve, is the Mystery present? Or if a Greek Orthodox family went to a Pentecostalist church for Easter, how could they be certain about the matter? Or how far is the Mystery present in a school assembly which may be led by agnostics?

If worship, rather than being a mere occasion for distributing 'dollops' of grace, is in fact co-involvement in the events of Christ, then we need to be able to say what counts as worship – what kind of activity counts, and what kind of community? Otherwise it is difficult to claim any objectivity to the Mystery-presence – it will be everywhere and nowhere, or will appear according to its own whims, and we will only be able to try and 'tune in' to it at a subjective level, a situation in which we lose the incarnation. One solution would be to say that only officially authorized worship led by authorized ministers and fulfilling all due requirements are the Church's liturgy. This used to be the position in the Roman Catholic Church before the Second Vatican Council. Even in the Council documents this attitude still emerges very strongly. It can be seen, for instance, in the *General Instruction on the Liturgy of the Hours*, where only celebration by the clergy of the Roman Breviary or its authorized equivalents count as the Prayer of the Church, the daily office. In subsequent documents there has been a gradual movement away from this, even though there is still a very strong tendency for official pronouncements to speak as if 'The Church' were a tightly definable Roman citadel. Such a model can only work by ignoring the wide Christian diversity in the world today.

## WHAT COUNTS AS LITURGY?

If it is not possible to take the view that real Christian liturgy only takes place when it follows the authorized forms, celebrated by authorized ministers, and yet we wish to take seriously the notion of the Church as Mystery, then we still have to find some way of defining what counts as Christian liturgy.

We cannot define precisely how God acts, or indicate where he does this or that, or where he does not. All we can do is try and be reasonably sure of his intentions in fundamental areas, knowing that in the end God makes his appearance where he wills. The model here could be the nebula, which has a clearly recognizable centre, and then going out from it are areas of decreasing clarity. We have to let God be God, and accept that the way he in fact operates will never coincide neatly with our maps of it. We are not in the business of prescribing, but of mapping, establishing a map which will follow God's movements sufficiently closely for us to be able to regard it as the most reliable map to hand, and enough for us to allow it to guide our action. A suitable parallel to illustrate this would be the wind. The wind blows where it wills, and its actions, capacities and ramifications are so complex and unpredictable as to be beyond our grasp. The meteorologist, however, can usually operate with a reasonable degree of certainty by relying on the vast amount of scientific knowledge now available, and although there will be some embarrassing mistakes, in a majority of individual instances he or she will be on the right lines, and in the long term over the years will stay in touch with general trends. Weather forecasters will be only too aware of the lurching, hectic, risky nature of the game, but if they hold on tight and keep a clear head and a sufficient grasp of the overall enterprise, it works. The parameters hold, but only with a flexible spirit. If we absolutize them, we lose track of the wind.

## A NUANCED ECCLESIOLOGY

The Mystery-doctrine of Odo Casel forces us to examine our ecclesiology, for while it is possible to make a 'tight' ecclesiology workable if we concentrate on the 'validity' of the sacraments, this becomes much more difficult if we increase their number, and increase the acreage of their location. By this I mean that, for instance, in the eucharist the scholastic concentration of 'presence' almost exclusively in the bread and wine is broken open by Casel to become a presence which embraces all the participants and the action they are engaged in, even if the presence in the gifts remains unique (and all of this was the understanding of the early Church). Writers in this school frequently say in addition that the Mystery-presence varies in intensity and in emphasis, so that, for instance, in the celebration of a feast the particular 'mystery' of that feast is especially intense, but never at the expense of the whole range of the acts of our redemption.

Mystery-theology therefore demands a much more nuanced conception of the Church, perhaps along the lines of that proposed by Edward Schillebeeckx in his book, *The Church with a Human Face*.[22]

For Schillebeeckx, apostolicity is a fundamental criterion for identifying the Church. It is the unique mystery present in the apostles' own lived experience, a mystery handed on through the history of the Church. The word for 'handing on', *paradosis,* has come to be translated by the technical word 'tradition'. The apostolic *paradosis* embraces the whole Christian way embodied in the Church, her Scriptures, sacraments and self-understanding. There are various things which show the presence of this tradition, and they include worship which is within this continuity, right belief, and right ordering of the Church. This tradition, however, is God's free gift. All we can do is spot it, like the wind, staying true to our 'maps', but accepting that our maps are imperfect. Apostolic succession is one of the conditions by which the presence of the apostolic mystery, the *paradosis*, may be tested. Various elements go to make it up: the Scriptures, baptism, episcopal ordination of ministers, right faith, right practice, and so on, but often one or more is missing, without seriously diminishing a church's apostolicity. It may be the absence of episcopal ordination, or diminution of the proper role of all baptized believers, faulty belief or inadequate liturgy. It is Schillebeeckx's view that through too much of the Church's history life and initiative have come 'from above' rather than 'from below', and he says this not to deny the importance of the orders of ministry and their due role, but rather in order to show that this has to be complemented by an acknowledgment that the 'validity' of a local Christian community is ultimately tested by identification in it of the presence of the *paradosis* of the apostles, which is a gift of God.

One difficulty with this view is that while Church life which works from the 'top' downwards has a tendency to ossify into 'system', Schillebeeckx's own 'bottom up' view of the people of God fails to recognize that the sin which can turn sacrament into system is present in all human beings, and is just as likely to turn a 'people's Church' into system. There is, in other words, a great danger of sentimentalizing the people of God, and Schillebeeckx's vision fails to give serious attention to this. His view does, however, have several great merits:

1   It does justice to the misgivings of those many Christians who find it incredible that the Jesus portrayed in the gospels intended to found a legalistic system.

2   It takes serious account of all those committed Christians troubled by the fact that the 'system' has, by all appearances, a long record of quenching the Spirit.

3   It puts the 'system' in a wider context which enables it to be what it is intended to be – not simply system, but sacrament.

4   It achieves this while remaining firmly within mainstream tradition.

Whatever we may think of the particular vision of Schillebeeckx, it is within some such articulated and nuanced model of the Church, and a model that is rooted in historical fact, that we are enabled to say something credible about where to expect the presence of the Mystery. The Lord is going to make himself present when and where he pleases, and our 'mappings' are more for guiding us on how to act, than for prescribing all the circumstances in which the Lord will act.

It is interesting to find Casel's pupil Salvatore Marsili lending some support to such a view from another direction. He was almost unique in his time in saying that the Church's popular traditions and folk customs are also the liturgy of the Church. Roman centralism has always thought in terms of a centralized, clerical liturgy, but Marsili wants to include those forms of liturgy that have evolved on the ground, amongst the people: devotions, pilgrimages, popular 'piety', in which European Catholicism is (or was) particularly rich. He quotes the great liturgical scholar Joseph Jungmann as saying that the liturgy is the Church's worship, and this means 'not the worship for which the Church has fixed the norms, nor the worship which the Church authorizes; above all it means the worship that the Church actually does. The "Church at prayer", or the Church gathered for the activity of worship, is the real expression of the liturgy'.[23] Christian liturgy is strongly defined by tradition and authority, but forms cannot simply be handed down from above, and when they are, people will inevitably make up the insufficiencies by creating their own usages for themselves.

In conclusion, if a more specific answer is required to the question, 'What *counts* as Christian liturgy?', then it is difficult to be more specific than I have been. We can say that the Mystery is present in daily life, and as such is present to some degree or other among any who gather for the specific purpose of seeking it. In addition Christ in his saving deeds enters into active encounter with Christians whenever they gather for prayer in his name. We know that there is a uniqueness about this presence in the liturgy of a Church which is sacrament, but we can only map, and not prescribe, Christ's mode of operation. We are dealing with two complementary manifestations of Christ's Mystery. On the one hand, although *people* are full of sin and self-deception, there is something in their lives which is *real,* and so important that we have to attend to it. On the other hand, although the *Church* is full of sin and self-deception, there is something there, particularly in its liturgy, which is *real,* and so important that we have to attend to it.

## NINE

# *How? – Time Machines,*
# *Wholeness and Butterflies*

WE HAVE BEEN examining the question, 'How can we realistically speak of the presence of the saving events?', but found ourselves needing to turn our attention to another query: 'Is the Church special?' Now we can pick up the first question again, on which there is quite a bit more to be said.

## TRAVELLING BACK

Imagine you had the chance to use a time machine, and decided to travel back to Golgotha. You make the journey, and there you are. You are in the incredible situation of seeing Christ on the cross. There is his mother, and there are the friends standing by. There too are the thieves, the soldiers, the crowd. You feel overwhelmed and almost paralyzed by the scale of the drama, for you become starkly aware that this scene is the object of the attention of millions of souls down the future centuries, millions of individuals, thousands of communities, hundreds of nations. As you stand here this sense bears upon you with extraordinary weight. All those crucifixes, all those eucharists, all those prayers, gather at this one point where we are standing, at the foot of the cross on Golgotha. From the catacombs to the great basilicas, from the millions of humble parish churches to some of the great momentous occasions of history, the conversion of Constantine, the rebellion of Luther, the Second Vatican Council. So many eyes, so much weight of the history yet to come, looking intently to this scene, and to the scenes which precede and follow. There you stand, witness to terrible events. And this man on the cross, this broken, brutalized scrap of humanity, is a king enthroned in glory in thousands of icons, stained glass windows, and innumerable prayers. What a mountain of prayer and ceremony converges on this painful scene!

The cross and resurrection of Christ have been the subject of such a degree of attention that as we follow in awe and behold the burial of the Lord and, shortly after, the women going to the tomb, we might be tempted to think, on turning our thoughts back to Odo Casel, that he ought to have spoken of ourselves being present to the mystery-events rather than vice versa. As we stand at the foot of the cross, all the future ages are present, travelling back not by time machine but through their attention, their entering prayerfully into the Scriptures, and supremely through the liturgy. Might it not be easier to think of our participation in worship being like this? – a journey back through the ages: we are transported to the events, so that we are present to them. One thing is certain: if we had made such a journey through time and then returned to our parish in Luton or Liverpool, we would never be the same again. Every time we went to church we would relive the journey. The 'travelling back' would be so natural as to be almost automatic. In our mind and heart we would go back, joining the millions of whom we had thought, participating ourselves in that vast throng in its attention to this scene. If we look at this from the perspective of humanitas, then encounters with people's suffering too will 'take us back' to our visit to Golgotha. The phrase is interesting; we do not say, on visiting the mock-up of a 1950s shop interior in a museum, 'it conjures it up', but rather, 'it takes you back'.

It is not difficult to see from this imaginary journey that the thought of travelling back to the saving events is a potent one, and that when the Fathers, and the Jews before them, spoke of participating in the events by means of the liturgy, what they were really trying to put into words was an experience of travelling backwards to the events, rather than the events travelling forward to us. This point has been made by some commentators on Casel's theology, especially Viktor Warnach, and, more lately, Cesare Giraudo.[1] Such an approach has several merits. First, it makes the notion of encounter between ourselves and the saving events thinkable in a very vivid way. We only have to imagine ourselves at Golgotha to realize how all that attention of future generations will be for us a powerful and moving presence. Second, it emphasizes the historical nature of the events, and avoids turning them into an omnipresent abstract myth. Third, it is in harmony with the Jewish tradition of *anamnesis* out of which the Christian liturgical practice was born. Those who keep the Passover are passing through the Red Sea themselves.

However, we have to take note of the fact that this theory has major drawbacks. First of all, 'this is my body' speaks of a present reality, and tradition believes that insofar as the bread and wine at the eucharist can be spoken of as the body and blood of Christ, it is in terms of Christ coming to us rather than us going to him. Second, belief that we travel directly to the saving events cuts out the whole of intervening history – it puts two separate moments in connection, rather than seeing history as an organic, unfolding process of God's self-revelation – 'the Holy Spirit will lead you into all truth'. Third, because of this it also cuts out the Church as a continuation of the incarnation and resurrection. We behold the cross and the resurrection, but cut out the pipeline through which they have been held before people throughout history. Fourth, it plays down the physical dimension of the *present* moment, which becomes a mere means for our 'time-travel', rather than the very circumstances in which Christ makes himself present – in cutting out the present moment, worship can hardly fail to be a flight from the present. Humanitas is well and truly left behind. Fifth, *anamnesis* is made not just of the past, but also of the future. The saving events include the *parousia*, Christ's second coming. It is much easier to think of all times converging on the present moment, than of trying to direct our attention all ways at once. Christ would not be coming to Charing Cross or the Bronx – they would be left behind as we chase after him. These are hefty criticisms, and if they hold water they might be thought fatally to undermine the idea. Truth, however, like three-dimensional vision or stereophonic sound, repeatedly asks us to hold differing things together and try to enter a third dimension of seeing. The 'time machine' model is too fruitful and too vivid to us to be entirely wrong. If all times are his, and all the ages, then it could be said that we can only gain a feel for God's time by travelling up and down it in both directions, or, in liturgical terms, by letting the manifestation of the Mystery come to us at the same time as we are in turn transported to it.

## AN OBJECTIVE PRESENCE

'Travelling back' needed at some point to be mentioned, but there are quite a few things still to be said about 'travelling forward', and it will be good to begin by taking up the notion of 'presence'. If 'presence' seems an inadequate term to use, it is nevertheless the one used by most people, not least Casel himself, and as we continue to explore his thinking we shall find ourselves inevitably returning to it. Casel insists that the presence is first of all *objective* (rather than a subjective experience of the believer, although it will also be that), and that it involves the dimension of the physical. There is a common tendency in commentators on Mystery-theology to speak in terms of something 'spiritual' which is presented in physical form in the symbols of the liturgy. Sometimes it is said in effect that the inner *essence* of the saving events can be separated from the original events and re-attached to the symbols of the liturgy. Even Casel himself can use similar terms – in several places he says the presence is beneath the 'veil' of the liturgical signs. Elsewhere he emphasizes with great force the physical nature of the presence, and we are left wondering quite what he means in all of this. The problem is a real one, for if our salvation rests in an abstract 'essence', then the incarnation is undermined, and the Western delight in exalting the abstract and the mental above the physical will triumph once again, and the Hebrew understanding of the 'flesh' bite the dust. If, however, we overplay the idea of physical presence, we are in danger of claiming what is patently untrue: we see no real, bloody Golgotha in our parish churches – that would seem more appropriate to seances than to Christian worship. We see no centurion, no disciples, we hear no shouts, and see no physical violence. How can we make sense of these apparent contradictions?

## ACTION

First of all, the liturgy for Casel is *action:*

> When we talk today about the mysteries of Christianity, we immediately think of theological doctrines . . . But the ancients understood the Christian Mysteries to be something quite different . . . [they are] the liturgical accomplishment of the Christian saving events, the sacred *Mystery-action,* a concrete, visible, tangible and audible entity, whose reality consists not only in concrete things, but also in an *action,* which is carried out before the eyes of the beholders, and in which they themselves join through their own action.[2]

Engagement with the Mystery involves physical things and people, and physical action, but this only lives through the power of the Holy Spirit:

> Contact with the Godhead through the sacrament does not rely simply on being subjectively 'spiritual': it is objective and physical. This is no 'religious materialism', but rather the highest triumph of the Spirit, where matter is here a totally obedient servant of the Spirit, while on the other hand the spiritual power raises up the material to itself and fills it so that it becomes spiritual.[3]

Again:

> The promise 'I am with you always until the end of the world' is to be fulfilled not merely by the moral or spiritual protection of grace in the abstract, but in a concrete yet Spirit-filled presence, of an objective nature. Therefore the Lord left behind him for his Church not merely faith and Spirit but his Mysteries.[4]

And again:

> Because we are flesh and blood God has given us in addition the visible sign of the Mysteries. They attest for us, in a way we can touch and see, the reality of our faith. This has always been God's way with us. Christ himself became visible, and when his human form was taken away we continued to see him in the visible signs of his Mysteries. Scripture itself gives us proof that God communicates himself to people by means of visible, tangible things. We have only to think of the Lord's

healing of the sick: his restoration of the sick body was a sign of the healing of the soul ... Now Christ is risen, it is no different: he lets himself be known to his friends in visible signs; he has Thomas touch him, he eats with the disciples; they recognize him at the breaking of the bread.[5]

In another place he says:

If in itself the life of faith could still be conceived as a purely intellectual or moral bond, yet the Mysteries show us that Christianity involves an endlessly deeper, physical incorporation into the mystic Christ.[6]

If Casel has to emphasize the physical, he makes clear too that the Mystery involves not part of us, but our entirety. 'Faith in its fullness is no mere act of obedience on the part of the intellect, but the gift of our whole self to the divine life'.[7]

## THE WHOLE OF OURSELVES

What is meant by 'the whole of ourselves'? We can readily conjure up the elements which are popularly considered to make up the 'whole person': (a) the body, (b) the senses, (c) the thinking mind, (d) the feelings, (e) the intuitive and perceiving faculties, and (f) the various unconscious 'layers' of the human personality. All of these elements are usually in operation, but always with one or two predominating: the blacksmith will rely heavily on (say) a and b, with a certain amount of c and e, the opera singer on a, b and e, with some occasional quick use of c, the theologian on c and e. And yet this does not do justice to what is going on: when a person acts with the whole of their being there is more to it than simply an aggregation of elements. Take an extreme case: when Beethoven was writing his ninth symphony the autograph score shows that this was a very physical operation – it was bursting with feelings too, sensuousness, searching vigour, thought out with great cogency, while also welling up from Beethoven's unconscious being: it was an intuition on the grandest of scales. When we hear the music, however, we have to say that these elements were not operating separately: the whole of his being is one with itself and with the creation which is issuing from him, while at the same time it is an almighty struggle, often threatening to slide into chaos, and miraculously all coming together again in a unity beyond our comprehending.

That is not reserved to great composers: in varying degrees throughout the day we too are living like this with the 'whole of ourselves'. It is the way the person thoroughly enjoying cricket throws the ball, the way children play an engrossing game, the way we sometimes talk with each other, love each other, argue with each other, burst out in anger, act cunningly in a sticky situation. This takes place sometimes with more, sometimes with less of the 'whole' of ourselves. In addition it is part of the human experience to enter moments when all that is in us is fused into a single movement and we realize in a greater way than is usual the wholeness of our humanity. A really good laugh can be as near to it as a symphony: these are moments when our self gets in the way less than usual, because we are momentarily lost in self-giving. Our poor old self, in fact, spends a lot of its time getting in the way of being itself. Heightened inner consciousness of ourselves is a great gain, but brings with it a great loss.

## MORE THAN OURSELVES

To that crude sketch we now have to add something more. There are two aspects to it: the communal and the transcendent, and they are linked. The communal aspect might not seem very obvious, and so it is especially important to draw attention to it. The reason I am here is that the human race physically produced me. It also provided me with my genes. That sets the scene for all that follows: from a community I receive my language, my capacity to think, my education, my culture; my character is affected by those responsible for my upbringing, and my daily bread, food, shelter and safety all depend on society and family. While there are both communal and individual dimensions to the human person, it is a fact of life that community is 'prevenient', as it were, in our formation. The community, our culture, was there before we were, and the things in other people which have marked us in life flow through us in all that we do, intimately united with our real and unique individuality. Had Clint Eastwood been a Yorkshireman, acting with the 'whole of himself' would have brought some very different results. Had Alf Garnett been adopted at birth by an arty, liberal university lecturer, the same individuality would have some possibilities denied to it, and others opened up. And even before that particular twist of community influence on him, there is the *historical* fact that the human community is prevenient. Every human person emerges into personhood from community. Another way of recognizing this is to speak of co-inherence. This term is familiar in theology to those who have studied the doctrine of the Trinity. The three persons are distinct, but they also co-inhere in each other. We can also say that people co-inhere in each other, in all the ways we have mentioned. The community and its traditions, our language, our relations and friends, our culture and its representatives, such as Beethoven, Augustine, Elvis Presley, all co-inhere in us, they are thoroughly a part of what we are.

To that community within and without, there is a further dimension: it can sometimes seem to us that our actions have been 'inhabited' by something – perhaps it may be something like that 'love which moves the sun and the rest of the stars' of which Dante speaks. Some would put it in terms of God, some would be agnostic about it, some would seek to rationalize it partly as projection, and partly as a concept like John Robinson's 'ultimate reality'. The way we interpret it does not much matter here. What concerns us is the very common and ancient perception that there is 'more', more than the whole of ourselves, more than all of those people who 'co-inhere' in us, something more which summons, and which is of a life and depth extending beyond our horizons, or coming to us from beyond them, we are not sure, and which can leave us feeling, as when we are with those we love, or listening to Mozart, that we are not just the whole of ourselves, but more than ourselves, and reaching out to still more.

It is in such terms as these that we must envisage what is at stake in Christian worship. It summons the body, the senses, mind, feelings, intuition and all our unconscious layers to be involved, engaged in concert as a dynamic unity, 'swooping', forgetful of ourselves, going out beyond ourselves. Occasionally something like this may actually take place in worship, but more often it will be partial, with instalments here, instalments there. Its perfect realization is the end towards which we look, that perfect humanity which is at unity with God. To repeat Casel's words, 'Faith in its fullness is no mere act of obedience on the part of the intellect, but the gift of our whole self to the divine life'.[8]

## PRESENCE IN DAILY LIFE

Our purpose in looking more closely at the meaning of the phrase, the 'whole of ourselves' was to put the physical in its fuller context. The divine presence we encounter in the liturgy is integral, involving the whole of our being, of which the physical is a part which must not be minimized.

We can now return to our main inquiry, and the search for responses to the question of how the saving events become 'present' in the liturgy, this time taking as our starting-point everyday life itself. Christ is present in our neighbour, and he is present in the life around us. In all the suffering we see in others or endure ourselves, in all the darkess and evil buried in the human spirit, and in the certain triumph of death over us all, we come to know the cross of Christ. In this we do not see the crucifixion as a tragedy like any other human tragedy, but quite the reverse: all our darknesses are an engagement with the eternal now of Christ's cross. In all those situations, on the other hand, where life triumphs and evil fails to take the upper hand, we are glimpsing the resurrection. The pain of joy is different from the pain of darkness, for in joy we find pleasure in something that will never please us enough. Like an early day of spring, it can even be so beautiful that we can hardly bear it, realizing the fact that we are not large enough to receive it. We cannot cope with too much celebration – and so our encounter with the resurrection brings home to us that in the short term resurrection leads to waiting, to hope as a way of life, rather than hope fulfilled. If, in the light and dark of life we are not after all encountering Christ's very cross and resurrection, then life is less than we thought it was, and the gospel more remote. 'I bear in my flesh the marks of the Lord Jesus' (Galatians 6.17) is a vivid description of such an identification. Our only ultimate response in the face of the atrocious sufferings that come before our helpless eyes by means of modern communications is to acknowledge that our tongues are silenced. Christ suffers in his people, and shares with them all their darkness and all their light.

## PRESENCE IN THE LITURGY

If it is possible to speak in this way of daily life, this opens the way for us to turn our attention to Christian worship. First of all, worship, however esoteric it might be, is a part of life. These truths about everyday life apply here too. But there is more. We go into church and take our place, waiting. The liturgy comes into action. In some ways it is part and parcel with life outside: language, music, clothes, seats, light-fittings, walking, sitting, standing. But it is also unique and different. It is a particular ceremony or game following its own rules. But even here there are parallels with the world outside. The Christ of salvation history is met in people co-operating together in an action. The passion, the cross and the resurrection are all there in them. But they are also there in people's gifts, great and small, and in physical objects, in the dance and play of the liturgy. In the bread and the wine without any doubt. But this is extended to all the visible paraphernalia, even the candles and the servers who are holding them, the books given out, and the helpers giving them. All is sacrament, all is the Mystery. It is, as it were, 'concrete grace'.[9] A little boy who was being got ready for bed once asked, 'Daddy, what does God wear?' – a very profound question, as we can often expect from the mouths of children, who are more in touch with the basics than adults often are. God wears all the things we have been talking about, and his clothes are concrete grace. God wears the liturgy, he wears the baptized.

## DRAMA

God 'wears' us in the enacting of his drama. Greek drama in its origins was religious, and European drama has religious origins too. Drama is a natural constitutent of liturgy, because liturgy is the drama of dramas. The Greeks believed that in their plays the characters were co-actors with the gods. In Christian liturgy we are co-actors with Christ. Odo Casel believed this passionately:

> Believers . . . unite themselves in the closest possible way with the action of their Lord and saviour; they offer themselves as a sacrifice with him and through him, and unite themselves to that redemption which by Christ is objectively accomplished; they become creative out of the deep sources of the Redeemer. They suffer with him, rise with him, are glorified with him, and enter with him into his heavenly nature. In this way they perform with him a holy, grace-bestowing drama . . . every participant in the celebration of the eucharist is a co-actor

136

with Christ the divine protagonist; indeed, he or she in a certain degree plays his very person.[10]

Following the principle of interillumination, we can furthermore say that this is true of daily life. We are co-actors with Christ in the world. Through the grace which we receive in the liturgy it is possible to see all of life as part of the drama of God. Outside on the street the cross and resurrection are acted out in the things and people we see and touch. The whole point of immanence is the divine presence in the very physical things themselves as they are – in the pensioner mugged at night, the naughty boys stealing fruit, laughter at a party. If this can be said of the liturgy, then we seem to be forced to a conclusion of dramatic simplicity. All the events of salvation history have come and gone. History is past, and cannot be repeated. The scene on Golgotha, the crowd, the centurion, have all gone and will never be seen again: the saving events have died. But they died as a seed died and, passing through that cosmic interface which is the resurrection, they continue to live in the sacramental order of the Church. Just as the seed dies to bring forth the plant, the Church is that new order in which the Mystery is carried forward in the epiphany of the liturgy. The visible liturgy is the very presence of the Mystery; it is the space in which we engage with the whole of ourselves in the whole of the Mystery, or, in Casel's preferred language, in the saving events.

Now, in all honesty a parish eucharist does not look much like Golgotha or the empty tomb. Nor does it always look inspiring. Does all this really happen in the midst of candles not put in straight, grubby servers in albs and trainers, half-hearted singing and unspeakable sermons? And even if the liturgy is beautiful and inspiring, are we *really* supposed to believe that something so visibly different from the bloody scene on Golgotha is its visible presence? In order to throw light on this, it would help to discover some commonly experienced area of human living where there is a similar discrepancy between a reality we know to be there and the outward circumstances which bear it.


## MUSIC

We have such a field in the world of music, which gives us not a direct parallel, but one close enough for our purposes. Music normally does not describe the appearance of anything. Unlike painting or sculpture, whose roots lie in representation and have found some of their greatest power there, and unlike poetry and literature, the trunk of whose tree is the description and discussion of things as we know them in daily life, music's foundation is pure sound. Occasionally it can be used to represent sounds in daily life (such as in Prokofiev's *Peter and the Wolf*) but such things are peripheral to the main stream of music, and rarely rise above the merely entertaining (that is not to despise entertainment). The strange mystery of music is that it takes nothing out of everyday life, it imitates or represents nothing we can recognize or put into words, apart from rough-and-ready descriptions of mood, or sometimes approximate evocations of sounds and associations. A Mozart symphony can take us to the height and depth and make us feel utterly and profoundly human, and yet the sounds relate to nothing. Shakespeare's *King Lear* excavates our inward parts through the persons and events of a story which we can follow and describe to others, a story which reflects pathos and exaltation knowable in our own life. Rodin's sculpture 'The Kiss' opens to us the spiritual physicality of human loving, and gives us a picture of human life as it is or can sometimes be. Beethoven or Schumann, however, leave us electrified and we cannot say why.

If we turn back to Casel's reading of the Fathers, we find them saying this: the saving deeds of Jesus, and especially the incarnation, cross and resurrection, gave birth to something which is at the heart of the gospel; they gave birth to the Body of Christ, which immediately began evolving its liturgy. The disciples' involvement in Christ's life, death and resurrection becomes an involvement *to us too*, but in the form of the liturgy. The liturgy in certain ways, but not all, is like music, in that it does not exactly represent either the life and deeds of Jesus nor our own daily life. If anyone participating in the Holy Week liturgies were looking for representation, they might say that a passion play would do it better than this. The 'passion-play' element was indeed introduced in the later Middle Ages, with a greater emphasis on tying the liturgy more closely to the sequence of historical events, but the general opinion is that this only succeeded in reducing the obliqueness and profundity of the liturgy. The liturgy is something all its own, a 'music' born out of the cross and resurrection. Or in fact perhaps we should say that the cross and resurrection became the liturgy. As Leo the Great put it, 'What was visible in the Lord has passed over into the mysteries'.[11] The liturgy is a symphony of signs, the physical presence of the Paschal Mystery.

## THE BUTTERFLY

Another image may help us to take this a little further. When W. R. Inge (Dean of St Paul's, 1911–34) was once asked whether he had any interest in liturgy, he is said to have replied, 'No: nor do I collect butterflies'.[12] Our business here is to redeem such a poor understanding of the liturgy, but it is also possible perhaps to redeem Inge's image of the butterfly. The liturgy emerged from the events of those three days in Jerusalem just as a butterfly emerges from that which goes before it, totally different, and yet the same being, the same material. A butterfly is an interesting image, not only because it is a traditional symbol of the resurrection, but also because it makes us realize the enormous advantage of such a 'translation' of the saving events. The caterpillar is slow and restricted, confined to one small piece of earth, while the butterfly, like the Spirit, blows where it wills: the world lies at its feet, and the scandal of particularity is eliminated. The culturally determined, temporally and spatially marginal, almost parochial events of the life of our Lord are by this translation made readily accessible to every parish church and Christian community the world over, and are made contemporary with them, because of that contextualization ('inculturation') which is fundamental to the nature of liturgy.

It might be thought that if this theory is correct, then only a small core element of the liturgy can be involved, such as the water in baptism, or the actions and words of the last supper in the eucharist. It is sometimes said that the liturgy is built upon 'deep structures' which indicate its essential, minimum content. So the liturgy of the eucharist acts out the four actions of taking ('offertory'), blessing (eucharistic prayer), breaking (fraction) and distributing (communion), and the eucharistic prayer itself contains a range of standard elements, which go to make up the 'deep structures'. But our 'translation', our 'butterfly', cannot involve just these basic patterns. It has more to it. The liturgy in actual use is always contextualized, filled out, beautified, endowed with symbol and gesture which arise out of the local culture. The basic structures never exist on their own, any more than the branches of a tree can have been created without the leaves. It is impossible to celebrate the eucharist simply in terms of its 'four actions' in the abstract. They have to be expressed in commonplace and local details. To say otherwise is to end up with the medieval problem of what to do with all the bread in the monastic bakery if a priest walks in and says, 'this is my body'. It is important for our understanding of worship to identify its deep structures, but that is not enough. *Inculturation* is so native to the liturgy that it is rarely satisfactory or, it might even be said, possible, to limit worship's essence or 'soul' to those inner structures alone. So, when the eucharist is celebrated in Africa, it would be a travesty of the liturgy to say that the saving Mystery-presence is to be identified simply with its most basic actions: the hearing of the Word, the taking of bread and wine, giving thanks and distributing, and so on; for on their own they are a mere skeleton which cannot become eucharist unless they are enfleshed. Rather are we to identify the 'translation' with the whole liturgy, including the dancing, the marimbas, the drums, the rich, syncopated African choral singing. Truly contextualized liturgy is a fleshing-out and extending of the fundamental core until the core *lives*. Without that, it is a lifeless shape, the famous 'shape' of the liturgy, but lifeless. Casel comes close to this when he says:

> The content, and so the essential form of the mysteries, have been instituted and commanded by our Lord himself; he has entrusted their performance to the Church, but not laid down to the last detail what is necessary or desirable for a communal celebration. By leaving the Spirit to his Church, he has given her the ability as well, to mint inexhaustible treasure from the mystery entrusted to her, to develop it and to display it to her children in ever new words and gestures.[13]

This liturgy, the people who make it up, the style of its performance, the choir, the servers – all these things constitute the presence. In one sense, dare we say it, it is as simple as that. If, while playing my part in the worship, I ask myself, 'how can I get in touch with the Mystery? How can I perceive its *presence?*', one answer is, 'look no further than what you can see, hear and touch. This is it. God's workings in us cannot always be perceived, but his presence is always before our eyes'. It helps to remember that Mystery means sacrament. It is the Mystery-sacrament. Even when vicar and curate sit down to say the daily office together, what we see, hear and perform is the Mystery-sacrament. The solitary commuter, too, saying the Church's evensong on the train, is embodying the Mystery-sacrament; all around too, in the surrounding passengers, in their tiredness, hopes, angers, worries, in the baby's cries and the quiet conversation, the Mystery is hidden there. The Mystery-sacrament can be perceived as entirely objective, purely on the surface of things. Where is the Mystery? There to be seen and touched in the people and the book and the silent words. When we look at the entire situation, however, we have to say that it involves not less than the whole, the outward and the inward, the actions, bodies and movements, but also the thoughts, intuitions, emotions and that inner language in which 'heart speaks to heart'. Without that, worship is mere mechanism, an outward routine; but we do have to learn that without the external liturgy the interior journey is severely handicapped, or even doomed to failure.

## SUMMARY

At this point in our journey it will help to sum up the ground we have traversed so far. The question of how the saving events become present has always to be seen in the light of the word 'Mystery' which itself has to be held in tandem with the word 'sacrament'. We have seen several ways in which it is possible to talk of this presence which is not simple presence, but engagement and involvement:

1   It is unquestionably the case as far as *subjective* experience is concerned – enough people have spontaneously spoken of this sense of being in the presence of the cross and the resurrection during the liturgy for it to be accepted as a natural experience of Christians.

2   The quasi-sacramental *kerygma* proclaimed in the New Testament comes upon us in the liturgy in the Scriptures.

3   Christ's ministry is present in the form of conflict.

4   The people in church bring the saving events with them from their daily lives.

5   We are taken to the saving events, travelling, as it were, back through time.

6   The saving events are present physically and spiritually

141

in the liturgy as it is, in all its details, majestic or mundane. What we see is a 'translation' of the foundation-drama so that we also can become actors in it.

If this were all, perhaps we could be happy, but questions continue to press upon us. We can attend the worship in our local church and come out thinking all these theories to be very fine, but, really, that is not how it feels. Our worship does not rise sufficiently above the mundane for us to say categorically, 'this is so'. It just does not seem like that when we are worshipping. There is a lack of 'empirical fit'. Is it in fact credible when we are faced with worship in our own parish church?

# TEN

# *Is it Credible?*

## WHAT WE ALREADY KNOW

CASEL'S THEOLOGY SETS out not to add to our experience, but to put in traditional Christian language things that we already know. Such language will always mislead until we see what it is talking about. This is true of the whole of life, and not only of theology. For example, if a friend told you that an unidentifiable foreign body had lodged in one of the vital tubes in her husband's body, and this had set off powerful convulsions during which he momentarily lost his hearing and his balance, you might be alarmed. Only when you saw him sneezing would you recognize the experience that the words were attempting to fit. I once made a journey to Poland at a time when there were riots against the Communist government. Many friends were concerned that I should cancel my journey. This illustrates well the over-simple way in which we read information. On another occasion when I was in Budapest, all the news media were full of pictures of violent riots in an English city. I was asked by people in the hotel whether it was safe for me to go home until they had stopped. The danger in presenting the theology of Casel is one of failing to enable the hearer to get beyond the theories to the living thing of which they are a poor imitation.

Mystery-theology can seem to ask us to expect from worship something more dramatic than we are used to. Casel then seems to be like the people in the Budapest hotel, not a person to be taken seriously. If we have problems with him, however, it is we who are the Hungarians in this story. Casel proposes nothing dramatically new – rather does he attempt to put better things that we already express, but badly. Our usual language about what happens in worship is in many ways inadequate, as all language must be. Casel tries to show that we need to recover a way of looking at it which we once had, but have lost. The language about the saving events is a kind of 'template' which, when held against our worship, shows up in it things which we have probably not before considered. I remember a children's game where a piece of paper was covered with a whirling mass of meaningless coloured shapes. With it came a piece of coloured cellophane. When you looked at the paper through the cellophane (say it was red) the shapes in certain colours disappeared, and there became visible a ship or a flower or some other object. Reading Casel and reading his patristic texts colours our sight, so that we see the liturgy in a different way: but still the same liturgy and the same experience. The language of Mystery, arising out of the New Testament and developed by the Church Fathers gives us (a) a more adequate way of describing what we already experience and know in worship, and (b) a more adequate theology for speaking both about that and about all in worship which is beyond our experience and our sight. And (c) it gives us a way of seeing the connections between eternalism and humanitas.

## SINKING IN

In worship we are dealing with things which are not simple, but have all the complexity of life itself. An act of worship can often leave us with feelings more mixed than we would like, for we want its effect on us to be simple and straightforward. If the saving events are present, then it ought to be obvious. God, however, tends to work on the gradual principle.

We are in fact gradual beings. We do not like shocks or sudden changes, and we take time to adapt to drastic alterations in circumstances. Often there is a process of 'sinking-in'. Sometimes we respond by double-take, while at other times we can only cope through an involuntary delayed reaction. This can take many forms. Say, for instance, you are knocked over by a car while shopping. Scrambling up immediately, you assure the gathering crowd that you are all right. People collect up the bits of your shopping, put the shattered eggs in a bin, brush down the soiled coat, and help you into a shop to sit down, while the driver of the car, as white as a sheet, stands there looking helpless. You insist you are fine, and get home on the bus. A few hours later you become very ill, and have to be put to bed. The doctor is called. 'It's the shock of the accident', he says, 'a case of delayed shock – she'll be all right'.

Such experiences as that come within the category of the psychosomatic, affecting both our mind and our body in a way which shows how closely both are connected. There are many ways in which this phenomenon of delay shows itself, not least in the realm of the affections. Dramatic events in our personal life can be strangely unreal at the time. When we are parted from someone close to us, perhaps by death, or by the equally traumatic experience of a marriage break-up, the events themselves can take place quickly and without much drama – on the outside, appearances retain their normality and ordinariness, and on the inside, we cannot at this stage register the earthquake which has taken place. The furniture looks the same, the plants are still there with their dusty leaves, the papers strewn on the settee, the sun shining through the window – all is normal to the eye and ear. We feel much the same, we speak in the same way; and yet the other person has gone and our world, although we are nowhere near taking this in, will never be the same again. We have no good reason for accepting it, for in the world of our own experience the person is alive to us in the way they always have been. The awful reality now present in this house is belied by appearances, and by the continuing vividness of my relationship to that person. At odd moments I have a flash of knowledge, however, that not only has my spouse or parent gone, but I myself have disappeared, for I have not known myself as a separate person in this way for a long time, if ever. I have no idea yet what this is going to mean. There is much that is unknown, much that cannot be taken in. I know with my mind that the truth is as real as it can possibly be, and yet it is invisible. In such a situation as this, while we can understand with our mind what the consequences are, this understanding is like a cardboard cut-out – I am unable to *register* it yet, it has not so far become real life, however much my body may be telling me through aches and pains that a terrible thing has happened.

When Stalin, Roosevelt and Churchill gathered at Yalta to

decide on the future shape of Europe none of them can possibly have *felt* what they were doing as they drew lines on maps. They cannot have felt with the folk of Poland, whose country was being moved bodily away from territories they had thought their own. Nor can they have felt with countryfolk whose village fell a kilometre inside the Iron Curtain, while Churchill tapped some ash from his cigar. The meeting took five days. Little more than a weekend at the seaside, and yet what was done there unfolded into a historical drama of such magnitude that the individual cannot begin to take in the scale of what was set in motion.

It is because of the difficulty we have in *registering* with the whole of ourselves things of which we are aware in theory that people constantly ignore the risks of doing what is openly acknowledged to be harmful: smoking or overeating during pregnancy, driving recklessly on a motorway in fog, locking emergency exits in cinemas, leaving the bow doors open on a ferry, going out into the frost when we have a touch of flu, employing people to do work we would never risk doing ourselves. Human beings can be painfully slow at registering at the felt-level the true reality of things they know to be the case at the head-level.

A slightly different example are moments of 'ontological passage' when we pass from one state in life to another. A wedding service cannot make a fully established marriage: it is a starting-point. At ordination the candidate in technical, legal and theological terms becomes a priest, but in every other respect is just the same person as the day before. The priesthood has yet to grow in them.

In the New Testament too, the significance of Jesus was not tumbled to at the time of his ministry – it was with hindsight that that happened, and the process of discerning the significance of Christ has no end to it – it goes on in our own day and will do so into the future.


## WORSHIP

The phenomenon of delay is part of the very nature of Christian worship. Claims to religious experience always bristle with problems. How far was it imagined? How far was it self-induced? How far simply an emotional experience? Why use the word 'religious', and what do we mean by it? It is difficult to put great weight on the methodical documenting of 'religious experience' which has been undertaken in this century, not only because of these questions, but also because there is a very strong and healthy strand in the Christian tradition which places 'religious experience' low down on the scale in talking about prayer and worship. Such experiences are unreliable, and anyway are not to be sought in themselves – any importance they may have is only as an element on the road towards true religious experience which almost always operates on the gradual principle. The theological tradition known as *apophatic* states this most clearly: we know God better in emptiness than in fullness, in thirst rather than in satisfaction, in constancy rather than in the immediate. The soundest and most reliable religious experience, if any is reliable at all, is rarely instantaneous: it is delayed and gradual. There may be moments when we are moved, moments when we are impressed, or come to understand in a new way, or meet something which can in no way be put into words. But *real* religious experience cannot be coped with instantaneously. Just as Moses had to hide in the cleft of the rock while God passed, and was only granted a sight of him from behind, so we, whether we like it or not, respond to worship mainly by delayed reaction. The profundity of God can only be sounded gingerly and in retrospect, in growth in simplicity and wisdom, in conversion of heart. This gradual process may have 'stripes' in it, oblique flashes which have disappeared almost before we catch a glimpse of them. This is how it often is with poetry or music. At the concert everything is happening at once. The music may affect us deeply, but much of its power emerges in retrospect, as we go over certain moments again and again. We attempt to relive the concert, the play or the film, and one reason for this is the deep disappointment we can feel that it is over. We were not big enough to receive all that was being given at the time.

Sometimes the experience itself is tremendous, and our sense of failure lies in the inability to retain the tremendous thing that has come at us. Sometimes it is the other way around. A great work of art such as a painting by Leonardo can be so familiar to us from reproductions that standing at last in front of the real thing comes as an anticlimax. It looks too vulnerable, too approachable, part of our ordinary world, it has been disenchanted and come down to earth – our preconceptions and expectations completely get in the way. They have to be over-come before we can be open to its mystery. In either case, one thing is needed, and that is day-to-day familiarity with the work of art itself, so that bonds begin to grow up and something different starts to seep through.

In worship we can often be vacant, neutral, or even bored – there certainly may be nothing we could call 'religious experience'. It is in the aftermath that we gradually live more fully what was largely hidden; and it is by living with worship day by day, rubbing shoulders with it, having it as part of the furniture, that we begin to find that the secrets of its life are being tapped. The best religious experience is one that we would never think of calling by that name: the unquantifiable sediment laid down in the daily round.

When I was a child the Sunday service in our local church was Solemn High Mass. I used to be ravished by it; the candles, the incense, the music, the priest, deacon and subdeacon dressed like kings, and on a greater festival clothed in gold and crimson. In the words of a seventeenth-century poem,

> Then are th'Priests words like thunderclaps when he
> Is lightning like rayed round with Majesty.[1]

It was heaven on earth, and yet for me as a child and as a teen-ager, more often than not it was at the same time tedious. In ret-rospect, curiously, it was always a wonder, it always thrilled, and however boring it might often have been in the actual per-formance, I could never say in between times that it ought to be replaced with something simpler, or that I would like to stop going. I would not have minded it being shorter, but certainly not simpler. So it is, it seems to me, with countless Christians in church on Sundays and daily through the week. The service may console a little, or help, or strengthen, but nothing dramatic, nothing much to show. The ordinary round of life follows, and there, by accumulation over the years, the underlying strength emerges, the recollection becomes more powerful than the event itself. A fine example of this can be found in the christening of babies. When asked what was the most wonderful day in his life, Michael Ramsey is said to have replied: 'My baptism'.

Worship in this sense is like a spot of ink falling on a sheet of blotting-paper. A small round mark forms. Ten minutes later we find it has been spreading and enlarging itself. Because worship is like this, and life is too, we have to treat the question of religious experience with reserve. It is not difficult to find groups of Christians who set great store on making worship a religious experience. Most of it on close inspection can just as well be put down to Dionysiac self-stimulation. The depths of what is going on in any relationship, however, are far more likely to manifest themselves in retrospect, through the long aftermath, while our gaze is obliquely turned away.

> One moment weighs like another.
> Only in retrospection, selection,
> We say, that was the day.[2]

Artists often find their work is a retrospection on events already lived – an experience which has passed is reflected on, and a poem or painting is born from it. For William Wordsworth poetry 'takes its origins from emotion recollected in tranquillity'.[3]

Coming back to Casel's Mystery-theology, we may say that his patristic vision is impressive, but when I am in church I find it difficult to see how it can be. He is claiming too much. It is overblown. Casel, however, was at great pains to insist that we are not dealing with a presence which we can expect to perceive or sense – we are dealing with a reality which is objective, and independent of our capacity to sense it. The Mystery-presence, if it is to be perceived at all, will most of the time be revealed in inklings coming upon us in retrospect. That is how life works, and the same is true of worship.

## THE USE OF THEORIES

There remains one more thing to be added about apparent lack of 'fit' between theory and reality. Any attempt to give a systematic account of what happens in worship is bound not only to be a diminishment, but also potentially a travesty of it. Theories, in other words, need to know their place.

It is important to be clear in our minds about the level at which Odo Casel's Mystery-theology is valid. It is valid:

1   As an attempt to analyse ineffable mysteries *which we know already* – it is less than the real thing, and valid only after the event, descriptive, not prescriptive. We

should not expect to work our way from Casel's theories to encounter with the Mystery – the theories may
be of some help, but may get in the way.

2   The theology of the Mystery has an objective standing
as a measuring-rod insofar as it reflects what is found
in Scripture and the Fathers. In other words, it is something against which to measure our worship.

3   This kind of theology needs to be absorbed and then
forgotten or put on a back burner – its proper work is
done in our unseen layers.

These are three ways of saying that it all needs to be taken
seriously but also with a pinch of salt. That to which it points is
greater, and theories must always decrease that Christ may
increase.

## GNOSIS

If the Mystery has proved controversial, one of the reasons must
be that by constant repetition, phrases such as 'the saving events
are made present in the liturgy' become evacuated of vitality and
reduced to jargon, on a par with the empty slogans trotted out
by totalitarian regimes. Casel was right to insist that there is no
ultimate answer to the question, *how?* We are small, attempting
to comprehend something big, and beyond a certain point words
can take us no further. Casel also used another term which I
have not referred to so far to because of potential misunderstanding, but we cannot avoid all mention of it. There is a
knowledge of the Mystery of Christ which can only grow in us
through worship. For this kind of knowledge Casel used the
term *gnosis*. The term is found amongst the Fathers, but is better known in connection with a shadowy fringe of Christianity
in the early centuries which perhaps has some affinities with
modern 'cults' – it is therefore very difficult to use the term *gnosis* without arousing suspicions of élitism and claims to esoteric
knowledge.

Christianity is not esoteric, but open to all, and all have direct
access to the Father in Christ, so there can be no élite ones with
privileged access to him. Nevertheless, there is a strand in the
New Testament which seeks to identify the stages people are at.
In Mark 4.10f., 'those who are about' Jesus and the twelve are
distinguished from his other hearers: 'To you has been given the

mystery [RSV: 'secret'] of the kingdom of God, but for those outside everything is in parables.' In Colossians 1.26f., those to whom the Mystery is made known are the saints, and in 2.2 it appears that it is through being knitted together in love that the saints will have 'all the riches of assured understanding and the knowledge of God's Mystery, of Christ, in whom are hid all the treasures of wisdom and knowledge [*gnosis*]'. In 1 Corinthians 2.6 it is the 'mature' who are able to receive this knowledge. In 3.2 Paul makes particularly clear the need for maturity in the Spirit (cf. 2.10): 'I fed you with milk, not solid food; for you were not ready for it; and even yet you are not ready, for you are still of the flesh.' Raymond Brown has analysed this theme carefully, both in the New Testament and in the preceding Jewish tradition, and concludes that it is characteristic of the Semitic concept of mystery,[4] and that the Pauline writings and the gospels reflect Semitic literature when they allude to divinely imparted knowledge restricted to those who are ready for it.[5]

The purpose of raising this here is not to seek to identify who might or might not be in possession of this gnosis, nor to attempt to say what form it takes. The reason for raising it is that Casel rightly points out its importance in the New Testament and the Fathers as a concept closely associated with that of Mystery, and he sticks to the Greek word *gnosis* as a technical term because we are speaking of more than is implied by our word 'knowledge' – it is nothing less than a personal acquaintance through the whole of our personality with the one whom we encounter in worship, that is, Christ himself. Casel says:

> We need first of all to acknowledge Christ by *faith*; then this truth, which initially we accept obediently in faith, needs to be explored more deeply with the help of prayer and absorption in Holy Scripture, in the study of which we can use all the scholarly and critical means available. However, any merely intellectual examination of the truths of faith is totally inadequate on its own. The theological student has to grow up in a living way into the reality of Christ. In this way Origen connects theology with the life of devotion. Gnosis grows as we grow in unity with Christ.[6]

Casel comes back again here to his famous and repeated stress on the fact that knowledge of Christ is not first of all private and inner, but practical and objective: gnosis is a practical knowledge gained through the action of the liturgy celebrated by the people of God.[7] Casel's gnosis is not esoteric, but open to every-body: it grows in us by means of that process of conversion of heart which takes place in the liturgy. Aidan Kavanagh hints at this in his book *On Liturgical Theology*, where he speaks of the gradual conversion wrought in us through regular participation in worship.[8] This gnosis, which is more than knowledge, and has more to do with relating, with others, ourselves and God, is a prerequisite for listening to Casel; and it is one of the main keys to all he has to say about the presence of the Mystery. The objection to such a notion has been pungently expressed by a commentator on Heidegger, W. D. Hudson, who observes that John MacQuarrie

> dwells on Heidegger's contrast between 'scientific' or 'calcu-lative' thinking and 'true' or 'meditative' thinking, which 'is more likely to be found among poets than among scientists' . . . As MacQuarrie points out, Heidegger conceives of think-ing as 'close to worship'. All this, no doubt, sounds congenial to Christian ears but does it really put worship in a clearer, or in a fraudulent light? The notion that religious worshippers are 'one up' on investigators in their apprehension of objec-tive reality is surely as misleading a comment about religion as it is about science.[9]

## WORLDLY ANTENNAE

Here is a clear expression of the suspicion of many in the humanitas tradition that eternalism lays fraudulent claim to privileged knowledge. In practice, however, the same claim to special knowledge is there in our humanitas too – a claim to privileged insight. Just as in prayer and worship we can speak of the growth of a special knowledge or gnosis in the believers, so also the humanist in us will want to say that there is a gnosis of ordinary life, giving a feel for 'where the world is at', a stand-point akin to so-called 'common sense', which is aware of what makes sense for people in our society as a whole, and of what tunes in with the world as they really experience it. We are obvi-ously faced with something difficult to define: the best way of approaching it is probably by showing it in operation. The development of doctrine is an area where the gnosis of both eter-nalism and of humanitas can be seen operating. When Newman spoke about the development of doctrine, he saw it as an unfortunate necessity: the faith was intuitively understood 'in the bosom of the Church' (i.e. eternalism), and development of doctrine came about through the continuing need to defend that faith, and proclaim it to succeeding generations in their changing societies. Henri de Lubac put it in terms of 'cashing' the unchanging faith into the coinage of each generation.[10] If that speaks about the preoccupations of eternalism, I have not come across anyone who has sought to describe the other side of the bargain, no doubt because it is such a difficult thing to speak of, that all-round understanding of life which is found not in the 'bosom' of the Church but in the 'bosom' of society. Most members of human society inevitably have it in their bloodstream already – we could hardly fail to. Even in the make-up of the late Archbishop Lefebvre there moved the values and attitudes of modern Europe. They could be divided up into three categories: (a) fundamental human attitudes which are found in any age, (b) attitudes and values which are inherited as part of our history and culture, and (c) contemporary attitudes which reflect the spirit of the times. They are always a rag-bag of good and bad, and it is always difficult at any one time to discern the good from the bad in them, making the development of doctrine a tricky business at the best of times; but the effort has to be made to discern what is of God in the contemporary scene, and the reaction of this with the received faith of the Church is a chemical process through which development of doctrine takes place. The reason we have to be wary of any claim to insight by 'daily life' is well expressed by Lord Acton, who stresses the importance of a historical perspective in our discernment: 'History must be our deliverer not only from the undue influence of other times, but from the undue influence of our own, from the tyranny of environment and the pressures of the air we breath'.[11] All of that can just as equally be said of the world of the Church – all too often a rallying to flags goes together with a poor sense of history.

A good example of the process of development can be seen in the doctrine of the atonement. The early medieval vision of a God who by a cunning manoeuvre wrested from the Devil his fiefdom, and therefore his jurisdiction over mankind, could not survive the demise of a heroic and feudal society. Other visions of what it is to be human came along to challenge it, and so as an expression of the doctrine of the atonement it had to change.

Some modern writers such as Dennis Nineham would like to take this to its logical conclusion, claiming that the faith held in any age is so determined by that age that there can be no continuity between it and what went before:[12] each age invents a Christian faith for itself forged out of the spirit of the times. While many find Nineham's extreme approach unconvincing, it is an incontrovertible fact that each age and each society brings its own insights and basic, spontaneous attitudes to bear on the inherited faith, and out of that comes a 'development' – change.

If these are valid 'stabs' at the question of secular gnosis, our next question is to ask who are the best representatives of it? Whose antennae are best attuned to society's view of life? It is difficult to see how this question can be asked without being invidious or even offensive. However, if either side, the gnosis of eternalism and the gnosis of humanitas, are to be able to respond to accusations of fraudulence, then it is worth trying to look for some objective, entirely practical bench-marks. For testing the credentials of my gnosis of daily life, one obvious question to ask myself would be, 'how wide and deep is my experience of the modern world?' The answer would be something like a *curriculum vitae,* listing where I had been and what I had done. It would be of superficial worth, but it would be something, a start; something to help see my viewpoint in perspective. A corresponding question for my eternalism would be, 'how wide and deep has been my participation in Christian prayer and worship?' The answer would likewise need to be entirely objective, listing all my activities, disciplines, reading and so on in that area. It might be objected that someone may go to church a lot and practise extensive private prayer and yet be foolish and churchy: but these data are still *something,* for if I criticize eternalism, but cannot show that I have great experience of the *practice* of it, then that will put my comments in proportion. This is a feeble start, but it is well worth trying to find ways of self-examination which can make us more aware of where our strengths lie. It may be possible to evolve some kind of basic bench-marks such as those used in the 'discernment of spirits' in the Ignatian tradition; its questions could cover such areas as temperament, experience (of Church and of society), strengths and weaknesses, personal history, awareness of personal preferences. The aim is to identify two types of gift: a feel for the 'soul' of society, and a feel for the 'soul' of the Christian Church; and the aim is not to identify who has the best understanding, but to see more clearly how each understanding may attend to the other.

We need, naturally, to beware of unthinking canonization of gnosis, whether it be that of eternalism or of humanitas. Christians can betray their relationship with God, assuming knowledge of him when in reality they are far from him. Secular societies too can misunderstand their own life badly, and the whole notion of 'real life' has to be treated with great caution, something that can hardly be done without recourse to the eternal dimension of the Christian faith. There is, however, an obligation to attend to the voice of God which comes via ordinary life. For the Word 'enlightens every human being who comes into the world' (John 1.9). So the students at Kelham in 1916 were studying 'what God was doing on the Somme, and at Westminster, and at Tilbury Docks', though we at the other end of the same century would have some very agonized questions to ask about the Somme and how it all fits with God;[13] so we have the important caveat about the danger of canonizing our gnosis.

I have suggested we search for some guidelines for cross-border 'attending' because each area of living has a gnosis or knowledge which the whole body corporate needs. It is time for some examples. First of all, a tale of two cathedrals. Milan cathedral underwent a revival in the time of the great Cardinal Schuster who was Archbishop of Milan in the years immediately following the Second World War. He had a vision of the cathedral as the focus of the local church, as a spiritual centre and place of prayer. He saw the heart of the cathedral's life to be the worship. The fruits of his vision can be seen even today, for there are few Italian cathedrals quite like Milan for popular feel, with vast numbers of local people (by British standards) going there to pray and attend its services. For all the beauty of its liturgy, for which it is justly proud, this is very much a people's cathedral (witness Cardinal Martini's extraordinary Bible-study sessions with thousands of young people), and there is no doubt that the heart of that popular participation is prayer and worship.

Now to Britain. Derrick Walters, Dean of Liverpool's Anglican cathedral, was interviewed for an article in *The Tablet* in which we read:

> The dean's view is that the cathedral's mission in Liverpool is 'to help people to deepen their knowledge of themselves. We're in a service industry and we're trying to meet human

need.' Strikingly, the worship of God does not come top of his list, although 'introducing people' to that worship is high on it. He trained as a sociologist and 'I always come to theological questions by asking what function religion has in the life of society', he says.[14]

For Schuster, the cathedral's primary role was deepening people's knowledge of God, but for Walters it is 'deepening their knowledge of themselves'. For the one its role is service of the local church, for the other it is the service of local society. There are serious questions to be raised about Walters' low estimate of people's need for direct access to God (and God's desire for them) in worship. But we also have to ask whether enough 'antennae' are out in Milan towards the baffling, worldly and troubled civic and social life of that great metropolis. Here are two cathedrals who could attend to each other. For other examples, we could look to the sharp differences between Pope John Paul II and the German theologian Hans Küng, or in Britain the different stances taken by, say, the Church Union and David Jenkins. Confrontation can be transformed into attention if eternalism and humanitas will realize that their differences represent not alternatives but two different sightings of a more complex and baffling state of affairs. We need to be prepared for the fact that God can be mind-boggling.

## OBJECTIVITY

If the Mystery makes itself known to us in retrospect, and depends on a growth in us of gnosis, this simply underlines the fact that first and foremost we are speaking of something objective. When Odo Casel speaks about gnosis he insists that it is not simply concerned with internal dispositions, but is practical and physical. In worship we tend to look for immediate experience of an interior kind, which we might call 'deep'. Deep inner experience. There is a tendency in our culture only to be able to see depth in things we describe as 'inner'. The human sciences, however, and the wider traditions of human culture are now telling us with increasing insistence that practical activities in which the 'inner' engagement may seem to be slight are whole and 'deep'.

We can see this from our daily lives, where the depths are sounded through the apparently negligible activities which fill our day. The subconscious mind processes the signals our neighbour sends (often unwittingly), and also produces our own response, of which we can be largely unaware. David irritates Mike, but Mike cannot think why. Mike behaves brusquely and coldly in response, and David is surprised. Even if we ignore the content of the conversation, the body-language of both people says it all: one has a twitch round the eyes, the other sits unconsciously swinging a foot back and forth. Outward phenomena of little account are letting the cat out of the bag. The same truth confronts us in our dreams. Apparently superficial occurrences can be immediately forgotten, only to dominate a dream that same night – or even weeks or years later. As we become older we can have an increasing tendency to look back rather than forward, and often this will include remembrance of events long left behind and forgotten. We simply cannot tell from all the host of occurrences and actions which fill the day what is being put into store in the layers of our subconscious. Between friends, the fabric of trivial activities together has no depth at the objective level, and yet can constitute, express and nourish the strongest bonds of mutual belonging. Fergus Kerr in his *Theology after Wittgenstein* has a good deal to say on this, and at one point comments on some interesting words of Nietzsche: '"Those Greeks were superficial – out of profundity!" The depth of the world is on the surface, so to speak.'[15]

We could put this in another way and say that if you are looking for depth, then the surface is the place to start. John Cornwell, in an article in *The Tablet*, brings corroboration of this from an unexpected quarter – Don Cupitt.[16] According to Cornwell's record of his conversation with Cupitt, the latter has become fascinated by current discoveries in computer science and artificial intelligence:

> 'The surface!', he started, with the daunting emphasis of absolute certitude. 'It is *all* on the *surface*'. The brain, he wanted me to know, is just a business of 'electronic waves of excitation'. What we are used to calling the 'mind', he told me, is entirely on the surface of our heads and bodies, for understanding finds its origins in the 'motor nerves' that give rise to language and speech and a sort of 'fluttering' that occurs in the soft palate and ends up in the ear.

It is a characteristic of heresies to fasten on to a truth and expand it out of proportion, so we do not need to agree with

Cupitt's conclusions to be able to see that he is on to something. He seems to conclude that all is *merely* on the surface, whereas the Judaeo-Christian tradition speaks more in terms of the surface as the only way of approaching the depths – for they can only be approached obliquely. Cupitt is close to our point, even though he comes to a completely opposite conclusion.

'Look', he said, 'I want to convince you that my mind is here on my face, in my field of vision, in my speech, and so on; it's not *inside* my head'. Conjuring up a series of images and repetitive reflections, Cupitt now laboured to persuade me that there was no such thing as 'inwardness', inner self-consciousness, inner privacy. '*It is all on the surface!*' No deep inside; no interior; no depth; no private self; no inner secrets known only to God and oneself. Just the skin, the self-conscious 'public language realm'.

There is a danger that these simple assertions (as they are reported) will incline us to dismiss the truth hidden in Cupitt's caricature. The 'surface-ness' of our daily round, and of our body and our face, does not so automatically diminish the grandeur of the human mystery – on the contrary, by showing how many-layered our humanity is, it reveals the grandeur. When we meet each other, when we have a conversation, or when we enter upon the Church's worship, we are coming in sight of icebergs. Nine-tenths of an iceberg is hidden below the water, but there is a straight continuity between the seen and the unseen. The iceberg is a very good metaphor for the way symbols work: true symbols point beyond themselves, but also participate in that to which they point. We often speak of the 'externals' of worship as if they were superficial decoration, or mere indicators like a sign pointing to a street, when they are in fact symbols, outcrops of a far greater reality of which they are a part. If we think outward dress is of little account, we should imagine what life would be like if we only ever wore the minimum that was practically essential. Dress is a very powerful and subtle symbol in human relating and self-expression.

However fair or not the article in *The Tablet* may be to Cupitt, it gives a good idea of the way in which our relating to life is through objective actions. We can thank Cupitt for his insight about the surface while keeping our own counsel about the depth. There is more to the trivial actions of every day than we realize. Furthermore, many people continue to believe that at times we become aware that we are more than ourselves. The Christian liturgy needs to be allowed to happen – we just need to get on with it. We do not need to look for extraordinary things – on the contrary, we should expect the same kind of unselfconscious 'layering' which we take for granted in everyday life.

This is yet another way in which daily life throws light on worship, and worship illuminates daily life. It also helps us to see in what way our insights (gnosis) of God's holiness and of daily life can be described as 'practical knowledge', a knowledge that grows gradually, starting at the surface and working its way inwards by the steady digestive processes of our human make-up. Conversely, the mysteries implanted in us from before the day when we first crawl bubble up to the surface by their own natural energy – the culture which has formed us, and the Holy Spirit who is our life are at work in a two-way process whose normal way of working is a gradual one.

# ELEVEN
# *The Great Code*

Now for something a little different. The Bible seeks to make sense of life, and it does it by means of a saga. Great interest has been shown in recent years in an obvious truth which we are apt to overlook: understanding is impossible without narrative. Alasdair MacIntyre gives an illustration:

> I am standing waiting for a bus and the young man standing next to me suddenly says: 'The name of the common wild duck is *Histrionicus histrionicus histrionicus*'. There is no problem as to the meaning of the sentence he uttered: the problem is, how to answer the question, what was he doing in uttering it? Suppose he just uttered such sentences at random intervals; this would be one possible form of madness. We would render his act of utterance intelligible if one of the following turned out to be true. He has mistaken me for someone who yesterday had approached him in the library and asked: 'Do you by any chance know the Latin name of the common wild duck?' Or he has just come from a session with his psychotherapist who has urged him to break down his shyness by talking to strangers. 'But what shall I say?' 'Oh, say anything at all.' Or he is a Soviet spy waiting at a prearranged rendezvous and uttering the ill-chosen code sentence which will identify him to his contact. In each case the act of utterance becomes intelligible by finding its place in a narrative.[1]

The way we come to understand things is through knowing the story of which they are a part. We can say of an unknown object, 'what is it?', when really we are interested in more than that – we want to know what story it belongs to. There is a British TV programme about antiques which is very good at this. Someone appears with an unusual object, and an expert will be able to say not only what it was used for, but when and where it was made, what hopes might have been invested in it, what kind of household it would have been used in, how it turned out not to be a great success, but proved rather good at being used for something entirely different later on. People want the whole story in order to understand an object, event or situation.

This fact is of great interest in the matter of making comparisons. Two dentists each have a hundred patients on their list. One is euphoric that she has a hundred patients, but the other is plunged in gloom at having the very same number. The difference is accounted for by the fact that six months ago the first dentist only had twenty-five patients, while the other then had two hundred and fifty. The important thing to know about these dentists is not simply the statistics on their register, but where they are coming from and where they are going. It is the same with the football league table, with success in gardening, or with any other human enterprise, and what is true of artifacts and of activities is true of people themselves.

We can only understand others and ourselves in terms of the story and stories of which we are a part. An inhabitant of the Ukraine is likely to have a particular picture of Margaret Thatcher as prime minister, probably overflowing with admiration. A member of the British public, however, who has lived through the saga of the Thatcher years, could not be guaranteed to have such a view. This particular prime minister's name conjures up vivid images and atmospheres which could almost be tangible, good or bad according to your point of view – it evokes the story which makes Margaret Thatcher what she is for the British public, something people in the Ukraine would find difficult to grasp.

The analogy of the two dentists can be taken further. Each of them has a secretary who is bad-tempered with the clients, and clients, in comparing notes, might conclude that they are two of a kind, the one no better than the other. However, while one secretary is habitually impatient with people, and lives life on a short fuse, the other happens to be going through a bad patch in her marriage, and rows and lack of sleep make for tiredness and irritability. The one kind of bad temper needs to be faced up to (granted that it *also* needs help in identifying what might lie at its root), while the other deserves more compassion and understanding. Before we return an eye for an eye or a tooth for a tooth, we need to give thought to the possible story out of which people's behaviour comes. Similarly, psychologists will be quick to tell us how important it is to be aware of our story and to have told it (in some part) to others. The telling of our story is so important that a person may not be able to listen to other people's stories and take them in because he has not yet told his own, which, imprisoned within him and struggling to get out, simply stands in the way. Whenever we try to understand a person, situation or event one thing we need to know is the story of which the present moment is the latest episode.

If individuals constitute a continuing story, then so do communities, and the two cannot be separated – every individual story has a place in a communal story, and is in effect a sub-plot in something larger. So we find the great narratives of cultures, foundation-myths, and stories of heroic deeds, disasters, tragedies and victories. Then also as civilization progresses we find the increasing importance of the study of history, for that tells us who we are, where we have come from, and why things are as they are.

In the Church, narrative functions in various ways. The Scriptures preserve for us the story of roots and beginnings, and their continual retelling holds this narrative before our eyes. Then there is the history of the Church itself. Like our dentist, the Church of the present moment can only be understood if we are aware of where it has come from. There are forms of Christianity which happily repeat the mistakes of the past, or wander from one failed inspiration to the next, because of a lack of any adequate sense of the community's continuity. Then there comes the celebration of the story in the liturgy, and not least in the Church's year, where vignettes of the total story come round one after the other to engage our attention. This continual story-telling in Church can sometimes seem fruitless – we have problems gaining anything from many of the Scripture readings, or from texts like the Creed or the eucharistic prayer, which repeat the story's main headings with monotonous regularity. There are various possible reasons for this. Too often we cannot for one reason or another find the opportunity to study, discuss or read about the Scriptures and Christian doctrine. Our culture, while it is mind-bendingly repetitive (for example in the repeated news bulletins and advertisements on television), makes us so dependent on vivid stimuli, especially visual, that repetition of texts has become an uncongenial exercise. We know the story, and have heard it so many times – what on earth can be gained from hearing the parable of the sower or the story of the crucifixion yet again? One reason for our problem may be that we expect to *receive* from the story, when the exercise is asking us to *give*, to have within us already a rapport with the whole Christian story which will make us warm to a reading of the parable of the sower in the same way that good friends are happy to hear the same old thing over and over again. This is one way of appreciating the Mystery in Christian worship: the text is read in the context of celebration, waiting for us to breathe our faith, to breathe our selves, into it. Gregory the Great refers to this more than once: in one of his sermons he says, 'The words of God advance at the pace of the reader'.[2] The words of Scripture and of the liturgy can be empty to us if we have not become attuned to the Mystery. Our own personal (and family and community) story and the story of Christ need to court each other and 'get engaged' as it were, so that eventually ours may merge with his, and his with ours. This can only happen if participation is with the 'whole of ourselves' – it cannot come about merely through trading in words; it has to be *lived*, in the liturgy, and in the living of life as a follower of Christ.

If narrative is fundamental to us, equivalent indeed to the blood supply of our psychological body, then the modern world's problems with narrative will lead to inevitable problems with the gospel. Today we do not want to inhabit a narrative, for fear that it will constrain – rather do we seek freedom and 'authenticity'. So we throw off the shackles of inherited traditions of relationship and behaviour, in the belief that they constrict us and limit us. The rebellion is a false one, for in abandoning the ancient narrative of the Western tradition, all we succeed in evolving are lame and halting substitutes, for real innovation, imagination and creativity can only arise in a living tradition or, as we might say here, in a full-flowing narrative. For all of this, the reader is referred to Alasdair MacIntyre's *After Virtue*, especially Chapter 15, and to N. T. Wright's *The New Testament and the People of God* (*passim*).[3]

## TRUE TO TYPE

While there is not the space here to give an adequate account of the function of story in the whole matter of being human, it has been necessary to sketch an introduction to it because of one particular insight into the relation between salvation history and the Bible which has been significantly recovered in recent years. This begins with the assumption that the whole salvation narrative from Genesis to the Apocalypse is a story evolved by God hand-in-hand with his people, a story in which we believe God is more than just fumbling his way forward in the dark. In other words, does God know what he is doing? Does he know what will be the consequences of the events which he has an active part in shaping? Do the different parts of the story relate to each other logically? Or, to put it another way, is God consistent? When he caused the Hebrew people to end up (by whatever were the means) with the story of the exodus from Egypt, what were his intentions? We do not know what actual events lie behind this story, but we have seen that it is of a type – it belongs among events and experiences of escape and liberation in daily life which can be 'disclosure situations' of the divine. In leading the Jews to have such a tradition of disclosure as the exodus, was God aware that in the fullness of time Jesus would be crucified? If God is omniscient, as any God worth believing in must be, then he must have been aware of that, and of the connections between the two, for both are 'disclosure situations' of escape through suffering which show remarkable similarities in matters of detail, and he must have been aware that people would draw such a conclusion. Does God allow his revelations of himself to follow a random course? Or are we not constrained by our understanding of the omnipotence of God to take seriously the suggestion that the whole of salvation history is basically consistent, its parts relating organically to each other and to the whole? The more we ask such questions the more our attention is drawn to an approach to salvation history which takes seriously the notion of God's consistency. Such a notion of consistency implies that in the exodus story Christ is already hidden (note yet again the notion of the Mystery hidden in creation), and in some way the crucifixion is already present. This leads us to something which can be revealing today in opening doors that seem locked – the method of interpretation which works on the basis of typology.

Typological interpretation is unfamiliar to most of us, and if we have come across it this will probably have been in medieval art. It is generally understood as an inventive twinning-up of events from the Old and New Testaments in a way sometimes seen in stained-glass windows where under a portrayal of the crucifixion there is a picture of Abraham's sacrifice of Isaac, or under a picture of baptism there is another of Noah's flood. It is thought, in other words, to be a picturesque and fanciful method of connecting Old Testament and New Testament stories in order to show that the one was intended by God as a foreshadowing of the other. The most common criticism is that it is fanciful and arbitrary, and even such encyclopaedic works as N. T. Wright's *The New Testament and the People of God* (cf. pp. 381, 389) and A. Thiselton's *New Horizons in Hermeneutics* (cf. pp. 163f.)[4] seem to misunderstand it. It is, however, crucial to our understanding of the New Testament. Typology has in recent decades received considerable attention in such works as Northrop Frye's *The Great Code* and Avril Henry's edition of the *Biblia Pauperum*, and has been more recently presented with cumulative power by the Hungarian Lutheran Tibor Fabiny in his little book *The Lion and the Lamb*.[5]

The first point to make about this way of interpretation is that it is thoroughly biblical. We find a ready example in 1 Corinthians 10, where Paul speaks of a group of saving events in the Old Testament. He refers to the rock which followed the Israelites in the wilderness, and goes on to say that that rock was Christ. He explains this by saying in verse 6 that these Old Testament events were 'types' (*typoi*). The word 'type' in Greek means 'pattern' or 'mould', of the kind into which clay or metal is poured, so that from it might emerge a corresponding form. A contemporary parallel would be the photographic negative, from which is made something which is exactly the same but different. According to this terminology the mould is the 'type', while the finished object which emerges from it is 'antitype'. In 1 Peter 3.21 this is stated explicitly in regard to baptism, which is described as the 'antitype' (*antitypon*) of Noah's flood. Fulfilment of the Old Testament is thus understood literally as a 'filling up', a coming to a fullness (*pleroma*). The mould (type) is filled up to produce the antitype. The notion of 'fulfilment' occurs very frequently in the New Testament, for example in the phrase 'the Scriptures are fulfilled' (e.g. Luke 4.21). Fabiny asks,

'What is the meaning of this frequently mentioned but often mis-understood expression? It involves the notion that Scripture . . . was powerless or "empty" in itself but by the new eschato-logical event it is again "filled up" like an accumulator so that the Word is once again at work, it is able to radiate anew its creative power'.[6] Here then we have a claim to see organic con-sistency in the ways of God with his people. Events, people and places in one age are a mould which, when filled up, issue in something which is both the same and yet 'more', in a step-by-step self-revelation of God. This is a process which can happen not only once, but many times – in fact it has a propensity to repeat itself. Noah's flood is a type to which the crossing of the Red Sea is antitype. This in turn serves as type to Christ's bap-tism (say), which again in its turn becomes a type to the Chris-tian baptismal liturgy, which emerges from it as antitype. Fabiny sees this repeated progression from type to antitype as an extremely rich and fruitful way of characterizing God's revela-tion of himself to his people within the organic framework of the created order. This scheme is not simply a fanciful man-made concoction of correspondences (even if it is not immune from being turned into that, as has often been the case – as when the red cord used by Rahab to protect her house was interpreted as referring to the blood of Christ at the crucifixion!) – it is a com-plete way of seeing the world.

Such a brief introduction to typology runs the risk of selling it short, and I encourage the reader to read Fabiny's brilliant book in order to gain an adequate feel for a way of thinking which is part of the fabric of the New Testament, and whose writers took it so much for granted that we are guaranteed to misunderstand them if we ignore it. 'This typological way of reading the Bible is indicated too often and explicitly in the New Testament itself for us to be in any doubt that this is the "right" way of reading it – "right" in the only sense that criticism can recognize, as the way that conforms to the intentionality of the book itself and to the conventions it assumes and requires'.[7] Northrop Frye gives an impressive list of fundamental typological connections in the New Testament:

> Moses organizes the twelve tribes of Israel; Jesus gathers twelve disciples. Israel crosses the Red Sea and achieves its identity as a nation on the other side; Jesus is baptized in the

Jordan and is recognized as the Son of God . . . Israel wanders forty years in the wilderness; Jesus, forty days. Miraculous food is provided for Israel and by Jesus for those gathered around him (see John 6.49f.). The law is given from Mount Sinai and the gospel preached in the Sermon on the Mount . . .[8]

And so it goes on. The pointing out of such correspondences is familiar to us in biblical commentaries, where they are interpreted as deliberately intended to make a point. These correspondences, however, were intended not simply to make a point to the hearers, depicting the status of Christ in the form of familiar paradigms: that way the sermon on the mount would *replace* Sinai, Easter would *replace* the Passover. The one does not replace the other, it fulfils it as part of God's consistent process of salvation. The New Testament does not replace the Old, it 'fills it up'.

## TYPES AND THE LITURGY

Not only is typology important for the interpretation of the New Testament, however: it is also a key matter for any who would seek to understand the liturgy as it is presented to us by the Fathers and the continuing tradition which derives from them. At a very formative stage before the latter part of the fourth century this was the way in which people sought to explain what was happening in worship and in particular in the sacraments. In relation to the liturgy however a wider range of terms is used, a terminology both richer and more subtle.

### Type – antitype – shadow – image

We have seen that the Old Testament provides the type, to which Christ is the antitype. This is relatively straightforward. Christ is the fullness of the Mystery, whose 'mould' is found in the Old Testament.

In the Greek Fathers, not only Christ but also the sacraments are called 'antitype', and this is precisely because the sacraments were seen as constituting the same reality – both Christ and the sacraments are antitypes. Sometimes the Fathers make a finer distinction in seeking to show how the two may be distinguished. Then they continue to speak of Christ as the antitype, but for the sacraments they switch to the word 'image'.[9] In the

Eastern liturgies the eucharist is often referred to as the antitype of Christ, so we develop a slight sense that these terms are going round in circles, when in fact we are seeing the terminological leapfrogging in full swing. Christ is the antitype foreshadowed in the New Testament, while the eucharist is again in turn the antitype of him.

Hence the use of the word 'image' (*eikon*). In Colossians 1.15 Christ is the 'image of the invisible God': this is not intended to mean any mere picture or representation – the image, rather, is the reality of God himself emerging in our own dimension. The ancient understanding

> does not limit image to a functional representation present to human sense but also thinks of it in terms of an emanation, of a revelation of the being with a substantial participation in the object ... It has a share in the reality. Indeed, it is the reality. Thus *eikon* does not imply a weakening or a feeble copy of something. It implies the illumination of its inner core and essence ... In the New Testament the original is always present in the image ... [and in Colossians 1.15] all the emphasis is on the equality of the *eikon* with the original.[10]

In John's gospel it is put in these terms: 'He who has seen me has seen the Father' (John 14.9). This is language which the Fathers use in describing the liturgy too – it is antitype, and the nature of its relationship to Christ the type is *image*, just as in its turn, the nature of Christ's identity with the Father is 'image'. So we could say that whoever has seen the liturgy has seen Christ. Once again we are in the territory of icebergs.

The image is an emanation of a reality which it does not merely represent – it shares in its being. Perhaps there is a parallel in the human face. The human face is often noticeably shaped and sculpted by the experience and character of the person to whom it belongs. There are exceptions, when appearances deceive, such as the comedian whose face when he is not entertaining looks deceptively miserable, but on the whole we can frequently look at a face and say 'I can confide in this person', or 'this person will not be good company'. Our face is to some degree or other an emanation of what we are, and what we have been.

I have avoided saying much about the notion of the real presence in the bread and wine of the eucharist because of the complexity of the question, but it is worth pointing out that in this typological context we meet the fullest realism in the Fathers in seeing the bread and wine as the body and blood of Christ, which is yet expressed not as static presence, but with the 'lively' terminology of *antitype* or *symbol* or *similitude*, all terms which in slightly different ways refer to a relationship between two realities filled with life (Christ and the eucharistic gifts) in which each inhabits the other in a manner which is not static, like a wall painted with emulsion paint, but rather like a Monet painting which is all in one colour and yet alive – these terms describe not a state but a happening. In this sense the medieval and scholastic definitions of real presence were a diminishment. 'Real happening' might be a better term. Medieval scholastic theology, says Johannes Betz,

> looked first and foremost at the *effect* of the sacrament or, which is the same thing, at the *person* who received the sacraments. Casel however opened the way to a consideration of the *sacrament* in itself, a consideration more in coherence with the economy of salvation and directly founded on Christ . . . so that there results from it an organic vision of the sacrament. That which in the ancient Church was something natural, as a completely established fact, that is, the *memorial* presence of the saving works of Christ in his mysteries, has once again been brought to the attention of modern theologians. It is a great achievement, which needs to be acknowledged.[11]

We shall see that this kind of sacramental realism is no less categorical than our more recent tradition of the real presence, but has regained its *life*, founded in the person of Christ and the acts of God.

*Shadow*

In Hebrews 10.1 we meet another pairing of categories similar to that of type and antitype. 'The Law has a shadow of the good things which were about to come, but it does not have the image itself of the accomplished deeds'. Here the word 'shadow' is paired with 'image': the old covenant is the shadow of Christ cast backwards into time. Now however we have left the shadow behind. The reality is here, and this reality is called 'image'. In relation to this passage Theodore of Mopsuestia says:

> A shadow implies the proximity of a body, as it cannot exist

without a body, but it does not represent the body which it reflects in the same way as happens in an image. When we look at an image we recognize the person who is represented in it – if we knew that person beforehand – on account of the accurately drawn picture, but we are never able to recognize a man represented only by his shadow, as this shadow has no likeness whatever to the real body from which it emanates. All things of the law were similar to this.[12]

Theodore emphasizes the difference between shadow and image, but perhaps many would want to recognize more in the 'shadow' of the Jewish religion than he gives it credit for.

### Other faiths

It is perhaps of more than passing interest here to suggest that we may have a fruitful basis in this language for relating to other religions. It only needs a further step to see the other world religions as a part of the shadow which is reflected by the person of Christ. In his *The Mystery of Christian Worship* Odo Casel says of the old pagan mystery-religions, that they 'were only a shadow in contrast to the Christian mysteries; but they were a longing, "a shadow of things to come"; the body whose backward-reaching shadow they were was "the body of Christ", which showed itself beforehand in the types of the Old Testament'.[13] In another place he says,

Christ is God's acceptance of all creation; his refusal is reserved for evil, for what has turned from him; all that is positive he takes up. It cannot be right, then, to talk of the taking over of empty forms; rather what has taken place is acceptance, completion, the implementing and perfecting, the glorification and upraising of human form ... When the sun's rays fall on a diamond they bring out all that rested in it before as a mere possibility.[14]

Some would be unhappy with a model which cast Christianity as the reality and other religions as its shadow, fearful of the arrogance of Christian triumphalism. People of other faiths, however, do not usually have much respect for such relativism, while they do have respect for a Christianity which is as confident in its own faith as they are in theirs. Here is a possible basis for interfaith dialogue and worship on a strong theological foundation which, in a more generous way than Theodore of Mopsuestia was able to do, understands the shadow in terms of the hidden presence of the Mystery. It is then but a small additional step to begin to see that all that is good in our secular and agnostic world can also be thought of as part of the shadow, the hidden presence of Christ's mystery, waiting to be made manifest. Again, there is often greater respect in the world at large for self-evident Christian commitment than for the inclination of some Christians to appeasement. The recovery of an understanding of the faith in terms of the Mystery may also be of help in making sense of 'folk religion', and in teasing out priorities over questions such as baptismal policy. Typological interpretation encourages a frame of mind which is open to the identifying of connections.

### Christ in the Old Testament, and both in the liturgy

When the Fathers use the language of type and antitype, shadow and reality, in reference to the liturgy, they use it in a direct way. The type is so much one with the antitype that both are inseparable parts of one reality, and this is a relationship that works in both directions. For John Chrysostom the lambs' blood painted on the doorposts in Egypt saved the Israelites not simply because it was a pre-arranged signal, but also because it was the type of the blood of Christ, it prefigured it. It is because of Christ's blood that the Israelites were protected by the lambs' blood in Egypt.[15] Or we might want to say, in the light of critical scholarship, that the story of the lambs' blood as the Jews received it, whatever its actual origins, is a disclosure of the Mystery which was yet to be fully revealed. Its origins may lie in ancient practices of a pastoral people, which were a partial 'disclosure situation' of Christ's cross. The lambs' blood and the blood of Christ are 'isomorphic'. This approach, the more we look at it, has a capacity to make greater sense not only of Scripture but also of God and the consistency of his ways – it reveals a deep unity between the Old and New Testaments. To dismiss it entirely is to believe in a God who, when he acts, ignores his future intentions.

This typological approach in the Fathers is applied to the liturgy too, not only to what we know as the sacraments, but also to all the other rites and ceremonies in the liturgy which become, as a result, 'sacraments' in their own right. So for example the renunciation of Satan in the baptismal liturgy is understood as a full-blown 'mystery'.[16] Ambrose in the West takes a similar approach when he speaks of the action of the Holy Spirit in baptism taking its origin from the brooding of the Spirit on the waters at the creation of the world. 'Consider . . . how ancient this mystery [of baptism] is, that was prefigured at the very beginning of the world'.[17] Again, in the Milan baptismal liturgy there was the rite of 'opening', or *ephphatha*, when the senses of the candidates were touched with spittle. This derives from the New Testament episode of the healing of the deaf-mute (Mark 7.31-end), which Ambrose calls a *mysterium*. He establishes 'an ontological identity between the rite of the church and the action Jesus performs on the deaf-mute'.[18] Enrico Mazza shows that in this understanding 'the events comprising the history of salvation are objectively bound together to form a coherent whole', and that they form a procession of phases, 'a movement from the lesser to the greater, from sketch to full reality', the final climax of which will come about at the end of all things. 'As a result, the various stages in the history of salvation refer to one another and are mirrored each in the others in a kind of ontological correspondence . . . Thus, the characteristics of the ritual action can be predicated of the historical event, and the characteristics of the latter can in turn be applied to the liturgical celebration.' What he is almost, but not quite, saying is that when the candidate is receiving the *ephphatha*, there before us is Christ healing the deaf-mute. 'The two events that are thus brought into reciprocal relation by means of biblical typology end up constituting a single reality in which each merges into the other . . .'[19]

This unity of the divine plan can be seen in many places once it has been pointed out. These texts come very little short of actually saying (as Paul did about the rock) that the washing of the feet *is* Christ washing his disciples' feet at the last supper, the priest who baptizes the candidate in the water *is* Christ himself. All these things are neither mime nor reproduction nor simple imitation – they are *image*. The words of Ambrose are worth repeating here: 'We are no longer in the shadow, nor in the figure, nor in the type, but in the reality; O God, not by mirrors and enigmas, but face to face have you revealed yourself to me, and I find you in your mysteries'.[20]

The Fathers see the relationship between these things to be so close that each can be explained in terms of the other. Indeed, when seeking to explain a rite or sacrament, they simply assume the correspondence, and are content to do an appropriate exegesis on the Old or New Testament. For instance, in showing the sacramental nature of the footwashing which at that time took place in baptism, Ambrose discusses not the rite but the biblical story. All he feels ultimately obliged to do is to show that Christ's washing of the disciples' feet was an action which sanctified. That is all he needs to do, for when he washes the candidates' feet what is taking place is the washing of the disciples' feet by Christ. 'Hear, then, the proof that it is a mystery and a sanctifying action; "If I do not wash your feet, you have no part in me"'.[21] The radical, transforming significance which Christ saw in this action is represented in the liturgy.

## DIFFICULTIES WITH TYPOLOGY

This way of thinking which was so powerful for the Fathers is not so easily taken on board by us, who naturally incline to more 'rational' attitudes. The typological approach can never be for us the only way of understanding things as it was for them, but we need to receive it and make it our own as one of the wide range of approaches which the history of Christianity has handed on to us. And whether we can cope with it or not, our brief examination of it has given an idea of the degree to which in the patristic period sacramentality was understood in terms of saving history. And this was understood to be alive, involving us with itself.

If we still have any further doubts about typology when it is used with the right seriousness, then we should hearken to the secular disciplines who see in it a revealing instrument in the quest for truth.

> With the great capitalist revolutions of the eighteenth century, typological thinking entered the secular arena. For believers in progress in the democracies, contemporary events are proceeding toward their own antitypes in the future, toward a state of human existence that will make what is now happening intelligible as a series of signposts pointing in that direction. For Marxist and other revolutionaries, a worldwide revolution is the central future event that will constitute the antitype of history as a whole . . .[22]

Serious typology is a way of describing the organic nature of the world as a whole, not simply extruded evenly like toothpaste from a tube, but by phases, each of which constitutes an evolution in which a mould gives birth to something fuller.

## WRITING OUR OWN NARRATIVE

We can return at this point to the question of the narratives we inhabit and which we continue to write by our daily lives. N. T. Wright, although he seems to misunderstand typology, gives an example of the way a narrative rolls forward which is nothing if not typological:

> Suppose there exists a Shakespeare play, most of whose fifth act has been lost. The first four acts provide, let us suppose, such a remarkable wealth of characterization, such a crescendo of excitement within the plot, that it is generally agreed that the play ought to be staged. Nevertheless, it is felt inappropriate actually to write a fifth act once and for all: it would freeze the play into one form, and commit Shakespeare as it were to being prospectively responsible for work not in fact his own. Better, it might be felt, to give the key parts to highly trained, sensitive and experienced Shakespearian actors, who would immerse themselves in the first four acts, and in the language and culture of Shakespeare of his time, *and who would be told to work out a fifth act for themselves.*
>
> Consider the result. The first four acts, existing as they did, would be the undoubted 'authority' for the task in hand. That is, anyone could properly object to the new improvisation on the grounds that some character was now behaving inconsistently, or that some sub-plot or theme, adumbrated earlier, had not reached its proper resolution. This 'authority' of the first four acts would not consist – could not consist! – in an implicit command that the actors should repeat the earlier parts of the play over and over again. It would consist in the fact of an as yet unfinished drama, containing its own impetus and forward movement, which demanded to be concluded in an appropriate manner.[23]

The model of the unfinished play offers rich possibilities for understanding the relationship between the divine economy and human freedom, and between the various stages of salvation history, not to mention the Christian liturgy itself, within the setting of the whole Christian life, as a 'fifth act' of salvation history which is both spontaneous and divinely 'filled up' from within.

## THE COSMIC MYSTERY

Typology is about things being 'filled up', becoming in a sense what they already are, but more so. The Mystery, we have found, is similarly concerned with a 'before' and an 'after', in which what was partly known becomes more adequately known. The history of this, and its new proclamation in modern times, now lead us to press home our claims. I have tried to show how in the liturgy the saving-events-in-Mystery become actively present, and we become involved in Christ the Mystery; but if we are content simply to describe it in terms of the liturgy, then it is in danger of being little different from pulling a rabbit out of a hat. It might have been little green monsters or Snow White and the Seven Dwarfs that become present, but happened to be the story of Jesus of Nazareth. The story itself, however great, and even though its particularity is essential to it, cannot be left to its particularity. If this liturgical re-presentation of the Mystery is so great, then it must concern things which correspond in some essential way to fundamental patterns in the universe. Nothing else will suffice if we are aiming to take it seriously.

The story of Jesus is not simply a story which might have been different, but happened to take this form. There is something about this story, this person, these saving deeds, which connects them with the foundations of creation. It is, as it were, something like DNA, the element which scientists have identified as a fundamental building-block of life on earth. In Christ's birth, life, death and resurrection an epiphany takes place which shows fundamental truth about the way life in the cosmos is structured. When we celebrate the liturgy we are uncovering the roots of life. If Scripture and the liturgy can be interpreted in the light of this Great Code, then so can life itself, to boot. The intuition of the ancients, that type relates to antitype, is only another way of saying that God's way with his creation is consistent, that he is not concerned with conjuring tricks, turning it into something quite different, but with drawing out from it what has always been latent in it. For this reason those Christians are right who say daily life is to be valued and taken seriously, while those other Christians are also right who say that the particular tradition of the Church is to be valued and taken seriously, because in both places the Code is to be found in a unique and essential way. What in fact we need to recognize is that 'secular' life and the life of the Church are complementary *loci* or places where we witness the breaking-forth of a Mystery which is so part of the roots of life that it can be called elemental. The progressive revelation and fulfilment of this elemental reality gives us an inkling, in turn, both of the organic nature of the world and of the consistency of God. In the words of Maximus the Confessor, 'Whoever knows the mystery of the cross and the tomb knows the meaning of things. Whoever is initiated into the hidden meaning of the resurrection knows the purpose for which God created everything in the beginning'.[24]

# TWELVE

# *Where Did it Go?*

NOW WE TURN to one of the most obvious questions of all: if all I have said about the Mystery is so important, why did it seem to disappear for a millennium and a half? Protestantism is sometimes criticized for assuming that Church history between the New Testament and the Reformation can be written off, and yet a similar criticism seems applicable here.

We need to remember first of all that Odo Casel has held up for our attention a theology. Theology is not the truth itself, but an endeavour by the limited means of human language to point towards the truth. Such a theology can only arise out of what is actually lived by the Body of Christ. One of academic theology's main roles is that of guidance, showing Christians how it is possible to live and believe. But if theology alone has the right to do that, then we fall into the trap of imagining we can be objective observers of the Church, thinking our way to the truth. The observer participates in and reacts reciprocally with that which he or she is observing, as the human sciences are now very eager to tell us. There is no purely 'objective' observation: we cannot come to the task of observation without presuppositions which destroy our claims to objectivity – such presuppositions reveal a preceding and unacknowledged relationship with the object to be observed. In a small quarry in the Canadian Rockies in 1909 a geological deposit known as the Burgess Shale was discovered to contain abundant fossils of a very strange nature.[1] Contemporary investigators were constrained by their Darwinism to fit these forms into the standard biological categories established over the preceding two centuries. Only very recently has it been realized that they forced these fossils into categories that will not fit. Scientific 'laws' have had to be abandoned in order to understand these weird and baffling animals – Darwin's theory in the simple form in which it had been received had to be drastically modified in order to accommodate them. So it became apparent that here were life-forms with no evident relations before or after them, and which in geological terms arrived and disappeared again very suddenly. Some of them are so weird as to leave scientists deeply puzzled. For the first investigators, the 'scientific' truth could not be seen because of the Darwinian presuppositions which were getting in the way. It still cannot be seen in its entirety, and at that level we have to admit that we never will have the purest truth about the universe, because we always look at it through tinted spectacles, never through clear glass – something of which we are incapable without relinquishing our humanity.

This illustrates the difficulty of claiming to observe the Christian Church from an objective standpoint, and of calling such observation 'theology'. Theology can only emerge out of what is actively lived by the Church, and that life is so complex, manifold, and, in a sense, so infinite in exceeding our capacity ever to encapsulate it in clear characterizations, that ultimately it is very difficult if not impossible to say what is going on in the soul of the Church, any more than we can pin down what is going on in the universe. The nearest we can get to finding out what is happening in the spiritual life of the People of God is probably by such rough-and-ready methods as are traditionally used in the 'discernment of spirits'. In the end it is exceedingly difficult to sit in judgement on the Church as regards her inner life. The fact, therefore, that certain truths are not adequately expressed in the *theology* of any one period does not automatically mean that those truths are not being adequately *lived*. So in Chapter 10 I suggested that Mystery-theology seeks to describe what Christians already know and always have known – always imperfectly, but always known in some way.

In many, if not most, areas of its life, the Church began from the fourth century onwards to veer from what was until then a (relatively!) straight road. Whether it be the Scriptures, worship, church government, or almost any other area of the spectrum, we find a gradual compartmentalizing of the Church, leading above all to clericalization of worship, church government and the other important aspects of its life. The original vision became obscured. It might be compared to a train travelling into a tunnel. For some time the bright light of the entrance remains behind us as we look out of the rear window. But the train meets a curve, and now the light of the entrance bends away out of view. The tunnel begins to curve this way and that, and we lose a sense of our direction of travel. In many fields, today, there-fore, we are finding it necessary to rediscover the mind of the early Church (which stood near the 'entrance') by digging back to it a straight tunnel of our own, bypassing the curve. Over the centuries Christian life has in many ways veered off the main track (for instance, the laity lost their full part in worship, and sacraments became distorted: only the eucharistic bread was given at communion, anointing of the sick became a rite for the dying, and so on). The reforms of the twentieth century have sought to return to roots, back to the lost 'entrance' of the tun-nel in the interest of returning to the main track. The 'curving' journey travelled has on the whole been right enough. Christian people have always known the relation between the Paschal Mystery and the liturgy, they have always lived it (in the falter-ing way which characterizes all our doings with God), and they have known Christ in the living of it, even though this has not often been formulated in categorical statements. Christians know it in their bones, even if it has not always been tackled in their heads or issued from their mouths. It is only now, when practice of the faith is being so sharply challenged by the mod-ern world, that we are experiencing the need to analyse and for-mulate what before has been practised and formulated inad-equately. We can see some of the implications of this by examining the fate of the word 'mystery' in Christian history.

## 'MYSTERY' IN LATER CENTURIES

For the primitive Church, as we have seen, the Passover of the Lord (or *Pascha*), comprising his suffering, death, resurrection and exaltation, was an all-encompassing glory, beauty and truth, a deep source out of which poured that life of the Spirit which bore them along in power. Each Sunday was not only a little Easter, but a little Holy Week. The Paschal Mystery was at the heart of all worship, and for many centuries this remained quite clear in the writings of the Fathers. However, the Middle

Ages were to see an unravelling into separated threads, the beginnings of which can already be seen quite early. Enrico Mazza shows abundant signs of it as early as the fourth century. The 'mystagogical catecheses' of Ambrose of Milan, Theodore of Mopsuestia, John Chrysostom and Cyril of Jerusalem show that it was becoming increasingly difficult to meet the needs of the time by speaking of the sacraments in the old way by means of typology (see Chapter 11). A steeping in the Scriptures could no longer be taken for granted, and a Christian Church now becoming well established in a formerly pagan world was encountering difficulties in staying faithful to its early vision. In explaining the sacraments, there was an increasing need to call a spade a spade, to analyse with boldness and clarity, and point with greater sharpness and less subtlety and nuance. So the trend was towards realism, and towards 'the connecting of sacramental efficacy, not so much with the saving actions of Christ (of which the rite is the sacrament) as with the sacramental rites considered in themselves as having a power of their own . . . [so that they come to be] looked at more in themselves than in the light of the saving historical events in which they participate'.[2] Theodore of Mopsuestia is the first of the Fathers not to be content to speak in general terms of the presence of the *Pascha* - he goes on to link its individual stages with successive moments in the liturgy: at the offering of the gifts Christ enters on his passion; the deacons are the angels accompanying him and appearing on the Mount of Olives; the altar becomes the tomb, over which the deacons wave fans, just as is done at the funerals of the great of this world (the fans are still carried in the Orthodox liturgy, and were once used also in the medieval West). This kind of interpretation was to have a long future in the allegorical schemes of the Middle Ages. In the West, various schemes of allegorical interpretation came into vogue, the most famous being that of Amalarius of Metz (c. 780–850), who allegorized the liturgy, the ministers and the building down to the smallest detail, turning the worship in effect into an elaborate representational drama.[3] This led to a trivialization of the connection with the saving events, by making the Mystery describable, little more than a biblical strip-cartoon. This affected also the Holy Week ceremonies, which in the early Middle Ages were turned from a unitary celebration of the *Pascha* into a glorified passion play, each detail remorselessly followed by the next in ever more literal representation, rather than the oblique and frequently overlapping intimations of the old organic mystery.[4]

A more fundamental problem from the fourth century onwards is a split between revelation and dispensation: the revelation recorded in Scripture becomes separated from the ongoing dispensation of the Church. Revelation is something firmly in the past, and the Church becomes less a continuation of it, and something more like an egg laid by it. The effect of this is that the Church's life, worship and sacraments become merely a present consequence of a past that is no more. The revelation has come and gone, the sacraments dispense its fruits. This inevitably led to a separation between belief and history. While in the New Testament the *kerygma* consists of telling the events of Christ, climaxing in a call to enter into those events in baptism, this creed-as-story came to be replaced by creed-as-eternal-truths. Revelation became an object for study, while worship turned into a means of meeting God and receiving helpings of grace. For this the saving events (now lost in an irretrievable past) were the authorization and inauguration. The baleful effects of all this are still with us in an inability, for instance, to connect liturgy with theology, which goes back at least to the scholasticism of the Middle Ages. Or again, our difficulty in being able to see the Church as holy – a sacrament, and not simply a convenient structure for organizing the doing of good. This separation between revelation and dispensation always remained partial among the churches of the East, where apprehension of the liturgical Mystery was never lost to the same extent, so that revelation has remained integral to dispensation, the Mystery of salvation lives in the liturgy.[5]

## The word 'Mystery'

Although from the fifth century onwards the understanding of the relation between sacraments and saving events became narrowed down, the term 'mystery' itself continued in currency through the medieval period and right up to our own day, and, most importantly, it retained its association with salvation history and with the sacraments. Individual saving events, for instance, have continued to be known as 'mysteries' in the saying of the rosary, in a meditation on the 'mysteries' of Christ's life, death and resurrection. Theology came to talk of the 'mystery of the cross', or of the incarnation, and so on. The problem with this use was that the saving events came to be seen as abstract truths rooted to such a degree in the transcendent that the greatest emphasis is on their inaccessibility. Then there is the practice of referring to sacraments, and the eucharist in particular, as 'the mysteries'. The full scope of what is meant by 'mystery' was dismembered and parcelled out in two ways in particular: theology on the one hand and private meditation on the other. Use of the term in theology

> was concerned with two series of problems: (1) the ontological nature of the man-God and the interpretation of Chalcedon, and (2) the salvific value of the death of Christ and soteriology . . . In this area the death of Jesus was without doubt seen in terms of mystery; but speculative theology did not meet the need that existed for a theology of Christ's Mysteries in their totality . . . The mysteries were therefore abandoned to the spiritual writers, who produced many writings on the theme . . . Since the end of the middle ages [these] have tended to follow a separate path from dogmatic Christology, and their vision has remained too exclusively psychologizing or moralizing, which is their great limitation.[6]

The notion of the Mystery-presence in the liturgy never completely disappeared, however. A strong strand of it survived in medieval theology in the form of the presence of the *passion* in the liturgy.[7] Here we perhaps come closest to the old understanding, but it has been fitted into the narrower frame of the medieval obsession with the passion.

Participation in the mysteries of our redemption has remained a favourite theme among spiritual writers. It is well known in the methods of structured meditation that matured at the time of the Counter-Reformation, familiar to students of Ignatius of Loyola. A writer who was particularly noted in this was Pierre de Bérulle (1575–1629). Bérulle believed that the saving events were living and present[8] 'and he stresses that they have a universal presence and efficacy because a *concrete* achievement has been universalized'.[9] A. Colombo has said that Bérulle's concept of the living presence of the mysteries of Christ in the believer is taken up by the eighteenth-century French liturgist J.–B. LeBrun (1661–1729), who shows that this comes about through the action of the liturgy.[10] I have been unable to find anything so explicit in LeBrun, but it was certainly in the air in the liturgically-conscious Gallicanism of seventeenth and eighteenth-century France. An example is a book published in Paris in 1691, *Treatise on the parish Mass, where are revealed the great Mysteries hidden under the veil of the ceremonies of the Public Solemn Mass*, by Petrus Floriot. The author defends ceremonies, stating that we are composed of both bodies and souls, and the body must have its part in worship. 'Through the ceremonies we acquire knowledge (*intelligence*) of the Mysteries'.[11] We cannot perceive the spiritual with our bodily eyes, 'and this is why we are not offered the naked mysteries as they are in themselves, but under the form of certain ornaments which lead us to perceive them as full of majesty, and our spirit receives them with profound respect'.[12]

## The Reformation

Luther did not often use the word 'mystery', but he understood it to have the same meaning as 'sacrament' and, good Bible-man that he was, he knew it to be intimately connected with the person of Christ. Wilhelm Stählin goes so far as to say that Luther in effect developed a Mystery-theology without actually using the term.[13] Luther insists that the Scriptures are a mystery[14] and so is the Church:

> Luther rounds on those who say in regard to Christ and the Church, 'it is neither a mystery nor a deep work of art, but a spoon filled with wisdom, which they would like to gulp down . . . Christ would be for them neither a mystery [*Mysterium*] nor a secret [*Geheimnis*], but an empty nutshell, and long before the kernel has given birth they have winkled it out and thrown the shell away. We on the other hand, want to suck like a child at the breast of its mother, until we get something from it – we don't want to be weaned from it so early, as these big people wean themselves out of shame at sucking their mother's breast; for they are able to walk before their legs and feet have properly grown.[15]

Luther says in another place that Christ is *opus Dei in mysterio* (the work of God in Mystery).[16] Such language of Luther's was bound to recede into the background with the advance of the Enlightenment, and it is only in this century that German Protestants (with encouragement from Odo Casel) have begun to talk again in these terms in any serious way.

In Anglicanism the terminology was guaranteed a secure place through its use in the Book of Common Prayer, where the eucharist is described as the 'holy mysteries', and baptism, marriage and the Church are qualified as 'mystical'. The language was common currency, and can be found in many Anglican writers between the seventeenth and ninteenth centuries. Here is a good example from William Law's *A Serious Call to a Devout and Holy Life*:

> The Christian's great conquest over the world is all contained in the mystery of Christ upon the cross . . . And all the doctrines, sacraments, and institutions of the gospel are only so many explications of the meaning and application of the benefit of this great mystery. And the state of Christianity implieth nothing else but an entire, absolute conformity to that Spirit which Christ showed in the mysterious sacrifice of Himself upon the cross.[17]

The realism of our participation in the Mystery is strikingly portrayed by Richard Hooker (*c*.1554–1600):

> The very letter of the word of Christ giveth plain security that these mysteries do as nails fasten us to his very cross, that by them we may draw out, as touching efficacy, force and virtue, even the blood of his gored side, in the wounds of our redeemer we there dip our tongues, we are dyed red both within and without, our hunger is satisfied and our thirst for ever quenched . . .[18]

Lancelot Andrewes (1555–1626) speaks of Good Friday as the day when Christ 'is lively described in our sight, and as the Apostle speaketh, is "visibly crucified among us"; when in the memorial of the Holy Sacrament "his death is shewed forth until he come", and the mystery of this His piercing so many ways, so effectually represented before us'.[19]

The non-juring Bishop Thomas Deacon (1697–1753) composed a catechism which is as explicit as we could wish:

> What is the meaning of the word sacrament?
> A sacred thing.
> Does it not also signify an oath?
> Yes, because an oath is a religious act.
> Which are the sacraments in both these senses of the word?
> Baptism and Eucharist.
> What are the sacraments called besides?
> Mysteries.

What signifies Mystery?
Something hidden or concealed.
Are Baptism and the Eucharist Mysteries?
Yes.
Why?
Because they are one thing, but represent and signify another.
What other things are Mysteries?
All the ceremonies of the Church, which have any spiritual
    significancy in them.
Why?
Because they represent something more to the understanding,
    than appears to the outward senses.
What are those ceremonies called beside Mysteries?
Sacraments.
Why?
Because they have an holy signification, and are applied to a
    sacred use.
Are Sacraments then and Mysteries the same?
Yes: both those words have the same signification in ecclesi-
    astical language.[20]

Deacon is so steeped in the Fathers as to corroborate our view
that sacraments, or mysteries, cannot be limited to two or seven:
'All the ceremonies of the Church, which have any spiritual sig-
nificancy' are mysteries.

In general the word 'mystery' and its cognates have four types
of meaning in Christian use, all of which we find in Anglicanism:

1    Individual saving events such as the crucifixion, and
     'mysteries' of the faith such as the Trinity.
2    The mystery of the Scriptures. This occurs frequently
     in Anglican writers, and refers to the typological inter-
     pretation of the Old Testament on the understanding
     that its hidden meaning is Christ.
3    The sacraments referred to as mystery – the usage in
     the Book of Common Prayer is rarely commented on,
     but must inevitably tie in with the mystery-language of
     the epistles, not least with the passage on marriage in
     Ephesians, where 'mystery' there becomes 'mystical' in
     the BCP wedding service, showing the interconnected-
     ness of the terms.
4    Mysticism. This word often has a pejorative sense out-
     side the Roman Catholic Church, but true mysticism is

also represented in churches of the Reformation. In England we have the mystic William Law and others, and in the twentieth century such outstanding writers as Evelyn Underhill and W. R. Inge. There is a similar mystical tradition in Lutheranism, of which Jakob Boehme is an outstanding example.

## The nineteenth century

It is with the Romanticism of the nineteenth century that the road begins to open towards a new appreciation of the Mystery, not yet in an explicit way, for that had to wait until Casel, but intuitively it was all there. Deep changes were astir in the spirit of the times, and in Christian circles one expression of this was a turning from rationalism and social revolution to outlooks considered lost since the Middle Ages. Radical changes were taking place in society: the Industrial Revolution was destroying communities and communal values, materialism was eating away at the old culture of Europe, and there emerged out of this a great yearning for deeper things. The reforming movements associated with Keble and Pusey in England, Guéranger in France and Möhler in Germany all began in the same year, 1833. All three represented a quest for a catholicism centred on community, the community of the Church – in all three countries in different ways the Church had fallen prey to rationalism, the gentry, state control of worship and doctrine, the rejection of monasticism (even among Catholics), and a low estimation of the liturgy, which was often performed in the most perfunctory manner. These reformers all wanted to bring the supernatural nature of the Church to light again.[21] All three movements also involved opposition to bishops, governments and academic establishments. We see in both Ultramontanism and Tractarianism a rediscovery of the liturgy, of Gregorian chant, of the sacramental and mysterious nature of the Church. Guéranger sent spies to England to see what was going on among the Anglicans, and his movement came to receive financial support from Anglican Tractarians.[22] In the Anglican orbit in particular, one fruit of this which still has much to say to us is the connection made between the holiness of the Church and the fight for social justice based on a markedly incarnational theology. Liturgy was now of great interest, and even if the interest was conservative, it was sowing potent seeds of revolution – apparent conservatism was to be the seed-bed for renewal, and out of it emerged the Liturgical Movement. Then Odo Casel finally appeared on the scene, speaking of a profound crisis in the human spirit, and of a 'turning to the Mystery' (*Wende zum Mysterium*). Rampant individualism, loss of community, the disorienting effects of the scientific and industrial revolutions, the unravelling of European culture, and so on, were all aspects of a profound crisis. Meanwhile the Church and her worship were in a state of decadence, and people were looking uncritically in any direction for some spiritual solid ground. This sense of crisis was dramatically heightened by the rise of the false 'mysteries' of Communism and Nazism. Casel was a man of the present moment, not just an archaeologist. At his first meeting with the sisters at Herstelle on his arrival as chaplain his opening words on sitting down were, 'we must attend to the signs of the times'. People were unconsciously seeking the Mystery – the time was ripe to reassess what this meant for Christianity.

## CONCLUSION

This very summary sketch shows us how the early patristic understanding of the Mystery became subject to fragmentation and dispersal in the Middle Ages. The reality to which it referred, however, the real participation in the saving events of Christ during the liturgy, was never entirely lost from sight, and there is abundant evidence to give us cause to believe that this is so fundamental to our humanity, and to the way we were made to relate to God, that it has always been there in people's instinctive response to him. It does not rely on grand theology inaccessible to the simple, it is 'not too hard for you, not too far off . . . the word is very near you; it is in your mouth and in your heart' (Deuteronomy 30.11, 14). The necessity of naming it for what it is has only come upon us with the modern erosion of the religious sense.

# THIRTEEN

# In the Parish

CHRISTIAN WORSHIP IS celebrated in all kinds of settings, but its home and hearth is the parish, the ordinary local church community set firmly within the matrix of society at pavement level. That presents us with a problem: can the web of thoughts which we have distilled from the word 'mystery' be expressed in 'pavement' language? Can the contents of this book be credible to clergy and ordinary believers? Can it *mean* something to us? This question has to be faced with realism, and anyone who is in tune with modern life and the people of today will sense that there are formidable difficulties.

Perhaps the sharpest representatives of the modern worldview are the young. They might lack the nuance that comes with experience, but the more simple view can spotlight issues with particular sharpness. We have material to hand here which is unexpectedly to the point. The German theologian Martin Klöckener has gone so far as to test the teachings of Odo Casel on seventeen- to eighteen-year-olds in school.[1] The school was in a Catholic area of Germany, and while the pupils were almost entirely Roman Catholic and had a positive attitude to RE classes, only a small number saw themselves as committed to the Church. Few had completely abandoned contact, however, and about fifty per cent attended Sunday mass.

No Church teaching or practice could be taken for granted among these students – indeed they had a pretty negative view of the Church as an institution, starting with its picture of God himself. Casel's picture of God as almighty and totally other was problematic – one of them said it does not fit, for 'today we live in a democracy'. There was an attraction to the mystery of God, less to the *mysterium tremendum*, and much more to *mysterium diligendum*: not a mystery, that is, which makes us tremble, but a loving mystery, at the service of humanity.[2] The youngsters sought freedom and self-determination, and such freedom would include an independence from rules, laws, and authorities set over them. It is difficult here to find room for God's Providence: the thought of God's Spirit working within us is foreign to most young people, and, rather than liberating, was seen as doing violence to freedom of choice and autonomy.[3] Nor can they connect God with the wider creation, or see it as his handiwork, or as a revelation of him. They cannot speak of love *for* God, except by equating it more or less with love of neighbour.[4] Not unexpectedly, these young people have serious problems with the word 'mystery'. For them it has negative implications: of something shrouded in darkness, inexplicable, not explainable through scientific methods, and therefore suspect. Klöckener comments that it 'is a difficult task to present such a negatively perceived term, and to help people take it on board'. In English the word is more congenial – mystery tours and mystery stories are inviting and intriguing. In a religious context, however, the difficulty with the word remains a real one. Furthermore, Klöckener comments that 'Any idea that God reveals himself to us in the liturgy, that the saving deeds of Christ become present, that Christ meets us, and makes his grace available to us, all of that is almost completely incomprehensible to the youngsters, totally foreign, from another planet'.[5]

As we might expect, the students find it most easy to relate to Christ as the one for others. While many today can have problems with Casel's vision of God's holiness, his powerful picture of Christ points to areas where a more positive response is possible. The students were also sympathetic to Casel's criticisms of modern society, of its crass materialism and consumerism. The theme of suffering likewise was very real to the students. There is a realization that it cannot be explained away, but also a conviction in many people that suffering is ultimately not meaningless. These are themes very characteristic of Mystery-theology with its centering on the saving events, and they are live themes for young people, dealing with things which for them are real questions.

Here we begin to move into more encouraging waters. There was sympathy for Casel's insistence that Christianity is not a 'religion', that is, a system of dogmatically established truths and moral commandments to be accepted without question. Christianity contains both of these, but much more. Nor is it 'religiosity' or 'piety', which to some extent or other depends on the individual's feelings. It is, rather, an *action* of God which takes place in Christ. Putting a priority on dogma and moral law cannot foster a living relationship with Christ. The students saw here a warning to the Church to put essential things at the centre, while it also implied they were not to dismiss the Church too lightly on account of its unsatisfactory appearance. 'Anyone today who wishes to live a Christocentric faith', thought the students, 'must be capable of a high degree of personal initiative and awareness, prepared to raise questions about church practice, something of which only a small proportion of believers seemed capable; yet for them the person and action of Christ could become a real source of life, which could then also fill the celebration of the "mystery of worship" with a new spirit'.[6]

The problems which the students have with Casel will not be found among all committed Christian adults, and the difference may result from a variety of things, such as adults' greater experience and maturity, or, more ambiguously, from disappointment of the hopes of their youth, with a resulting tendency to nostalgia. What is excellent about these data is that they come from classes involving the study of Casel texts, showing with great directness how the verbal articulation of the faith can fail to resonate with experience of worship, and consequently they point to the inadequacy of worship as these young people experience it and have been taught about it. These data therefore give us a good thumbnail sketch of where many contemporary people are, down in their foundations.

The responses of these German teenagers very usefully set the tone for looking at the wider Church and the world. It is clear first of all that the understanding of worship and life as articulated by Odo Casel and set forth in this book could not be presented as it stands to unbelievers and non-practising Christians. Nor would it be of much help with most people in the parish, even if a few could receive it with profit as it stands. Without corresponding experience it is mere dogma, and even with it, the language and concepts are not easily within people's grasp. It is not, and should never be, a system of truths to be propagated, but rather an attempt to put into words what is already known. In the parish, the priority is not to know *about* it, but to know it. The Mystery must be lived before it can be talked about, and Martin Klöckener's findings reveal a number of areas in the living of it which need our attention.

## THE OTHERNESS OF GOD

The modern situation is far from uniform, and it would be a mistake to imagine that we can talk in any simple way of modern people's attitude to God. With the otherness of God we immediately realize that modern society contains contrasting points of view. Some people are open to the transcendent, others seem oblivious to it. Many profess belief in God and actively participate in worship. There is widespread good will towards 'religion', and large numbers of people profess a belief in God, although some would say that this widespread religiosity shows all the characteristics of children who take their parents entirely for granted, expecting God to rubber-stamp their own perception of what is the good. For many people, God is a passive, transcendent endorsement of what we perceive to be good. There are, in other words, strong assumptions about God's *benevolence* in a Deist sense, without a corresponding vision of his consuming love and his judgement – there is no pursuit of God with *desire*. Then there are many in modern society for whom religious believers are something from another planet. They find it incredible that anyone can believe in such things today. This is endorsed by the basic world-view of our society, where God has ceased to be an objective point of reference – if God has any place at all, it is in the democratic queue.

While many would be unable to think in terms of *mysterium tremendum* (a mystery which makes us tremble), there is a strong and growing current in modern life which takes it very seriously. One form it takes is a reverence for nature. Pursuits such as bird-watching and mountain-climbing reflect reverence for something which has an integrity of its own to be respected, and even regarded with awe. There can be no doubt that modern men and women are open to the sense of awe, whether it be at a stupendous view of the Alps, or the behaviour of a bird. By no means is it easy, however, to connect this with the conception of the deity which they receive from popular tradition. The German teenagers could speak of a sense of wonder while walking

191

*loving*
*Mystery*

in the hills, but found any connection of this with God far-fetched. What is it, however, but a *mysterium tremendum*? It is more this than a *mysterium diligendum*, more an experience of awe than one of being loved. That this instinct is present in people is shown not only by the Green movement but also by those inchoate stirrings going under the name 'New Age'. Arno Schilson writes:

> There is clearly a new feeling for the mysterious nature of reality . . . In the place of the functional rationality of the Enlightenment we have a neo-mysticism which has many sides to it. A new inwardness tries by means of meditation and the discovery of the irrational powers of the self to uncover the secret of existence . . . A new mythology makes it its job to unlock the message of myths as manifestations of a God who is wholly other, a cosmic power . . . At the same time there are those who celebrate the breaking in of a 'New Age' in which the highest goal and ultimate fulfilment are found in becoming one with the powers of the Cosmos, entering into the rhythms of nature, feeling after the ultimate unity of spiritual and material, self-transcendence, and the crossing of the narrow border between consciousness of self and the extension of the self, through being at one with the unity of all things. It is not the individual but the 'whole' as an encompassing, cosmically conceived reality, which is in the foreground; this, however, bears traces of the divine and the religious. In order to find our true self, we must plunge into our own lifestream, and must let ourself be grasped by the cosmic mystery of life . . . We find little here in the way of learned theories or abstract speculation – everything centres on the carrying out of concrete practices, with direct experience as the only possible way to 'know' and to feel the secret of reality. Here belong a wide range of paraliturgical practices, which give wide scope to the mystical experience of the individual, and so confer on him or her a new identity, in the experience of the numinous and the divine.[7]

This bears striking resemblances to the ancient mystery-religions, which flourished immediately before the arrival of Christianity – at a purely human level they in their time were 'early warnings' of where the human spirit was yearning to go. There are also quasi-religious movements today which seek the *mysterium tremendum*, and while often cranky, they point to a shift taking place in the consciousness of society as a whole.

If the New Age movement is evidence of an inclination for the God who is 'other', the yearning is unbalanced, for a god who is simply 'other' is a pagan god: the Christian God has entered into our humanity and become God with us. It is interesting in fact that the two perceptions of God, as awesome mystery and as loving mystery (*mysterium tremendum* and *mysterium diligendum*), operate in complementary directions. With the mystery-which-loves-us we are in the receiving mode, but with the awe-inspiring-mystery we are drawn out of ourselves. Healthy relationships involve both giving and receiving, and a balanced Christian faith involves both. Perhaps the signs of our times point to a paradoxical conclusion: that people's inherited image of God leads them either to reject such a notion or to develop an unbalanced yearning for it. Either way, the presupposed image of God is the same, usually akin to the absentee landlord of Deism. This is simply assumed to be what is meant by the word 'God', and yet it is an image which Christianity itself rejects. The God which ordinary people often reject or treat with apathy is one that Christianity rejects too. The God of Jesus Christ is not the 'God' of atheism (i.e. that which atheism rejects), nor of New Age religion. Recent developments are interesting, however, for they suggest that the sense of the otherness of God is far from dead.

## THE AUTHENTIC CHRIST

The German teenagers, as we might anticipate, have tremendous respect for the peculiar authenticity found in Jesus of Nazareth. The status of the earthly Jesus is a complex one, for while he looms large in the gospels, the events of his life are hardly mentioned elsewhere in the New Testament. Some forms of later Christianity have homed in on the earthly teacher and healer, while for others the resurrection and all that followed loom so large that the earthly ministry fades into the background. While the faith of the apostolic Church was above all else a resurrection faith, this was not a resurrection in isolation, but a resurrection that arose out of the incarnation. It is unlikely that the disciples had any notion of the incarnation as such when they accompanied Jesus in his ministry. Their experience of the man, however, was a peculiarly impressive and converting experience, and as such would later be recognized in incarnational terms. The dramatic effect of the resurrection on the disciples is not due to resurrection itself – the resurrection of anyone else could not have had such an effect. It was that the things in Jesus that belong to the incarnation and the resurrection had already astonished people, and it was *this* astonishing person whose rising from the dead was so electrifying. Not only were they now surprised to find themselves fully confirmed in what they had always felt and thought about Jesus, but it was expanded totally beyond what they could have foreseen.

The figure of Jesus as he appears in the gospels is so impressive that even people who have negative attitudes to the Church and to religion in general can recognize his impressiveness. The Jesus of Galilee is by far the most accessible place to start in any presentation of the Christian faith to others, just as it was the most accessible place for the apostles. It is the same Jesus of Galilee who is also impressive to our German teenagers.

How did the first Christians live the Mystery? By meeting Christ. 'What we have seen, what we have heard, what we have touched with our hands . . . that we proclaim to you' (1 John 1.1). Just as the first Christians met Christ and their lives were changed, so must it surely be today. The first priority in the parish is Jesus of Nazareth. In exposure to the Scriptures, in teaching, in prayer, and in worship, Christ is the primary content of the Christian life. It is through engagement with him in parish life and in worship that we come to realize that Jesus of Nazareth is also Christ the exalted Lord, the Lord of the Church. For us too, as for the apostles, this confirms and vindicates what we sense in the earthly Jesus. In addition, this is one way of saying that we cannot know Christ without the story which belongs to him. The isolated Christ is a cardboard cut-out – we see him truly for what he is when he is the Christ of salvation history – and we get closest to Christ in those moments when salvation history is *present*, engaging with us.

## THE HOLY SPIRIT

Before there was any developed doctrine of the Holy Spirit, the Jews of the Old Testament already believed that God was involved and active in his world. This activity of God came to be understood as so intimate to us that Paul speaks of the Holy Spirit moving with our spirit, and of our action as part of the action of the Spirit, in such a way as to be almost elided with it. The German teenagers disliked this idea, feeling in it a threat to autonomy. Their ideal is liberation – this looks like slavery. Any idea of Providence is uncongenial for similar reasons, but such co-operation of God with his world seems incredible anyway. What is not realized of course is that freedom can never be found in isolation – it is always a function of community, of belonging, of self-giving. True freedom is free enough to give everything away, true individuality is born out of rich community life, and true autonomy can only be found in the climate of Providence. It is perhaps in this area of the Holy Spirit and the divine indwelling in us that the divide between these young people and the gospel (and indeed simple human maturity) is most stark, and the area where most difficulty will be met in contemporary Christian communities: not the (allegedly) remote Father, nor the more accessible Son, but the dispensation of the Spirit, in which Christ and the Holy Spirit work together in their divine engagement with the world. The Spirit challenges our supposed autonomy from within. The dislike of this idea is due to an illusion particularly characteristic of our age: the myth of the autonomous individual. It can be shown to be an illusion quite easily by simply looking closely at daily life. The same phenomenon of indwelling exists in human relations. If we can see that *people* indwell each other, then not only can we scotch the myth of the autonomous individual, but it will be easier to see how we can speak of God indwelling our lives and actions.

First of all, there is a communal co-inherence which is too familiar for us to notice. Our national culture, for instance, and its local variants, have formed us profoundly as persons. We have already touched on this with relation to Alf Garnett. In living out my Pakistani, British or Caribbean culture, in its local variant, I am giving voice to something evolved by thousands, or rather millions of people over many centuries. It indwells me. Exactly the same is true of our language, which is much closer to the ground of our being than we realize. Wittgenstein was absolutely right in pointing out that if we are to think at all, we need language. Without it we cannot get very far in attempts to think. And language is something outside us which becomes part of our very self, 'second nature'. We indwell each other in many ways. A more striking instance is found in the immediate family, whose members can not only share our facial characteristics, but modes of speech and gesture too, and even traits of character.

The family's members have all drunk at a common source, all contributed to the moulding of each other. Friends and acquaintances, teachers and even film stars, indwell us in a corresponding way. Children's language and gestures show a slightly unnerving propensity to imitate TV actors. In very close relationships there comes the ability to read the signals which come from the other person, having a sixth sense about their situation, being 'in tune' with them. In human co-operation as a whole, it is possible to speak of indwelling. In a football match, say, or a string quartet, the greatest excellence carries with it an uncanny degree of going-out of oneself towards the other, in a strange unity. Having discovered all of this, it is only a further step to discover the same with God – the greatest individuality and the greatest freedom are found in indwelling and being indwelt. Whatever people's objections may be to the notion of the Spirit working and praying in us, this truth faithfully reflects aspects of life itself, which today we try to suppress or ignore. We are at work in one another, and in the same kind of way 'God is at work in you both to will and to work for his good pleasure' (Philippians 2.13). The Holy Spirit dwells within us and is poised, ready to go forward, if we can enter into the Spirit's kind of co-operation.

## THE MYSTERY OF LIFE

We have already touched on modern reverence for creation, but there is something more to be said. Our contemporary concern for the environment has been dragged out of us by enlightened self-interest. It is self-interest that carries the political and commercial clout. Politicians and businesses are more aware than before that people do not want to be poisoned. However, there is also a reverence towards the things of the natural world which is more than simply that. There is for instance the nostalgia of many urban-dwellers for a nature from which they feel keenly separated. Those country-dwellers who are affected by it are on the whole those whose presence in the countryside is a recent one, often precisely as a result of nostalgia. Born country people are by no means devoid of a reverence for nature, but it is less self-conscious. There are signs however, that this urban reverence is more than mere nostalgia. As we have seen above, it can take forms which become quasi-religious, giving expression to a powerful need to restore lost unity with the universe, to breathe with the cosmos and to bring our awareness into line with its awareness.

People find it difficult, however, to accept talk of the Christian God being the Creator of the universe – the German teenagers were not alone in being unable to see the majesty and variety of the natural world as reflecting a God who made it. This does not reflect an inability to believe in God, but rather a problem with the picture of the Christian God they have picked up. If God is truly to be known in his creation, then once again there is something to be said for starting there, rather than with stereotyped hand-me-down images of God. In people's reverence for the mystery of the natural world God is revealing something of himself, and it may be that if the practice of the Church could effect a meeting of the Orthodox faith with modern people's intuitions about nature, a way may be opened for people to begin to connect the two. It is as if we need to make the Old Testament journey all over again. The natural world is the modern promised land – there we shall find our place in the universe. This will work not so much by capturing nature and bringing it into our churches (harvest festival originates from a very natural weekly practice in Orthodoxy, but the annual version of it practised in Britain has too much of the nostalgic about it) but by going where the 'action' is, as we used to do in the pre-modern world in the tradition of Rogationtide processions. The natural world needs to find its way also into our liturgical language and into formulations of the faith. The Christian doctrine of creation is fundamental in the Jewish-Christian way, and needs to move up alongside the story which people are weaving for themselves today about the natural world in which we are set. If we are to avoid the danger of pantheism and a sentimentalization of nature, however, our sights always have to be set on Christ, the cross and the resurrection.

## THE MYSTERY OF DEATH

In a society obsessed with success and fulfilment it is no surprise to find that there is evasion of suffering and death. There is a subtle difference here between attitudes to the two. Suffering in many ways is faced square-on today, and as the conversation with the teenagers revealed, is taken seriously as intimately concerned with what it is to be human. People today naturally live

197

their lives in terms of life, rather than of suffering: once the suffering of others impinges on them it may be avoided – not, however, without bad conscience. Help and support for others in their suffering is seen as a self-evident good, not a point that has to be laboured (even if we often turn a blind eye in practice, the more readily the further the suffering is away). In society as a whole efforts to help people come to terms with their suffering, and to play as full a part in society as possible, loom ever larger in our life, so much so that the contrast, say, with the 1950s is obvious. This is not to ignore ways in which our society has become more barbaric, or approaches moral problems with inadequate criteria, but simply to indicate the degree to which suffering is more on the public agenda than it has been before.

With death, the case is different, for while on the one hand we have developed a more healthy openness, so that it is more easy to be open about a person's impending death than used to be the case, this tends to come under the rubric of suffering, to which we have much more ready access – death in this way is translated into a form of suffering. The biggest problems arise after another's death – for we do not know what to do about it, or what to do with it, and this casts its shadow backwards. Terminal illness in this way differs from the straight issue of suffering, because of the dark shadow hanging over it which we find so difficult to cope with. In our society the reality of death is repressed. It is a neuralgic, foreign element in the fabric of our life, threatening to undermine its foundations – the only way we can cope is to expel it from our world, have it hustled out of sight by others.

A faith which has *suffering* among its component parts, therefore, can easily be seen as 'relevant'. A faith which includes dealing with *death*, on the other hand, repels us. This is not to say that Christian reflection on death cannot be appreciated by mourners – but again it will be as comfort for them in their suffering rather than facing up to death. Mourners will not tend to welcome talk about their own death, something which their equivalents would have taken naturally in the sixteenth century. Practising Christians are usually little different from anyone else here – we are part of our society and formed by it through and through, so that our worship and teaching and Christian life can fail to face death in a healthy way.

The resurrection transformed the disciples because of what they had already encountered in the earthly Jesus. There was something in the person of Jesus which made his obedient and confident relationship to the Father shine out, and inspired a new ability to be positive and even joyful. He filled people with awe and yet seemed to have an effect on them which made them want to throw their hats in the air. In the New Testament story, all this is followed by suffering, death and resurrection. What we must learn here is that we have a need to retell the story of modern life in terms of this story of Jesus. There is much in the modern attitude to suffering that echoes certain qualities in Jesus; there is also in the modern world a vision, continually disappointed, of a promised land, of exodus from all our troubles, and a new life which is already dimly reflected in our experiences of situations of resurrection. These things need a story which will string them together, restoring the category of death to its proper place in the process as *death*, but all in the light of Christ's resurrection: this story is the saving story of Christ. We need to see that we inhabit salvation history.

## STORY

The saving events are historical events, part of the fabric of daily life. Any ability to relate to them must start with the story of our own life – we need to be able to tell our story, and to recognize it for what it is. Many people cannot see their life as a narrative but rather a succession of unconnected events. We need to go through the experience of telling it, and in the telling of it the unity of the whole can begin to be seen. Only then can we see that the story of Jesus is a retelling of our own story in a different light, a light which makes new sense of it. We will never be able to relate to the Mystery of Christ if we do not have a preliminary sense of where we are in the mystery of our own story. We cannot begin to have an adequate vision of who we are as human beings without the category of narrative. The worst way to meet such a need is to blackmail people into giving unwilling testimonies before others – the traditional way is spiritual direction and confession, but other possibilities need exploring. Patrick Purnell, in his book *Our Faith Story* suggests, for instance, that in baptism and confirmation preparation the candidates should be encouraged to look for the moments at which God seems to have been at work in their own past lives. Recognizing perhaps for the first time this presence of God in their lives, they can then begin to make connections with the Christian narrative, and see how it fits with theirs.[8]

Once we start discovering the narrative nature of our own lives, we cannot fail to begin to be aware of the wider context of society's narrative, of which we are a part. We begin to discover in fact that the three narratives of self, society and salvation history are inseparable, and that any attempt to make sense of the gospel requires all three. In practical terms this means that growth in understanding of the faith will inevitably include some critique of society, not only comment on isolated aspects of its life, but also awareness of it as an enormous narrative of which we are a part. This is not something that can simply be taught – we have to be brought to a point where we see with our eyes, recognize it for what it is as story.

So much for the narratives of people's experience in daily life. The next element in the brew is a more straightforward matter of teaching – people need to be aware of the biblical story – salvation history. They need to have the simple information of what the events *are,* and of the bare fact that they are important in our life as Christians. This in turn needs to be connected with the content of the liturgy. A good example can be the use of oil in baptism. There are arguments for and against baptismal anointing, and this will be heavily influenced by cultural factors. Olive oil was an everyday thing in the ancient mediterranean world – used for lighting, cooking, cosmetics, washing, athletics, religion, and so on (this can still be appreciated in a country such as Italy). Today its use is more limited, and its symbolism has been altered by the results of the industrial revolution. The first thing we think of when oil is mentioned is cars, petrol, machines, and black unpleasant slime, difficult to remove. How can modern participants in a baptismal liturgy relate to it? One approach is to explain it as the baptism service proceeds. This, however, is almost completely destructive of its function, for the role of the oil is as *symbol.* Symbol points beyond itself, it sets off resonances greater than itself. The whole point of symbol is that it is needed where words fail. A true symbol cannot be adequately described or explained – it is killed in the process. So it may be thought to be a waste of time to use oil if it has to be explained. This too is to misunderstand what is needed. Anointing with oil not only arises out of salvation history, but is a means for putting us in touch with it.

Wherever possible, therefore, the answer to problems with a

symbol of the liturgy is not to attempt to explain it, but to put ourselves in touch with the associated elements in salvation history. Here the people to be involved in the baptismal liturgy need, over the preceding weeks, to have read to them the various stories from the Old Testament about anointings, of the sick, of kings, and of prophets. After that come the accounts of Jesus' baptism and references to him as the anointed one. All of this needs to be read without deliberate reference to the baptismal anointing. It could include seeing the coronation anointing of the Queen on video. The third stage would be about the early Christian practice of anointing at baptism. After that, all that needs to be said is that Susan, or John, or Craig, will be anointed. There should be no need to explain it. In this way we can see that salvation history 'fills out' what is going on in the liturgy, but also the liturgy puts us in contact with the contents of salvation history.

## THE CALENDAR

Christ's story dominates our worship: textually in the reading of the Scriptures and the Creeds, ritually in the eucharist and the other sacraments and 'Mysteries', visually in church buildings and in art. Not least is this so with the calendar, and this is one way of engaging with the Mystery of Christ which, while showing signs of improvement, is still under-developed in terms of present-day potential. A mere glance at Eamon Duffy's *The Stripping of the Altars*[9] will show how vividly this unfolding drama can find expression. When we have made due allowance for medieval distortion of priorities and for the way people may participate in worship today, it is possible to gain from such a book an idea of how the calendar may come alive ritually for our congregations in our own contemporary society. Such things can only evolve slowly, and it would be a mistake to try and create a scheme for the year as if we were sitting down to write a play. The full liturgical celebration of Holy Week and Easter is becoming increasingly common in parishes. Humbler practices such as Advent candles are also catching on, but in order to make an impact when the variety of such activities in the secular realm is enormous, we need to operate on a grander scale than this. We could ask ourselves, for example, how some of our church symbolism compares with Bonfire Night or seeing in the mew year in Trafalgar Square. Why are our symbolic acts in church often prim and lacking in boldness? Communal ritual enactment of the calendar is one of the primary ways in which worship becomes people's own (and it *must* become their own, so that they ask for it and do it off their own bat where necessary), and this touches on the heart of our problem – it is action and it is salvation history. Cyril of Alexandria says in relation to the eucharist, 'Christ does not say he is in us by a relation of an affective kind, but by physical participation'.[10] There is already material to hand in the Church of England in *Lent, Holy Week and Easter*, and *The Promise of His Glory*, and other material either already available or in preparation.[11]

## DAILY PRAYER

Teenagers are only one part of the population, and even among themselves they differ widely. From the enormous variety of the modern world it is not possible to take any one group or phenomenon as representative. I would like to add now something which comes from quite a different angle. It constitutes, this time, not a discussion of propositions, but a practical phenomenon. This is the fast-growing practice of celebrating the daily office.

There is a growing number of parishes in Britain where the offices are celebrated daily together by layfolk. The 'Simple Celebration' office in the new experimental office-book for the Church of England, *Celebrating Common Prayer*,[12] was evolved in an ordinary parish in Liverpool where it involves large numbers of people daily,[13] and has become a very significant part of parish life. In Dewsbury parish church in West Yorkshire, now renamed the Minster, the layfolk are entirely responsible for a fourfold daily office, mattins, midday office, evensong and compline. Many examples could be cited up and down the country. People are finding that the traditional prayer of the psalms and canticles in the form of the daily office is an unexpectedly fruitful and engaging experience. In addition there are interesting experiments in private prayer, such as the business rep who belongs to a parish group committed to praying evensong wherever they are at 6 p.m. each evening: at the end of his day he pulls into a convenient layby and says evening prayer, conscious that the others will be saying it at the same time.

This phenomenon is to be found in other countries too. At Bad Tölz in Bavaria between ten and twenty people sing vespers

202

every day. In Kremsmünster monastery in Austria youth vespers attracts between 600 and 1,000 young people on every third Friday of the month. Here there is no leader to the worship – 'people participate better when there isn't one'.[14] They have produced an office-book for daily morning and evening prayer which is widely used. In France I could cite various churches, several of them in Paris (including St Gervais, St Leu, Sacré Coeur, St Germain-les-Auxerrois). People do not always need much encouragement to embark on this – they could do far worse than simply read the introduction to the 'Simple Celebration' office (pages 281–3 of *Celebrating Common Prayer*). In this way, by worship based on community and recitation of the psalms and intercession, people can discover the Mystery amongst themselves.

For many centuries the psalms were the basic foundation of all Christian prayer,[15] and central to the psalms is the rehearsal of saving-history. The daily office is almost entirely composed of Scripture. We have already found that one way of characterizing the Mystery is as Scripture becoming present – engagement with the saving events is engagement with the very stuff of Scripture. The many layfolk and clergy who are rediscovering the daily office are in fact discovering an age-old way of engaging with the scriptural Mystery of Christ. Particularly when it is celebrated with some imagination, music and corporate participation this becomes very clear because then we are beginning to engage with the whole of ourselves. And what constitutes the *presence*? The people themselves as they are, as they physically see each other, as they speak and sing, look and listen. That is the top of the iceberg, completely one with the greater reality of the whole Christian Mystery.

## PRESENCE

Taking on board all that has been said so far, we now have to go on to say that at some point it will be necessary to articulate what has been experienced, by introducing people to the way the word 'mystery' is used in the New Testament, and connecting it directly with the resurrection. This can only be done, however, in a setting in which it is already alive to people. In addition, it all *has* to be connected up with the presence of Christ in daily life. We have to go on about this until people take notice of it – Christ is there in the people around us. There is little prospect of achieving anything simply by presenting Odo Casel's Mystery-teaching, even if in a suitably adapted form. We have to start with the real thing. We should not attempt to turn what is a mere formulation into a *recipe*. 'Concepts create idols. Only wonder understands'.[16] A lot of work needs to be done with people on recognizing Christ in daily life and in other people, particularly in the uncongenial ones. This shows up a failure in the formation of the laity which often results in an unhappy distinction between clergy and laity. Clergy have been trained to appreciate the humanity behind the bad behaviour of others, and so to have compassion even on the most unlovable. It is not unknown for the priest in a deprived urban area to be the only person in the parish to speak up for the local youth who have nothing better to do than vandalize the neighbourhood. Not all clergy have such sensitivity, and not all layfolk are without it, but there is work to be done here in enabling all members of the Body to have a sensitivity for Christ outside the church as well as in it.

## BOTH WORSHIP AND DAILY LIFE ARE SERIOUS BUSINESS

If these are some of the principal traits in contemporary attitudes to God, and if people need to come to an apprehension of the Mystery of Christ if their understandings are to change, we need to ask what practical steps can be taken in a parish to encourage this. The bread and butter of a Christian community's life is its worship, and encounter with Christ depends on how the worship is celebrated. For people to gain a whiff of his Mystery, worship has to be treated as serious business. It should not be necessary to say this, except that it is very clear that worship is often treated in the contemporary Church as if it were not serious business. This is a difficult area in which to establish criteria, as it really calls for conversion of heart. Christians can conduct worship in a way which is dead, trivial, like a circus, taking itself too lightly, taking itself too seriously – human ingenuity for elbowing God out is boundless. The conversion of heart that is needed, however, means taking God seriously, as part of a response so filled with wonder that reverence comes naturally and self-consciousness falls away. It is only within a climate of this conversion of heart that practical guidelines can be of any use. Without it they will simply be monstrous pretensions. A chapter on the parish needs at some point to descend to practicalities, but practical suggestions are worse than useless if the heart is hardened, superficial, or rooted in the self, in consumerism, in human autonomy. Rather than present detailed guidance, here are a few reserved and telegraphic headings for reflection:

1   The first necessity is a life rooted in prayer, and in reverent attention to God and to people. Such prayer needs to be done with others as well as in private. The only possible starting point for prayer is the recognition of our own utter inadequacy and frailty – in other words, repentance.

2   We have to seek to take seriously the *distinction* between the presence of the Mystery in daily life and the presence of the Mystery in the liturgy. They are not interchangeable: life and worship are intentionally distinct.

3   The worshipping community should be aware of the realities of society and respond to them. (The 'shrine', or the charismatic community, which lives for its own private life cannot be following Christ properly.)

4   We need to watch where our attention comes to *rest*. There has to be a balance between attention resting on human beings and attention resting on God (see Chapter 3).

5   Worship needs to be prepared with care; attention (sane and unfussy) will naturally be paid to its detail, both its practical accomplishment, and the people involved.

6   The liturgy *as* liturgy is larger than the people celebrating it. This should help us avoid drawing so much attention to the personalities of those taking part that the greater Mystery in which we are all involved is forgotten or trivialized. Clergy who behave like compères, take note! Christ is the celebrant.

7   We need to discover, and this will not be easy for our informal age, the difference between Christian joy and human jollity.

8   Worship needs to take suffering and death seriously (in daily life attitudes of reverence become particularly noticeable in these circumstances). We have to be able

to say the liturgy involves death for all concerned, whether it is talk about death, directing our attention to the death and resurrection of Christ, or dying to ourselves.

9 The worshipping community needs to have a sense that the worship *belongs* to all of us.

10 Real worship touches people in such a way that they can say they are engaging in something authentic and connected with their experience.

## PURSUING THE MYSTERY

Whatever we might want to say about the needs of the parish, there is ultimately only 'one thing necessary', and without it our best efforts remain robbed of vitality. Something is wrong in a Church in which there is little burning desire for pursuing the Mystery, pursuing the One who stands at the centre. The God of the Old and New Testaments desires to love and to be loved, and it is impossible for such a love to strike its goal through love of neighbour alone – it can go so far and no further without diminishing the neighbour we are called to love.

Fear wist not to evade, as love wist to pursue.

Love naturally pursues the object of its desires, but these words from Francis Thompson's *The Hound of Heaven* remind us to beware – who in fact is doing the pursuing? Any love we have for God is the work of the Holy Spirit within us, a sign of our entering into the circle of love amongst the persons of the Trinity. In this pursuit, who is subject and who is object? The love which circles among the divine persons is a pursuing love. And when the shepherd finds the lost sheep, or the father runs out to the prodigal son, who runs towards whom? Both parties end up pursuing, in the moment of encounter, as absence becomes presence. Until we sense the presence we are unlikely to pursue. In the words of one of the Church Fathers of the fourth century: 'You ask why on earth young people, when they grow up, drift away from the Church – but it is natural: it is like fox-hunting, where the hounds who have not seen him sooner or later grow tired, give up and return home, while those few who have seen the fox chase their quarry right to the end'.[17]

Parishes need pastors and congregations who have been caught up into the pursuit of the Mystery. They will be aware that in reality they are being pursued, that Love is pursuing them and desiring their response; and because God is not simply a God of the airwaves, their own desire can only be real if it loves the things of the Church: its worship, its Scriptures, its ministers, its paraphernalia. This has gained a bad reputation in the rich West, but if we go, say, to a South African township we will find that in many traditions black Africans love elaborate worship, delight in dressing up, and take the greatest pleasure in beautifying the liturgy. Such attitudes to worship are now among us in strength once again in Britain, in the many communities who trace their roots to various parts of the Commonwealth, and who take God and his worship seriously. European attitudes to the physical have been traumatized, and need to be made whole. Pursuit of the Mystery is likely to mean we will delight in church buildings, and in those things which are so naively called 'externals' (as if they had nothing to do with the fibre of our being). The Church as a place and as a people is a climate wherein we shall be surprised by the Mystery. Philip Larkin speaks for many people, practising and non-practising, when he says of the church building:

> A serious house on serious earth it is,
> In whose blent air all our compulsions meet,
> Are recognised, and robed as destinies.
> And that much never can be obsolete,
> Since someone will forever be surprising
> A hunger in himself to be more serious,
> And gravitating with it to this ground,
> Which, he once heard, was proper to grow wise in . . .[18]

So we will delight in pouring the best of our resources and reverence into parish worship, for ours is the God of the incarnation and of the sacrament of the Church which was born out of the resurrection. He is not simply on the airwaves – he is a God of pots and pans as well, of flesh and blood, bricks and stone. We will delight, at the end of the day, in two things: pursuit of the world's good through love of our neighbour, and pursuit of God in Christ through the Holy Spirit.

We will probably not get very far if we try to expound Casel's theology of the Mystery in the parish. The way forward is by getting on and living it. It will entail getting away from the fire-engine-ladder mentality of a frustrating, individual upward struggle; not that, but pursuit of the Mystery, in the power of the pursuing Mystery, coming to find as a result that our feet are on something more solid than we have known before.

## THE CONNECTION WITH RELIGIOUS COMMUNITIES

There is an aspect of eternalism which eludes all of us today, and this might be called a convinced piety. It is something which is perhaps most characteristic of Evangelical circles in Britain, but at one time was a natural part of all Christian living. It was out of it that monasteries arose, and certainly until the end of the seventeenth century the religion of the secular world and that of the monastic life were exactly the same in this matter. In modern society Religious Communities can find themselves to be puddles in a landscape of receding eternalism. But there is no reason why zeal for worship and a confident faith in divine Providence should be a monopoly of monasteries – they stand there as pools where the secular Church can refresh itself, refresh its memory that God is holy and believeable. This role goes back to monasticism's very beginnings, where it was a garnering of the primitive fervour of the early Church in times of change, lest that fervour should be lost. It is as if the brilliant light of the paschal beginnings was with the passage of time refracted through a prism and separated out into component colours. From the other side of the prism emerged the New Testament, ministry and sacraments, liturgy, calendar, analytical formulation of doctrine, varying degrees of fervour and commitment, and so on. Amongst the whole range of colours appearing, one is monasticism, custodian of something essential to the Church. This 'something essential' had in apostolic times been one element in a single, unitary experience; but now strands were being separated out, and this strand needed to be pursued in its own right as an act of stewardship of 'something essential' in the gospel on behalf of the whole Church. In this way it is possible to say that monasticism is an essential component of the gospel, and a Church which does not have it has a faulty gospel, as do those who have it but do not value it. And never was this role more needed than in the world of today.

It seems at first outlandish to make such a claim, and monks and nuns would be quick to say that they are not living the faith any better than anyone else, and are not living a part of the gospel but the whole of it. The New Testament is the rule above all rules, and their whole life involves being shaped and formed by the gospel. They would not claim, as has sometimes been claimed, that theirs is the 'most perfect' way, nor that they are giving more time to the gospel so that they may live it better than others. It is rather that these people have been called to live the gospel in this particular way, but the whole gospel, not a part.

On the other hand it is nothing new to claim a unique role for monasticism in preserving for the Church a particular perspective on life in the Mystery which would otherwise be obscured or even lost. So the seventeenth-century Anglican divine Herbert Thorndike could say that the Church is incomplete without the monastery. 'It is a perfection to Christianity', and 'it is certainly a blot in the reformation which we profess, that we are without it'.[19] While not all people would wish to say that monasticism is an essential element in the Church's life, it can certainly be said that the things which monasticism seeks to hold in trust are essential to the Church's living of the whole gospel. Often the Church loses sight of these things, and it falls to monks and nuns to continue proclaiming them. Sometimes monasticism itself loses sight of them and the vision goes underground until the Spirit renews them once more. Monks and nuns therefore have no monopoly on that which is their speciality. In a healthy Church these things are found in all believers, and the difference between monastery and 'parish' is not stark. Taking account of all these qualifications, it nevertheless makes clear an important point if we speak of monasticism holding in trust for, and sharing with, the whole Church a distinct band of that spectrum of colours which is the resurrection Mystery.

Monasticism is sometimes spoken of as a sacrament in the early centuries. It can really only be understood in terms of sacrament, and hence in terms of the Mystery, a place in the Church's life where the Mystery runs up its flag, often despite those at the bottom of the flagpole. The saving events are present in the house, where the daily life is lived. The incarnation, the witness, the conflict, the darkness, the transfiguration, the cross, the resurrection and the glory, are in the refectory, the kitchen, the garden, the brethren, the sisters, the guests, the newspapers that manure the community's prayers, the human encounters which continually touch on the harmonies and the dissonances of humanity. The Mystery is there in the house and in the worship in church. A monastery's church invades its house and the house invades the church.

If it is possible in any way to talk of the life of monastic communities as sacrament or mystery, it is as a gathering and a polishing-up of certain values and elements of the gospel that are found already distributed throughout the Church (and outside it), yet the communities are there to make sure these things are not forgotten, to encourage people in the pursuit of them, and to show by the godly folly of giving their whole lives to them, that these things are *real*. Monasticism is vital to today's Church for all these things, and yet at the same time it can lay claim to none of them. As for their unusual sense of community, even that is possible in any parish or family, with the sole difference that monastic brothers and sisters have the easier option, in standing apart from so many distractions, but if it is not done for and on behalf of everybody, then it is a total waste of time. Religious Communities are important to the pursuit of the Mystery in the parish because the encounter between monastery and parish generates a surprise for all involved that can enable God to catch us while we are surprised. Parishes and Religious Communities need contact with each other. There is much to be done, therefore, in making more of our Religious Communities, of increasing the two-way contact between parish and Religious brothers and sisters to the benefit of both parties. Each in a different way can make vivid to the other a vision of the Mystery which otherwise can easily grow dim.

I have put forward some random suggestions, and could well have included more. Some of what I have said may well be wide of the mark, but I hope I have given some idea of the possibilities. The best people to discover what the theology of the Mystery means in parish life are the people and clergy themselves.

## FOURTEEN

# *A Different Universe*

WE ARE TOLD the universe is curved, so that any journey towards its outer limits begins to turn back upon itself, and even at earlier stages of the journey the route is not quite as we imagine it. On the universal scale, a straight line is an impossibility. This is very difficult for us to grasp, but it is something we can appreciate a little more easily in the realm of human development and progress. Human history cannot travel in a straight line either, but curves away from itself in a way that can be demonstrated without too much difficulty. Were it a straight track, we would be able to look back and take in quite straightforwardly all that we could see. But we cannot – events left behind us quickly turn at an oblique angle to us, so that we will never again be able to see them as people did at the time. We can no longer see God as either side in the English Civil War saw him, neither can we see sexuality as the medieval Church saw it, nor understand how Stravinsky's *Rite of Spring* caused a riot at its first performance. History curves away from us, and those things which people saw as the obvious issues and choices facing them do not seem so to us – we can no longer imagine fully how they thought and felt. This also means that those issues and choices which are self-evident to us will not look at all so obvious to future generations: to some degree they are bound to be puzzled by our priorities.

Yesterday's passions can puzzle the actors on today's stage. Our choices do not fall in that alignment. The English Civil War was fought over certain clear choices which people saw to be

211

before them: those particular battle-cries, however, do not seem half so self-evident to us today:

> We cannot revive old factions
> We cannot restore old policies
> Or follow an antique drum.[1]

Were I transported back to seventeenth-century England, I could not be completely sure which side I would fight for. I would prefer one side for its religion and the other for its politics. But both the politics and the religion took forms I cannot easily relate to. The same can be true of modern situations in countries other than our own. We do not easily recognize the landscape of other people's passions, and they often seem lamentably tribal. We can only comprehend life in the terms that are available to us. The first chapters of this book tried to give an idea of how the terms available to us have shifted through successive revolutions which have left people changed in ways that cannot be undone. Our notion of who we are as human beings, and of the relation between the external world and our personal 'interior' life, have followed a curve of development which has taken us far from the position Plato or Augustine found themselves in. We can only look back through a warp which distorts, and one corollary of this is that we ought not to take our own current attitudes so much for granted as we tend to do. The quest for truth will include a preparedness to see our own standpoint as a moment within the warp of the universe. There is room to attempt to see things in a larger perspective than our present one.

## GAIN AND LOSS

Revolutions often represent an advance, but also bring loss. We are beginning to realize in our time that amongst the enormous changes taking place in the modern world we have lost some things to our detriment, and ways have to be sought to recover them. A good example of such ebb and flow in human development is the Reformation.

Eamon Duffy's book *The Stripping Of the Altars*[2] leaves the reader with a vivid picture of the medieval Church on the eve of the upheaval. Contrary to popular supposition, it emerges not as a hopelessly corrupt Church, but as in good order for its time, doing its job relatively well. The Reformation can consequently be seen as a tragedy, in which an alien way was forced on an unwilling population; a few misguided trouble-causers were responsible for the original upheaval, and other-wise the Church would have reformed itself in a more bal-anced way.

It is possible to accept this picture, and yet still be left with the question, 'Why?' There is never smoke without real fire, and although the Church might have been in good order, something burned in the hearts of some people which could not be held back. What was it? Partly it was the fact that material prosper-ity, the explosion in science and learning, and the emergence of humanism, printing, and the enquiring individual, all conspired to produce a gut urge to break away from the domestic apron-strings of the Church. Such independence had long been present in Lollardy. Something was now coming to birth in the human spirit which was too strong to be suppressed, signalling the pass-ing of a new threshold in the history of what it is to be human. It involved an embracing of the everyday, which was gaining respect through the achievements of science and commerce. Its force was like plants which push their way through tarmac, or trees knocking down walls – it was a new, little understood, and profoundly elemental urge. The Church either had to take it ser-iously or move out of the way. It seemed for a time that this urge was capable of positive chemistry with the inherited Church, but in one of those chaotic moments when a mere slip of the tiller can sink a ship, it went wrong, and created a havoc for which we are still paying the price. In a sense, no one party could take all the blame for this ecclesiastical Chernobyl – forces were at work which were larger and more complex than people's capacity to comprehend what was happening to them and in them.

The forces lifting up the paving-stones can have a colossal driving force, but so can the age-old tradition they seek to tear apart. We can find ourselves admitting that both sides need to be taken seriously. To a certain degree Luther's and Cranmer's guts were right, but the strength of their reaction against the tradition sent them off at a tangent, while Rome bounced off at another tangent, both parties then landing in separate trenches which they next had extreme difficulty getting out of. It needed four hundred years of waiting before something could move in the resulting landscape. When things did move, we find that they take the form of acknowledgement of positive gain, but also a pressure to restore great and fundamental areas of loss. Since the Second Vatican Council the Roman Catholic Church has come to take as normal many things which, in a different idiom, were slogans for the churches of the Reformation. Protestants, on the other hand, have been rediscovering the Catholic tradition, in what could without exaggeration be described as a new thirst for the sacraments and a sense of the Church.

The Reformation is only one example among many that I could have taken. This kind of ebb and flow, with both consolidation and recapitulation, is often to be found in the long-term history of revolutions. We might reasonably expect, therefore, that the history of human consciousness as outlined in Chapter 3 belongs in a similar perspective. As I wrote there, the baby which has been thrown out with the bathwater needs to come back through the window.

It is an easy temptation to depict the modern world and its problems in simple terms, when their complexity is in fact forbidding. We can better focus our thoughts if we narrow the field down to certain generally acknowledged archetypes, and I take the risk of oversimplifying here, by comparing two archetypical positions of our age. On the one hand we have a strong view of the faith delivered to the saints, the holiness and unchangeability of the Church, and a belief in the importance of responsible authority for deciding and ordering the things which lie at the centre of her life. Here is a powerful apprehension that the Church is a Mystery beyond the tamperings of mere human beings. It is beyond all our activisms, our self-will, our claims to personal inspiration, our desires to mould after our own image the eternal designs of God. This vision of the Church is part of a birthright which I myself took in from the time I was a child, the Church as Mystery, as sacrament, imbued with the holiness and transcendence of God, but close at the same time to the very fibres of life in the home and on the street, and in the human heart. It is 'Holy Church as his creation, and her teachings as his own'. This mystery is like a tree, branches and trunk forming a line of tradition which itself is sacramental, something caught, not taught. Either you see this, or you do not. Either you have gained this 'knowledge' (*gnosis*) or you have not. And this element in the Church today would pass inspection in just the same way as the late medieval Church does for Eamon Duffy – it is formally in good order.

But . . . there is something else. There are the guts. There are elemental forces moving in the human spirit. They are like elder trees forcing up the concrete – forces beyond our present comprehending, forces which threaten to wreak damage and chaos in their surging path. They are more complex than those which disturbed the late medieval mind, and much more widespread. It is incumbent on us to ask whether there lies hidden within these forces not only abundant human sin, but also something of the wisdom of God. He speaks to us through the Church, but also through the world. He speaks to us in the divine law, but also in the natural law. The truth about the planets established by Galileo is also truth about God and his desire for things. The common sense of folk is one of the measures with which we test our apprehension of the gospel. These two positions are not alternatives – we need to acknowledge that they are both there in all of us.

But that is not all. We need to add to this a further rogue ingredient. Contemporary society is undergoing a revolution in attitudes and self-understanding which we are hardly beginning to be aware of. This demands a response from the Church so that we can relate the gospel to the world we are bringing it to. The revolution demanded of us is so great, at least akin to that which gripped the sixteenth century, that individuals may find it impossible to take seriously both the voice of the Church's tradition and the voice of the world – they will feel a need to take sides. Unless, that is, we can find a language which enables real dialogue rather than shouting past each other in mutually incomprehensible double-Dutch.

Alasdair MacIntyre has shown in his recent writings the extent to which dialogue in modern society is impossible because there is no common language, no common starting-point.[3] All there can be is a Babel in which each constituency speaks its own language, operating on its own private terms: the result is a situation where people merely shout past each other. This problem is reduced in the Church, where some common points for orientation remain, such as the Scriptures and Church order. However, we are all aware of the degree to which positive dialogue becomes impossible because the plugs of one group are not compatible with the sockets of another, and so we are reduced to standing firm and loudly insisting on our particular point of view.

## A COMMON KERNEL

Angelus Häussling, in a retrospective article on Odo Casel, makes the interesting observation that the theology of Mystery differs from most other standpoints common today in that it provides a very simple but universally applicable kernel from which further developments seem to follow naturally in any direction we care to take. It is a small, concentrated deposit capable of infinite application and extension in any field. In this way it contrasts with most contemporary approaches to theology in that it works from the inside outwards, while theology on the whole starts at different points of the circle and endeavours to work inwards, piecing separate bits together in the hope of establishing an eventual unity. Häussling remarks that Casel 'is the first theologian for many generations who has once again recognized the need for theology to sum up in a single word the whole Christian life', a need that is as much pastoral as scholarly. 'Our world is less and less comprehensible, the actual forces which dominate contemporary history become ever more anonymous, the circumstances in which we are to proclaim the faith feel increasingly disoriented, and for the individual ever more hostile, to such a degree that this theological approach has become much more topical.'[4] Casel 'works outwards from the content of the saving word (*Heilswort*) itself, the single Mystery . . . [Casel says] "the Mystery is always complete" (*immer ganz*) . . . this "reduction" has, not least, made clear Christian spirituality's concentration on the *Pascha* [the mystery of the resurrection]'.[5]

Such a theological process asks us to risk being big enough for what seems not only impossible but at first sight repellent: to go beyond our visible horizon into a realm where truths about which we are fervent veer and bend, in ways which we could not have foreseen, not because the truths change but because we are changed, as they and we bend painfully round towards the incomprehensible Mystery of God.

For openness to each other there needs to be a common means of communication, and if the Creeds are right in assigning such communication to the Holy Spirit, then it is not something we can accomplish on our own. There is one thing which will definitely be of help to us, and another which may well also help.

First, there is that of which the theology of the Mystery speaks: a faith centred on the God of the incarnation, with whom we are brought into living engagement through all of our physical, mental and spiritual nature in *worship*. The practice of this with the whole of ourselves is the only way there can be proper communication among ourselves, and between different theological positions.

The second matter which may also be of help is Mystery-theology itself, as a common *language* capable of giving full expression to many Christian traditions. Because it is a kernel rather than a carapace, it is versatile without losing its central anchor.

## RECOVERING OUR BALANCE

If Plato, Augustine, Descartes, and Freud have all shown us truths about ourselves which we can never now leave behind, these truths also need to be brought together in the unlikely kaleidoscope of the truth of God. Quite naturally we assume that if I am right, then the person who seems diametrically opposed to me must be wrong. The larger context of the Mystery now helps us to see opposition differently – as witness. Three-dimensional vision cannot be conceived by one eye. A second eye is needed which sees things from a different angle. It is this difference which enables us to see in a larger, more unlikely, but undoubtedly more real, dimension. How could anyone who has never experienced three-dimensional vision believe that it works? Two differing pictures superimposed can in fact make a new kind of sense. Mystery-theology, and therefore the worship which it attempts to describe, encourage us to see the other not as opponent but as a witness. A Christian who is perceived by some as 'right-wing' is most likely being misunderstood, and this can become clear when we see him or her instead as a witness. The Christian who has marginalized worship in favour of unstinting service of the world may be seen as having sold the gospel down the river, but the Mystery enables us to see that that person too is a witness, fulfilling a greatly needed role. Heeding both of them is likely to open the door to a *via media* which is no longer merely average, but more like the royal road of Christ the exalted Lord. Archbishop George Carey coined a phrase for the ecumenical agenda which seems to express this well – he has spoken of a Church based on 'organic diversity',[6] a Church which is organic in gospel, order and worship, and yet doing justice to our great diversity in a way which builds up the unity rather than threatening it – a family of witnesses to the many facets of the Mystery. And what do these witnesses witness to? Not just two poles in the Church. They witness on the one hand to eternalism and the sovereignty of the transcendent God, and on the other they witness to what the modern world's 'corns' are telling it – often through people who profess no religious belief, strange people often, such as Pasolini the film director, or Francis Bacon the painter, and all those who give voice to the elemental cries coming from the heart of the modern world.

We are presented with hard questions about life in modern society as it is, and about the incongruity between it and the 'faith delivered to the saints'. The voices which arise from the heart of modern society cannot easily be dismissed as foolish voices, while a too unquestioning love of the 'things of God' can easily be a blinkered love. On the other hand, many Christians today need somehow to be helped to see that they have a blind spot (of which quite naturally they may be completely unaware): simply to treat the Church with wariness makes nonsense of the gospel, and sentimentalizes the 'world'. There is in all this some unrecognized sentimentality about 'ordinary people' and 'real life' which takes little account of the sin, perversity and evil present in every human being, so that if the Church loses credibility because of the Inquisition, humanity equally lost its credibility in Auschwitz and the debased life of consumer society, if it had not done so long before. All is corrupt, and all is holy. Both the Church and the world have to be treated with wariness and with reverent awe. With either tribe we are in danger of turning the gospel into a beautiful bag of abstract and high-flown ideals, when the gospel of Jesus Christ is both spiritual and physical, with all the inevitable paradoxes that that brings. It is to do with the guts of life, and is not to be idealized or sentimentalized in a way which imagines it can be refined off from sin. Both the Church and 'ordinary life' and 'ordinary people' are all implicated up to their necks in sin in a way that will not be redeemed until the end of all things, and we should steer clear of idealizing any of them. In the present age the cornfields will always have their weeds. But there is also much to learn from each other about reverence, and the particular senses in which the Church is holy and the world is holy.

The truth cannot change, and we cannot be disloyal to our own convictions: but we can make an effort to see that what is the truth for us is capable of being expanded. Three-dimensional vision does not expect compromise of the left eye's view with that of the right in an unprincipled betrayal: it brings instead a new order of seeing. Our truth is always too small, and needs to join hands with different truths which are not so false or alien as we think: the two are simply not reconcilable on our terms – only on terms which we are not capable of foreseeing.

## ODO CASEL AS A MAN

One of the things I have attempted to do is to introduce to a wider audience the thinking of Odo Casel. It is probably fitting, as we draw towards the end, to say a little about Casel the man. He was born the son of a Koblenz engine-driver in 1886, in 1907 he was professed as a monk in the abbey of Maria Laach in the Rhineland, and from that point on he led the hidden life of a monk, in 1926 becoming chaplain to the nuns at Herstelle on the Weser, a place which he never left again, dying there in 1948. Casel's life at Herstelle makes a fascinating story, for while on the surface there was nothing to tell, he and the sisters struck up such a fruitful relationship that from his pen (and from those of the nuns after his death) came the many writings which were to have such influence on the life of the Church. Casel's work was brought to an end by his unexpected and remarkable death. While carrying the Paschal candle into the church at Herstelle on the night of nights, having proclaimed the light of the risen Christ for the third time and climbed into the pulpit to begin the singing of the Exultet, he collapsed, and during Easter night passed into that Mystery which had been the focus of his lifelong attention.[7] During his lifetime he had worked together with the sisters for the renewal of their Religious Community life, and this impressive women's community continues today as a witness to the vigour of the insights which they discovered together with him. It is to be hoped that in the future his works may become more readily available in English, and in translations which are worthy of them.

Whether Odo Casel points to a language in which Christians can listen to each other in the midst of a chaos as great and as tense as the Church has ever seen, is for the reader to judge. What perhaps we see in Casel over and above that possibility is a sign of the times: indications of a turning-point in the history of Western Christianity. Ever since the first inklings of modern rational theological inquiry in the seventh and eighth centuries, the first flowering of analytical theological discourse in Anselm, through its great triumph in Aquinas, and on through the Reformation period into the Enlightenment the Western grasp of the Christian faith has increasingly separated the interior and the abstract from the exterior and objective, and rested the greatest weight on the interior. With the Enlightenment things began to go seriously wrong. Then from the mid-nineteenth century onwards the tide began to turn – the theology of the Mystery, rooted as it is in the liturgy, is perhaps the first clear and coherent signal that a consensus of many centuries is beginning to disintegrate. We are witnessing the passing of a picture of God which is no longer credible, the 'God of the airwaves', and rediscovering the God of the incarnation. The abstract and the interior (as we conceive them) are important, but there is still more to us than our over-simplified picture. With those things on their own we are missing out half of our humanity; and the interior journey to which we are all called can never be pursued without the other half, plus the other half of God's response to our humanity – the Body of Christ and its sacramental life. We are at last beginning to sense this truth. Not only are we rediscovering the created order as God's word to us – the universe, vast and stupendous as it is, is in fact even more yet than it seems, permeated within and radiated from without by the one who is abundant life, the Mystery of God, the person of Jesus of Nazareth, whose story is rooted in the story of Israel, in its turn rooted in the story of humanity. Mystery not as invisible, but as sacrament.

Books listed in the Select Bibliography are referred to by section and number (e.g. Crichton (B3)).

## Chapter 1

1. Augustine, *Tractate on the Gospel of John* 32.8, 9.
2. Gregory Nazianzen, *Discourses* 43.20.
3. See Kenneth Stevenson, *Nuptial Blessing*, London, Alcuin Club, 1982, pp. 62f., and *To Join Together*, New York, Pueblo, 1990, p. 49.
4. A. Wilkinson, *The Church of England and the First World War*, London, SPCK, 1978, p. 161.
5. Wilkinson, *The Church of England*, p. 163. The quotation is from *The Army and Religion* (1919), p. 57.
6. See A. Hastings, *A History of English Christianity 1920–1985*, London, Collins, 1986, pp. 174–6.
7. A. Wilkinson, *The Community of the Resurrection*, London, SCM Press, 1992, p. 307.
8. See Ronald Ferguson, *George MacLeod*, London, Fount, 1990, p. 238. I am grateful to Alan Wilkinson for this story.
9. Wilkinson, *The Community of the Resurrection*, p. 278.
10. D. Bonhoeffer, *Life Together*, London, SCM Press, 1954.
11. J. A. T. Robinson, *Honest to God*, London, SCM Press, 1963, p. 87.
12. *Church Times*, 9 March 1990, p. 4.
13. *Church Times*, 10 August 1990, p. 11.
14. *Church Times*, 29 March 1991.
15. Quoted in Eric James, *A Life of Bishop John A. T. Robinson*, London, Collins, 1987, p. 136.
16. H. Dawes, 'Theology in the parish – a lost cause?', *Theology*, March/April 1990, 117–24, pp. 123 and 117.

## Chapter 2

1. See J. Wilkinson, *Egeria's Travels*, London, SPCK, 1972, pp. 34ff.
2. T. Merton, *Conjectures of a Guilty Bystander*, Garden City, NY, Doubleday Image Books, 1968, pp. 156f.
3. W. H. Shannon (ed.), *The Hidden Ground of Love: Letters of Thomas Merton*, London, Collins, 1985, p. 155.

# Notes

## Chapter 3

1. Charles Taylor, *Sources of the Self: The Making of the Modern Identity*, Cambridge, Cambridge University Press, 1989. I am particularly indebted to Taylor's analysis throughout this chapter.
2. Taylor, *Sources of the Self*, p. 130.
3. Augustine, *De Vera Religione* 39.72.
4. Montaigne, *Essays* 2.17.
5. Taylor, *Sources of the Self*, p. 159.
6. See especially Taylor, *Sources of the Self*, pp. 161–74.
7. See Alasdair MacIntyre, *After Virtue*, London, Duckworth, 1981.

## Chapter 4

1. J. A. T. Robinson, *Honest to God*, London, SCM Press, 1963, e.g. pp. 54ff., etc.
2. J. Moltmann, *The Spirit of Life*, London, SCM Press, 1992, p. 34.
3. Ross Thompson, *Holy Ground*, London, SPCK, 1990, p. 246.
4. An accessible summary introduction to current thought on the subject is given in Tom Driver, *The Magic of Ritual*, San Francisco, HarperCollins, 1991.
5. Driver, *The Magic of Ritual*, p. 14.
6. W. D. Stacey, *Prophetic Drama in the Old Testament*, Manchester, Epworth, 1990, pp. 245f.
7. S. Weil, *Waiting on God*, London, Routledge, 1950, p. 92.
8. George Herbert, *A Priest to the Temple, or, The Country Parson*, chapter 14, 'The Priest in Circuit'.
9. D. Hare, *Racing Demon*, London, Faber & Faber, 1990, Act 1 Scene 12.

## Chapter 5

1. A. Adam, *The Liturgical Year*, New York, Pueblo, 1979, p. 36.
2. Ignatius of Antioch, *Ad Magnesios* 9.1–2.
3. Adam, *The Liturgical Year*, p. 42.
4. G. Bornkamm on *mysterion* in G. Kittel (ed.), *Theological Dictionary of the New Testament*, Grand Rapids, Eerdmans, 1967, vol. IV, p. 826.
5. See E. Mazza, *Mystagogy: A Theology of Liturgy in the Patristic Age*, New York, Pueblo, 1989, p. 22.
6. Marsili (D10), pp. 145f.
7. Leo the Great, *Sermons* 74.2.

# Notes

8. Theodore of Mopsuestia, *On the Eucharist*, ed. A. Mingana, *Woodbrooke Studies*, vol. VI, Cambridge, 1933, p. 83.

9. *On the Eucharist*, p. 103.

10. Theodore of Mopsuestia, *On Baptism*, ed. A. Mingana, *Woodbrooke Studies*, vol. VI, Cambridge, 1933, pp. 21 and 148. (Theodore is speaking about the Eucharist.) This is the translation provided by Mingana. A more literal translation would run: '. . . and by mystery we perform the signs in connection with our Lord the Messiah'. (I am grateful to Fr David Lane for this information.)

11. Gregory the Great, *Dialogue* 4.58 (PL 77.428); see Sartore (D18), p. 1285, n. 2.

12. Leo, *Sacr. Veron.*, ed. L. Mohlberg, Rome, 1956, p. 13, n. 93. The word translated 'made present' is *exeritur*. It was miscopied early on by copyists, changing to *exercitum* and later *exercetur*. Until recently, translations have therefore rendered the phrase as: 'the work of our redemption is completed'. This translation was still used in *Lumen Gentium* 1.3 (see A. Flannery, *Vatican Council II: The Conciliar and Post-Conciliar Documents*, New York, Costello, 1984, vol. 1, p. 351; see also E. Schillebeeckx, *The Church with a Human Face*, London, SCM Press, 1985, p. 159).

13. Ambrose, *Apol. David* 1.12.58.

14. Casel, *Mysterienfrömmigkeit* (E13), p. 104.

15. C. H. Dodd, *The Apostolic Preaching and its Developments*, London, Hodder & Stoughton, 1944, p. 94.

16. W. Temple, *Readings in St John's Gospel*, London, Macmillan, 1947, Introduction, p. xx.

17. Tom Driver, *The Magic of Ritual*, San Francisco, HarperCollins, 1991, pp. 24 and 16.

18. Filthaut (D3), p. 31.

19. From Newman's hymn, 'Praise to the Holiest' from *The Dream of Gerontius*.

20. See Brown (B2).

21. Rabbi Joshua ben Chananaiah (*c.* AD 90), *Mekilta on Exod.* 12.42.

22. *Baptism, Eucharist and Ministry*, Geneva, World Council of Churches, 1982. (See especially sections 5–13.)

23. See for example Casel (E21).

24. As a translation, *The Mystery of Christian Worship* (A) often leaves much to be desired, not least in rendering the vigour of Casel's German, and this sentence, which I have preferred to translate direct from the original, is barely to be recognized on p. 27 of the English version.

25. See note 22.

# Notes

## Chapter 6

1. For example, Casel, *The Mystery of Christian Worship* (A), pp. 17f.
2. G. Steiner, *Real Presences*, London, Faber & Faber, 1989, p. 230.
3. M. Eliade, *The Forbidden Forest*, Indiana, Notre Dame University, 1978, p. 68.
4. L. Wittgenstein, *On Certainty*, ed. G. E. M. Anscombe and G. H. von Wright, New York, Harper & Row, 1969, 62e.
5. From a manuscript in Herstelle Abbey, *Festkonferenzen 1943/44*, Pentecost 1944, p. 56. (Quoted in Krahe (D8), p. 23.)
6. See C. H. Dodd, *The Apostolic Preaching and its Developments*, London, Hodder & Stoughton, 1944.
7. Casel, *The Mystery of Christian Worship* (A), pp. 124 and 126.
8. Casel, *Mysteriengegenwart* (E16), pp. 208–10. The quotations are from: Paschasius Radbertus, *De Corp. et Sang. Dom.* c. 3 (PL 120.1276); Leo, *Serm.* 52.1 (PL 54.313f), *Serm.* 56.1 (PL 120.326B), *Serm.* 64.1 (PL 358AB); Proclus of Constantinople, *Sermon* (PL 54.508D).
9. I. T. Ramsey, *Models for Divine Activity*, London, SCM Press, 1973, pp. 4f: the quotations are from G. Jean-Aubry, *The Sea Dreamer* (1957), a definitive biography of Joseph Conrad, and George Adam Smith, *The Historical Geography of the Holy Land*, London, Hodder, 1894, p. 67.
10. Ramsey, *Models*, p. 7.
11. Marsili (D11), p. 125.
12. L. Cerfaux, *The Christian in the Theology of St Paul*, London, Geoffrey Chapman, 1967, p. 281.
13. Casel, *The Mystery of Christian Worship* (A), p. 123.
14. See J. Moltmann, *The Spirit of Life – A Universal Affirmation*, London, SCM Press, 1992, pp. 47–51.
15. D. Stăniloae, *Spiritualitate şi Comuniune în Liturghia Ortodoxă*, Craiova, 1986, p. 14.
16. *Lumen Gentium* 1.2 (see A. Flannery, *Vatican Council II*, 1984, vol. 1, p. 351).
17. W. Stählin, *Mysterium: vom Geheimnis Gottes*, Standa, Kassel, 1970, p. 191.
18. Stählin, *Mysterium*, p. 193–4.
19. P. Schellenbaum, *Abschied von der Selbstzerstörung*, Munich, Deutscher Taschenbuch, 1991, p. 175.
20. From the report *The Army and Religion*, p. 68 (see Chapter 1, note 5), quoted in A. Wilkinson, *The Church of England and the First World War*, London, SPCK, 1978, p. 161.
21. E. B. Pusey, *Monastic Rule*, para. 12.
22. Augustine, *City of God* 10.6.

# Notes

## Chapter 7

1. Ross Thompson, *Holy Ground*, London, SPCK, 1990, pp. 48ff.
2. Rowan Williams, 'Incarnation and Social Vision', the Gore/Scott Holland Lecture, 1989.
3. O. Chadwick, *Michael Ramsey, a Life*, Oxford, Clarendon Press, 1990, p. 22.
4. J. MacQuarrie, *In Search of Humanity*, London, SCM Press, p. 212.
5. K. Rahner, *Theological Investigations* 14, London, Darton, Longman & Todd, 1976, pp. 167f. (Translation adapted to correspond more literally to the German original.)
6. Rahner, *Theological Investigations* 14, pp. 169f. (Translation as above.)
7. K. Rahner, *Theological Investigations* 19, London, Darton, Longman & Todd, 1984, p. 142.
8. Rahner, *Theological Investigations* 19, pp. 142 and 143.
9. Rahner, *Theological Investigations* 19, p. 147.
10. Rahner, *Theological Investigations* 14, p. 295.
11. S. Maggiani, 'Rito/Riti' in D. Sartore and A Triacca (eds.), *Nuovo Dizionario di Liturgia*, Milan, Paoline, 1988, col. 1230, n. 1.

## Chapter 8

1. Hans Küng, *The Church*, London, Burns and Oates, 1967, p. 321.
2. E. Schillebeeckx, *Church: The Human Story of God*, London, SCM Press, 1990, pp. 13f.
3. Schillebeeckx, *Church*, p. 102. I have omitted here the phrase 'without Christianity being able to regard itself in a superior, let alone "imperialistic", way as the one true religion which excludes all other religions', because it can be read in two ways, and I can associate myself with only one of those ways (which I presume to be that intended by Schillebeeckx), i.e. as meaning that any 'feeling superior' to others on any ground whatever is contrary to Christ's example, and that while we will believe that the fullness of salvation is in Christ alone, we cannot regard ourselves as having a perfect grasp of that faith, and neither can we exclude the unique insights of those outside the Church, as if those insights were unconnected with Christ, who is all truth. A superficial reading of the sentence can give an impression of that relativizing of the gospel which I am not wanting to support.
4. G. Mensching, *Katholische Kultprobleme*, Gotha, 1927, reviewed by Casel in *Jahrbuch für Liturgiewissenschaft* 7 (1927), pp. 105–24; reprinted in Schilson (D23), pp. 126–43.

# Notes

5. Schilson (D23), p. 138.
6. David Jenkins, *God, Jesus and the Spirit*, London, SCM Press, 1988, p. 96.
7. *Il Regno*, 15 March 1992, p. 137.
8. O. Chadwick, *Britain and the Vatican in the Second World War*, Cambridge, Cambridge University Press, 1986.
9. Donald Nicholl, 'The Church and the Nazis – 2', *The Tablet*, 30 July 1994, p. 948.
10. Nicholl, 'The Church and the Nazis', pp. 947f.
11. See A. Thiselton, *New Horizons in Hermeneutics*, London, HarperCollins, 1992, p. 372.
12. Pope Paul VI, *Ecclesiam Suam*, n. 37.
13. Schilson (D19), p. 304.
14. Schilson (D19), p. 135.
15. D. Bonhoeffer, *Sanctorum Communio*, Munich, 1969, p. 174.
16. Schilson (D19), p. 305.
17. See Casel, *The Mystery of Christian Worship* (A), p. 166.
18. Cyprian, *De Unitate* 4, and *Epistulae* 45, 59, 69, etc.
19. *Lumen Gentium* 1.1 (see A. Flannery, *Vatican Council II*, vol. 1, pp. 350–423.
20. Schillebeeckx, *Church*, p. 213.
21. T. Goritschewa, 'Ich habe die Hölle erfahren', in *Rheinische Merkur/Christ und Welt* 3, 15 January 1988, p. 20.
22. Schillebeeckx, *The Church with a Human Face*, London, SCM Press, 1985, p. 116.
23. Marsili (D11), pp. 141f; the reference is to J. Jungmann, *Gewordene Liturgie*, Innsbruck, 1941, pp. 15–19.

## Chapter 9

1. See C. Giraudo, *Eucarestia per la Chiesa: Prospettive teologiche sull'eucarestia a partire dalla 'Lex Orandi'*, Rome, 1989, p. 610.
2. *Mysterium: Gesammelte Arbeiten Laacher Mönche*, Münster, 1926, p. 29.
3. Casel, *Die Liturgie als Mysterienfeier* (E13), p. 60.
4. Casel, *The Mystery of Christian Worship* (A), p. 58.
5. Casel, *The Mystery of Christian Worship* (A), p. 103.
6. Casel, *Mysterium der Ekklesia* (E1), p. 182.
7. Casel, *Mysterium der Ekklesia* (E1), p. 181f.
8. Casel, *Mysterium der Ekklesia* (E1), p. 181f.
9. The term is used by Schilson (D19), p. 141.
10. Casel, *Die Liturgie als Mysterienfeier* (E13), pp. 64f; see also Schilson (D19), pp. 175–8.
11. Leo the Great, *Sermons* 74.2.

12. Another version of the story speaks of postage stamps rather than butterflies.
13. Casel, *The Mystery of Christian Worship* (A), pp. 40 and 41.

### Chapter 10

1. Quoted in the frontispiece to G. W. O. Addleshaw and F. Etchells, *The Architectural Setting of Anglican Worship*, London, Faber & Faber, 1948.
2. T. S. Eliot, *Murder in the Cathedral*, 4th edn, London, Faber & Faber, 1938, speech of the Third Priest, p. 57.
3. From *Lyrical Ballads*, Preface to 2nd edn, 1802.
4. Brown (B2), pp. 430f.
5. Brown (B2), pp. 438.
6. Casel, 'Glaube, Gnosis und Mysterium' (E4), pp. 171f. See Schilson (D19), p. 118.
7. See Schilson (D19), p. 119.
8. See A. Kavanagh, *On Liturgical Theology*, New York, Pueblo, 1984, p. 73.
9. W. D. Hudson, 'Thinking close to Worship', review of J. MacQuarrie, *Heidegger and Christianity*, London, SCM Press, 1994, in *Expository Times*, March 1995, p. 190.
10. See Aidan Nichols, *From Newman to Congar*, Edinburgh, T. & T. Clark, 1990, pp. 200 and 202.
11. Quoted by John Briggs in *The History of Christianity*, ed. T. Dowley, Oxford, 1977, p. 14.
12. D. Nineham, *Christianity Medieval and Modern: A Study in Religious Change*, London, SCM Press, p. 14.
13. A. Wilkinson, *The Community of the Resurrection*, London, SCM Press, 1992, p. 278.
14. *The Tablet*, 24 June 1995, p. 803.
15. F. Kerr, *Theology after Wittgenstein*, Oxford, Basil Blackwell, 1986, p. 188.
16. J. Cornwell, 'Don Cupitt's Gospel', *The Tablet*, 6 August 1994, pp. 979f.

### Chapter 11

1. A. MacIntyre, *After Virtue*, London, Duckworth, 1981, pp. 195f.
2. Gregory the Great, *Homily in Ezekiel*, 1.7.8.
3. MacIntyre, *After Virtue*; N. T. Wright, *The New Testament and the People of God*, London, SPCK, 1992: much has been written on the role of narrative (or 'narratology'), and both authors in different ways provide a good introduction to the subject.

# Notes

4. Wright, *The New Testament and the People of God*; A Thiselton, *New Horizons in Hermeneutics*, London, HarperCollins, 1992.

5. N. Frye, *The Great Code: The Bible and Literature*, London, Routledge, 1982; A. Henry (ed.), *Biblia Pauperum*, Aldershot, Scolar Press, 1987; T. Fabiny, *The Lion and the Lamb*, London, Macmillan, 1992.

6. Fabiny, *The Lion and the Lamb*, pp. 23f.

7. Frye, *The Great Code*, pp. 79f. This was written before current debates about the relative importance of authorial intention, but the point still holds.

8. Frye, *The Great Code*, p. 172.

9. Marsili (D13), p. 68.

10. G. Kittel, article on *Eikon* in G. Kittel (ed.), *Theological Dictionary of the New Testament*, Grand Rapids, Eerdmans, 1964, vol. II, pp. 395 and 398.

11. J. Betz, *Die Eucharistie in der Zeit der Griechischen Väter*, I/1, Freiburg, 1955, p. 247.

12. Theodore of Mopsuestia, *On Baptism*, ed. A. Mingana, *Woodbrooke Studies*, vol. VI, Cambridge, 1933, p. 18.

13. Casel, *The Mystery of Christian Worship* (A), p. 33, author's translation.

14. Casel, *The Mystery of Christian Worship* (A), p. 171.

15. E. Mazza, *Mystagogy: A Theology of Liturgy in the Patristic Age*, New York, Pueblo, 1989, p. 137.

16. Mazza, *Mystagogy*, p. 134.

17. Ambrose, *De Mysteriis* 9.

18. Mazza, *Mystagogy*, p. 25.

19. Mazza, *Mystagogy*, pp. 25f.

20. See Chapter 5, note 13.

21. Mazza, *Mystagogy*, pp. 27f; Ambrose, *De Sacramentis* 3.5.

22. Frye, *The Great Code*, p. 86.

23. Wright, *The New Testament and the People of God*, p. 140.

24. Maximus the Confessor, *Ambigua* (PG 91.1360), quoted in O. Clément, *The Roots of Christian Mysticism*, New City, 1993, p. 40.

## Chapter 12

1. See S. Jay Gould, *Wonderful Life: The Burgess Shale and the Nature of History*, London, Hutchinson Radius, 1990.

2. E. Mazza, *Mystagogy: A Theology of Liturgy in the Patristic Age*, New York, Pueblo, 1989, p. 148.

3. See J. Jungmann, *The Mass of the Roman Rite*, New York, Benzinger, 1951, vol. I, pp. 87–91.

# Notes

4. See K. Stevenson, 'On Keeping Holy Week', *Theology* 89 (January 1986), pp. 32ff.

5. See E. Rufini, 'Liturgia: Comunicazione del Mistero', in L. Sartori (ed.), *Comunicazione e Ritualità*, Padova, Messagero, 1985, pp. 111–45.

6. See 'Mystères' in *Dictionnaire de Spiritualité*, ed. M. Viller et al., Paris, Beauchesne, vol. X, 1980.

7. See D. Power, *The Eucharistic Mystery*, Dublin, Gill and Macmillan, 1992, p. 209.

8. Bérulle, *Oeuvres de Pieté* 76.1.

9. P. McPartlan, *The Eucharist Makes the Church*, Edinburgh, T. & T. Clark, 1993, pp. 64f.

10. A. Colombo, 'L'Explication de la Messe' di P. LeBrun de L'Oratoire (1661–1729)', *Ephemerides Liturgicae* 101 (1987), 425–42, p. 441.

11. P. Floriot, *Traité de la Messe*, Paris, 1691, p 60.

12. Floriot, *Traité de la Messe*, p. 63.

13. W. Stählin, *Mysterium: vom Geheimnis Gottes*, Standa, Kassel, 1970, p. 39.

14. Stählin, *Mysterium*, pp. 39f.

15. Stählin, *Mysterium*, p. 40.

16. Stählin, *Mysterium*, p. 41.

17. William Law, *A Serious Call to a Devout and Holy Life*, 1728, chapter 17.

18. R. Hooker, *Laws of Ecclesiastical Polity* Bk V, 16.72. Hooker quotes the twelfth-century Abbot Arnold of Bonneval, believing the words to be those of Cyprian of Carthage. See S. W. Sykes (ed.), *Authority in the Anglican Communion*, Toronto, Anglican Book Centre, 1987, p. 106.

19. Lancelot Andrewes, *Sermons on the Passion*, in Library of Anglo-Catholic Theology, *Sermons*, 1841, Vol. II, pp. 120f. and 134. The references are to Galatians 3.1 and 1 Corinthians 11.26.

20. Quoted in W. J. Grisbrooke (ed.), *Anglican Liturgies of the Seventeenth and Eighteenth Centuries* (Alcuin Club Collections XI), London, SPCK, 1958, pp. 119f.

21. See R. W. Franklin, *Nineteenth-century Churches: The History of the New Catholicism in Württemberg, England and France*, London, Garland, 1987, e.g. pp. 58f., and also by the same author: 'Guéranger: a view on the centenary of his death', *Worship* 49 (1975), pp. 318–28; 'Guéranger and pastoral liturgy', *Worship* 50 (1976), pp. 146–62; 'Guéranger and variety in unity', *Worship* 51 (1977), pp. 378–99; 'The Nineteenth-century liturgical movement', *Worship* 53 (1979), pp. 12–39; 'Humanism and transcendence in the

nineteenth-century liturgical movement', *Worship* 59 (1985), pp. 342–53.

22. Franklin, *Nineteenth-century Churches*, p. 50.


## Chapter 13

1. M. Klöckener, 'Die Sakramentalität der Welt nach Odo Casel', in M. Klöckener and W. Glade (eds.), *Die Feier der Sakramente in der Gemeinde*, Kevelaer, 1986, pp. 403–15.
2. On *mysterium tremendum* see Rudolf Otto, *The Idea of the Holy*, London, OUP, 1923, chapter IV.
3. Klöckener, 'Die Sakramentalität der Welt', p. 408.
4. Klöckener, 'Die Sakramentalität der Welt', p. 409.
5. Klöckener, 'Die Sakramentalität der Welt', p. 411.
6. Klöckener, 'Die Sakramentalität der Welt', pp. 412f.
7. Schilson (D20), p. 28.
8. P. Purnell, *Our Faith Story: Its Telling and its Sharing*, London, Collins, 1985.
9. E. Duffy, *The Stripping of the Altars*, New Haven and London, Yale University Press, 1992.
10. Cyril of Alexandria, *Commentary on the Gospel of John* 11.11 (PG 74.560).
11. *Lent, Holy Week and Easter*, London, SPCK/Cambridge University Press/Church House Publishing, 1984, 1986; *The Promise of His Glory*, London, Mowbray/Church House Publishing, 1991.
12. *Celebrating Common Prayer*, London, Mowbray, 1992.
13. See G. Guiver CR, *Everyday God*, London, Triangle, 1994, pp. 63f.
14. See P. C. Haidinger, 'Erfahrungen mit der Jugendvesper', in *Heiliger Dienst* 1/2, Salzburg, 1987, pp. 65–71.
15. See G. Guiver CR, *Company of Voices*, London, SPCK, 1988, chapter 15.
16. This phrase is attributed by Jürgen Moltmann to Gregory of Nyssa (*Life of Moses* (PG 44.377)), but it can only count as an inspired paraphrase of what Gregory actually wrote. (See J. Moltmann, *The Spirit of Life – A Universal Affirmation*, London, SCM Press, 1992, p. 73.)
17. The saying is quoted in Enzo Bianchi, *Ricominciare nell'anima, nella chiesa, nel mondo*, Genova, Marietti, 1991, p. 53.
18. Philip Larkin, 'Church Going', from *The Less Deceived: Poems by Philip Larkin*, Hessle (E. Yorks.), Marvell, 1955.
19. H. Thorndike, *Works*, Library of Anglo-Catholic Theology, vol. V, 1954, p. 572.

# Notes

## Chapter 14

1. T. S. Eliot, 'Little Gidding', *Four Quartets*, London, Faber & Faber, 1944.
2. E. Duffy, *The Stripping of the Altars*, New Haven and London, Yale University Press, 1992.
3. A. MacIntyre, *After Virtue*, London, Duckworth, 1981.
4. A. Häussling, 'Odo Casel – Noch von Aktualität?', *Achiv für Liturgiewissenschaft* 28 (1986), 357–87; p. 367.
5. Häussling, 'Odo Casel', p. 368.
6. George Carey, 'What Kind of Unity?', Lecture at the Bucharest Theological Academy, Romania, September 1993.
7. Contrary to normal custom at that time, the Paschal Vigil at Herstelle was celebrated not on Holy Saturday morning, but in the night of Easter.

# SELECT BIBLIOGRAPHY

## Abbreviations

JLW    *Jahrbuch für Liturgiewissenschaft* (There is potential confusion in that the actual date of publication differs from that given on the spine, as follows: for the volumes 1925–30, publication date is one year later; volumes 1931–3, two years later; volumes 1934 and 35, three years later. Some authors cite the later date.)

ALW    *Archiv für Liturgiewissenschaft*

LJB    *Liturgisches Jahrbuch*

## (A) The only Casel text currently available in English

Casel, O., *The Mystery of Christian Worship, and other writings*, ed. B. Neunheuser, Westminster, Maryland, Newman Press, and London, Darton, Longman & Todd, 1962. (The translation is not always reliable, and fails to capture the vigour of Casel's style.)

## (B) Books and articles in English on Casel's theology and matters related to it

1. Bouyer, L., *Life and Liturgy*, London, Sheed and Ward, 1956.
2. Brown, R. E., 'The Semitic background of the New Testament MYSTERION', *Biblica* (Rome) 39 (1958), 426–48, and 40 (1959), 70–87.
3. Crichton, J. D., 'A Theology of worship', in *The Study of Liturgy*, ed. Cheslyn Jones et al., London, SPCK, revised edn 1992, 3–31.
4. Davis, Charles, 'Odo Casel and the theology of Mysteries', *Worship* 34.8 (1960), 428–38.
5. Empereur, J., *Models of Liturgical Theology* (Alcuin/Grove Liturgical Study 4), Nottingham, Grove, 1987.
6. Empereur, J., *Exploring the Sacred*, Washington DC, Pastoral Press, 1988, chapter 6.
7. Fink, P. E. (ed.), *New Dictionary of Sacramental Worship*, Dublin, Gill & Macmillan, 1990: articles by T. F. Koernke, 'Theologians, modern', and M. Skelley, 'Liturgical renewal'.
8. Hart, J. G., 'The Cult-mystery revisited', *Downside Review*, April 1973, 141–53.
9. Irvine, C., *Making Present*, London, Darton, Longman & Todd, 1994.

10. McMahon, L. M., 'Towards a theology of the Liturgy: Dom Odo Casel and the "Mysterientheorie"', *Studia Liturgica* 3 (1964), 129–54.
11. Neunheuser, B., 'Odo Casel in retrospect', *Worship* 50 (1976), 489–504.
12. Neunheuser, B., 'Masters in Israel: Odo Casel', *Clergy Review* 55 (1970), 194–212.

## (C) Bibliographies

1. Santagada, O., 'Dom Odo Casel: Contributo monografico per una Bibliografia generale delle sue opere, degli studi sulla dottrina e della sua influenza nella teologia contemporanea', *ALW* 10 (1967), 7–77.
2. Häussling, A., 'Bibliographie Odo Casel 1986', *ALW* 28 (1986), 28–42; 29 (1987), 189–98.
3. Klöckener, M., 'Odo Casel – Christ und Theologe fur unsere Zeit: Zu neuen Studien uber die Mysterientheologie', *Theologische Reveue* 84.1, Münster, Aschendorff, 1988, 1–18.

## (D) A selection of publications in other languages

1. Bernal, J. M., 'La presencia de Cristo en la liturgia', *Notitiae* 20 (1984), 455–90.
2. Dalmais, I. H., 'Le "Mysterion"', *La Maison-Dieu* 158 (1984), 14–50.
3. Filthaut, T., *La Théologie des Mystères*, Paris, Desclée, 1954. (This is basic reading concerning the early, controversial years.)
4. Gozier, A., *Odo Casel, Kunder des Christusmysteriums*, Regensburg, Pustet, 1986. (A German translation of the less accurate original French edn: *Dom Casel*, Paris, Fleurus, 1968.)
5. Häussling, A., 'Odo Casel – Noch von Aktualität?', *ALW* 28 (1980), 357–87.
6. Hoppe, R., 'Das Mysterium und die Ekklesia', in A. Schilson (ed.), *Gottes Weisheit in Mysterium*, Mainz, Matthias-Grünewald, 1989, 81–102.
7. Klöckener, M., 'Reformer aus Treue zur Tradition', *Christ in der Gegenwart* 38 (1986), 317–18.
8. Krahe, M. J., *Auf dass all eins seien: Die Mysterienlehre und der Dialog mit der Ostkirche – ausgewählte Texte von Odo Casel*, Würzburg, Echter, 1988.
9. Krahe, M. J., *Der Herr is der Geist*, St Ottilien, 1986.
10. Marsili, S., *Mistero di Cristo e liturgia nello spirito* (A cura di M. A. Abignente, Libreria Editrice Vaticana, 1986).

# Select Bibliography

11. Marsili, S., 'Verso una teologia della Liturgia' in B. Neunheuser (ed.), *Anamnesis*, vol. 1, Torino, Marietti, 1974.

12. Marsili, S., 'Das Gedächtnis des Herrn', *ALW* 22 (1980), 9–29.

13. Marsili, S., *I Segni del Mistero di Cristo*, Rome, Centro Liturgico Vicenziano (CLV), 1987.

14. Neunheuser, B., 'Neue Äusserungen zur Frage der Mysteriengegenwart', *ALW* 5.2 (1958), 333–53.

15. Neunheuser, B., 'Neue Beiträge im Gespräch um die Mysteriengegenwart', *ALW* 25 (1983), 297–307.

16. Neunheuser, B., 'Ut Mysterium paschale vivendo exprimatur', in *Traditio et Progressio* (Festschrift for A. Nocent, ed. G. Farnedi), *Studia Anselmiana* 95 (1988), 375–89.

17. Neunheuser, B., 'Lebendiger Gott: Zu den Büchern von Maria Judith Krahe OSB', *Münchener Theologische Zeitschrift* 38 (1987), 275–88.

18. Sartore, D., and Triacca, A. (eds.), *Nuovo Dizionario di Liturgia*, Milano, Paoline, 1988: articles by A. Cuva, 'Gesu Cristo'; S. Marsili, 'Liturgia'; B. Neunheuser, 'Mistero'; P. Sorci, 'Mistero Pasquale'; B. Neunheuser, 'Spiritualità Liturgica'; A. Pistola, 'Storia della Salvezza'.

19. Schilson, A., *Theologie als Sakramententheologie*, Mainz, Matthias-Grünewald, 1987. (A thoroughgoing introduction, essential reading for any serious study of Casel.)

20. Schilson, A., 'Die Gegenwart des Ursprungs', *LJB* 43 (1993) 6–29.

21. Schilson, A., 'Liturgie und Menschsein', *LJB* 39 (1989) 206– 27.

22. Schilson, A., 'Romano Guardini und die Mysterientheologie' in A. Schilson (ed.), *Perspektiven Theologischer Erneuerung*, Dusseldorf, Patmos, 1986), 63–79.

23. Schilson, A. (ed.), *Mysterientheologie: Ansatz und Gestalt*, Regensburg, Pustet, 1986. (Introduction and selected texts).

24. Schilson, A. (ed.), *Odo Casel, Gegenwart des Christus-Mysteriums: Ausgewählte Texte zum Kirchenjahr*, Mainz, Matthias-Grünewald, 1986.

25. Severus, E. von, 'Odo Casels Theologie des monastischen Lebens', *ALW* 28 (1986), 173–82.

26. Spital, H. J., 'P. Odo Casel OSB', *Archiv für Mittel-Reinische Kirchengeschichte* 38 (1986), 327–33.

27. Stählin, W., *Mysterium vom Geheimnis Gottes*, Kassel, Standa, 1970. (A Lutheran viewpoint).

28. Triacca, A., 'Odo Casel e il Movimento Liturgico', *Ephemerides Liturgicae* 101 (1987), 153–181.

29. Wegenaer, P., 'Heilsgegenwart: Das Heilwerk Christi und die Virtus divina in den Sakramenten unter besonderer Berücksichtigung

von Eucharistie und Taufe . . .', *Liturgiewissenschaftliche Quellen und Forschungen* 33, Münster, Aschendorff, 1958.

### (E) Principal published works of Casel

*(Casel died in 1948, and some of the following were edited by the sisters of the Abbey of Herstelle and published posthumously)*

1. *Mysterium der Ekklesia*, Mainz, 1961.
2. 'Die Eucharistie des hl. Justinus Martyr', *Der Katholik* 4 (1914), 153–76, 243–63, 331–55, 414–36.
3. *Das Christliche Festmysterium*, Paderborn, 1941.
4. 'Glaube, Gnosis und Mysterium', *JLW* 15 (1935), 155–305. (Also published separately in Münster, 1941.)
5. *Mysterium des Kommenden*, Paderborn, 1952.
6. *Mysterium des Kreuzes*, Paderborn, 1954.
7. *Das Christliche Kultmysterium*, Regensburg, 1932. (For English translation, see the first entry in this Bibliography.)
8. 'Katholische Kultprobleme', *JLW* 7 (1927), 105–24.
9. 'Zur Kultsprache des heiligen Paulus, *ALW* 1 (1950), 1–64.
10. 'Liturgische Bewegung', in *Die Religion in Geschichte und Gegenwart*, 2nd edn, no. 3 (1929), 1698–701.
11. *Vom wahren Menschenbild*, Regensburg, 1953.
12. *Die Liturgie als Mysterienfeier* (*Ecclesia Orans* 9), Freiburg, 1922.
13. 'Mysterienfrömmigkeit', *Bonner Zeitschrift für Theologie und Seelsorge* 4 (1927), 101–17.
14. 'Das Mysteriengedächtnis der Messliturgie im Lichte der Tradition', *JLW* 6 (1926), 113–204.
15. 'Mysteriengegenwart', *JLW* 8 (1928), 145–224.
16. *Das Christliche Opfermysterium*, Cologne, 1968.
17. 'Das Kultmysterium als Quell des neuen Lebens', *Liturgie und Mönchtum* 3 (1949), 8–22.
18. 'Religionsgeschichte und Liturgiewissenschaft', *JLW* 14 (1934), 197–224.
19. 'Neue Zeugnisse für das Kultmysterium', *JLW* 13 (1933), 99–171.
20. *Das Gedächtnis des Herrn in der altchristlichen Liturgie*, Freiburg im Breisgau, 6th edn 1922.
21. 'Älteste christliche Kunst im Christusmysterium', *JLW* 12 (1932), 1–86.
22. 'Art und Sinn der Ältesten christliche Osterfeier', *JLW* 14 (1934), 1–78.
23. 'Zum Worte "Sacramentum"', *JLW* 8 (1928), 225–32.

# Index

# Index

# Index

# Index